Responsive Democracy

Increasing State Accountability in East Asia

Jeeyang Rhee Baum

The University of Michigan Press | *Ann Arbor*

Published in the United States of America by
The University of Michigan Press
Manufactured in the United States of America
Printed on acid-free paper

2014 2013 2012 2011 4 3 2 1

A CIP catalog record for this book is available from the British Library.

Library of Congress Cataloging-in-Publication Data

Baum, Jeeyang Rhee, 1967–
Responsive democracy : increasing state accountability in East Asia / Jeeyang Rhee Baum.
p. cm.
Includes bibliographical references and index.
ISBN 978-0-472-11749-9 (cloth : alk. paper) — ISBN 978-0-472-02573-2 (e-book)
1. Government accountability—East Asia. 2. Government accountability—Philippines. 3. Transparency in government—East Asia. 4. Transparency in government—Philippines. 5. Administrative agencies—East Asia—Management. 6. Administrative agencies—Philippines—Management. 7. East Asia—Politics and government—21st century. 8. Philippines—Politics and government—1986– I. Title.

JQ1499.A58B38 2010
352.3'5095—dc22 2010030238

To Matt and Téa

Contents

Acknowledgments

This project began during my early days as a graduate student, when I encountered an observation by Will Heller, Phil Keefer, and Mat McCubbins that Korea had recently passed an administrative procedure act (APA). Having just read McNollgast's theory of APA passage in the United States, I was immediately intrigued about why Korea had passed such a law. Soon thereafter, a dissertation topic was born.

As I near the end of the journey that this book has come to represent for me, I have many individuals to thank. Because this project began as a doctoral dissertation at UCLA, I owe the greatest debt for its development to my academic advisers. From the outset, Kathy Bawn, chair of my dissertation committee, was genuinely enthusiastic about my work. No matter what factoid or underdeveloped idea I brought to her attention, I left her office in a much better place. Her patience, encouragement, and advice on a wide range of topics have been and continue to be an important source of guidance and inspiration.

Mike Thies, who took me under his wing as soon as I entered graduate school, encouraged me to return to my roots and pursue research on Korea. He mentored me throughout my graduate career by pushing me to place Korean politics in a broader institutional context. Had it not been for his constant support and enthusiasm, I might never have stumbled on this project. I learned a great deal about scholarly research during our many—and I mean *many*—conversations over coffee and pizza. I am forever grateful for his wisdom and encouragement.

I am also grateful to J. R. DeShazo for his enthusiasm, valuable critiques, and strong support. I especially appreciate his consistent encouragement and concern for my career, as when he gave me the opportunity to present my research at the UCLA Center for Governance Conference on External and Internal Governance of Public Agencies.

John Londregan, too, offered consistent support for my work. His enthusiasm was very contagious, and our conversations always sparked new ideas. Larry Diamond, Ron Rogowski, and Matthew Shugart offered valuable comments and suggestions early on in the development of my research. I also benefited a great deal from my interactions with a number of exceptional faculty, including Jim DeNardo, Barbara Geddes, Miriam Golden, Barbara Koremenos, Mike Lofchie, Tom Schwartz, Barbara Sinclair, and George Tsebelis.

At UC–San Diego, Gary Cox, Karen Ferree, Stephan Haggard, David Lake, Megumi Naoi, Sam Popkin, Phil Roeder, and Kaare Strøm read and offered valuable comments on various chapters or complete drafts of this manuscript. I am especially grateful to Mat McCubbins, who read and commented on multiple drafts of several chapters, helped me to frame my project, and offered constant encouragement and support.

More generally, I have benefited enormously from the outstanding intellectual environments at UCLA and UC–San Diego, in large measure because of my interactions with exceptional faculty members and graduate students. I thank my many colleagues who listened to my ideas or read parts of my dissertation project: Allyson Benton, Hanna Birnir, Eric Chang, Linda Choi-Hasunuma, Chris Jensen, David Karol, Mark Kayser, Kee-Seok Kim, Duncan MacRae, Woojin Moon, Chris Rudolph, Sanchita Saxena, Ross Schaap, and Elin Skaar. I also benefited tremendously from comments by the members of UCLA's Political Economy Workshop.

At UC–San Diego, I am grateful to Adam Brown, Jihyeon Jeong, Danielle Jung, and Alejandra Ríos-Cázares for outstanding research assistance and to Nathan Batto for his valuable insights into Taiwanese politics. I am especially grateful to Danielle for her valuable comments and suggestions on the manuscript.

Fieldwork was one of the most critical aspects of this project. For putting me in contact with key interview subjects, I am grateful to Richard Baum, Alex Brillantes, Choi Chul-Hee, Cora de Leon, Larry Diamond, Allen Hicken, Hoh Moon, Yuko Kasuya, Jih-Wen Lin, Yinsog Rhee, and Dennis Tang.

In Seoul, I am especially grateful to Park Kwan-Yong, Lim Woo-Yeong, Lee Kyung-Shik, Cho Paek J., Lee Seongman, Park Nam Hoon, Choi Jung-Il, Rhee Wang-Oo, Kim Duk-Oo, Kim Seung Hee, Lee Chae-Pil, Park Se Jin, Kwon Chul-Hyun, Kim Sung Hyun, Choi Byung-Sun, Rhee Zusun,

Kim Byung Kook, Joh Jung Jay, Lee Young Jo, Kim Byung Kook, Kim Suk Joon, and Im Hyug Baeg.

In Taipei, I profited greatly from my conversations with Yeh Jiunn-Rong, Yao Eng-Chi, Hsieh Chi Ta, John Huang, Cheng Pao Ching, Yuan Hsiao-Li, Chen Mei-Ling, Hwang Ching-Yuan, Chen C. H., and Kuo Chen-Lung. I am particularly grateful to Michael Lin, Roy Wu, and Carl Chang, who provided translation assistance and helped me get around Taipei.

In Manila, I benefited enormously from my meetings with Ledivina Cariño, Alex Magno, Juan Miguel Luz, Chito Salazar, Romulo Neri, Ruben Torres, Cecile Abella, Patricia Sto. Tomas, Celia Bernardo, and Carmencita Abella. Lala Macandog and Bombo Pasicolan deserve special thanks for making sure I got to my meetings on time. Finally, I express my appreciation to so many others who squeezed me into their busy schedules and shared their experiences and insights with me.

I thank the National Science Foundation (SES-0002288) and UCLA's International Studies and Overseas Programs for supporting my dissertation field research. The NSF grant enabled me to get translation assistance from the exceptionally thorough Tsai-Wei Sun and Jung Won Son. UCLA also supported the writing of my dissertation through the Dissertation Year Fellowship and Fishbaugh/UCLA Affiliates Scholarship. For supporting research on the last two substantive chapters of the book, I thank the UC–San Diego Committee on Research Grants and Hellman Faculty Fellowship.

At Harvard University, I thank the Kennedy School, Department of Government, and the Weatherhead Center for International Affairs, which supported the final stages of this project through research fellowships, and especially Jeff Frieden and Tony Saich, who offered support and encouragement. I also benefited from the helpful comments and suggestions of two anonymous reviewers as well as from the invaluable assistance of the University of Michigan Press's Melody Herr, Susan Cronin, and Kevin Rennells throughout the editorial and production process.

In addition, for valuable comments and suggestions on earlier drafts of various chapters, I thank participants in the following workshops and meetings: Stanford University's Department of Political Science's Comparative Politics Workshop and Shorenstein Asia-Pacific Research Center Korean Studies Colloquium Series, UCSD Graduate School of International Relations and Pacific Studies (IR/PS) Korea Seminar, University of Southern California Center for the Study of Law and Politics Symposium on Positive Political Theory of Law, Harvard University's Department of Government's Comparative Politics and Political Economy Workshops,

UCSD Department of Political Science and IR/PS and USD School of Law Conference on "Administrative Law and Process in the U.S. and Abroad: Cross-Disciplinary Perspectives," and annual conferences of the American Political Science Association and Midwest Political Science Association. I also thank Alberto Díaz-Cayeros, Mariano-Florentino Cuellar, Kent Eaton, David Law, Beatriz Magaloni, Mat McCubbins, Roger Noll, and Gi-Wook Shin for their helpful suggestions and critiques.

Portions of several chapters of this book were published previously in the *British Journal of Political Science* ("Presidents Have Problems Too: The Logic of Intra-Branch Delegation in East Asian Democracies," 37, no. 4 [2007]: 659–84), *Governance: An International Journal of Policy, Administration, and Institutions* ("Reining in the Bureaucrats: Democratic Transition and Administrative Procedural Reform in Korea," 20, no. 2 [2007]: 233–54), the *Journal of East Asian Studies* ("Breaking Authoritarian Bonds: The Political Origins of the Taiwan Administrative Procedure Act," 5, no. 3 [2005]: 365–99), and *Democratization* ("The Impact of Bureaucratic Openness on Public Trust in South Korea," 16, no. 5 [2009]: 969–97). This material is reprinted herein with the permission of Cambridge University Press, Blackwell Publishers, Lynne Rienner Publishers, and Routledge Publishers, respectively.

Finally, I am especially grateful to my family: to my grandparents, Kang In Sun and Choi Sang Ryong, for their inspiration; to my mother, Kyungwha Rhee, for always having so much confidence in me; to my father, Yinsog Rhee, who always talked about politics at the dinner table; and to my sister, Jeanne Rhee-Dechiario, for sharing her experiences while working on her dissertation. Richard and Steven Baum read and offered valuable comments on various chapters. Carolyn Baum, Kristen Baum Wilcox, and Karin Joffe have been incredibly supportive by letting me talk about my book project at every family gathering. My daughter, Téa, who was always asking me, "What's your book about, Mom?" not only got me through those tough days but also inspired me to imagine the impossible. Finally, I am eternally grateful to my husband, Matt, for always listening to the latest research development and for being by my side. In addition to reading and improving every chapter, his endless patience, support, and encouragement got me through this project. This book is dedicated to him and to our daughter.

1 | Introduction

From 1987 to 1995, South Korea's democratically elected government built dams along the country's major rivers and undertook other major public works projects without consulting anyone affected—not the local industrialists, not the local farmers, not even the local governments. As a former South Korean finance minister explained, consultation and deliberation take time, and "the main emphasis was on shortening the construction period and saving money" (Brull 1994, 1). According to one senior Korean bureaucrat involved in the projects, any opposition was "steamrolled."[1]

In 1987, South Korea's (hereafter, Korea) first democratically elected executive announced plans for the Imha Multipurpose Dam Project, which the government completed on schedule in 1991. Although the government forced almost 1,800 residents to relocate, offering some financial compensation in return, "no movements opposing to the dam construction itself were launched" (*Korea: Imha Multipurpose Dam Project* 2002, 8). Relocated citizens knew they had the right to compensation but had little or no knowledge of their rights to object to the project itself. The government essentially had license to overlook the project's environmental impact (Song 2004).

In 1997, the Korean government announced that a dam would be built on the Tong River at Youngwol. Civic, environmental, and even religious organizations immediately protested. Three out of four citizens in the affected communities of Youngwol and Jeongsun opposed the dam (Lim and Tang 2002). Two years later, the government had not started construction. Instead of steamrolling the opposition, the Ministry of Construction and Transportation responded to escalating public pressure by creating a joint government-civilian task force, including environmental experts, to determine the dam's feasibility. The task force recommended that the project be canceled; two days later, President Kim Dae Jung did so (Lim and Tang 2002).

Why did democratic responsiveness change so dramatically in a decade? Why could one democratically elected government steamroll its citizens and build a dam while another waited, listened, and responded to the citizens on a similar project, ultimately abandoning it altogether? In other words, when and why do democratic governments respond to their citizens?

Scholars and politicians typically explain democratic responsiveness in terms of maturation and consolidation, the strength of political parties, or the development of civil society. Though doubtless important, these broad concepts overlook the way that governments function and especially the ways that politicians create democratic responsiveness by changing the procedures guiding the operations of government. In Korea's case, a series of administrative laws passed in the mid-1990s dictates that the government cannot lay the first brick on a new construction project until it consults with everyone affected in any way, no matter how time-consuming the process. The party system, the constitution, and the citizenry did not change; however, administrative laws and procedures did change, dramatically altering the ways that politicians, citizens, and bureaucrats interacted.

Administrative procedural reforms "democratized" Korea's infrastructure construction process and made its government far more responsive. In 1987, citizens who disapproved of a dam had little recourse except to vote against the president who built it in the next election. In 1997, citizens could stop the dam. Citizens now have a say in the government's decision-making on specific projects, not just on which president should govern. This increasing popular voice is a measure of the transformation of *institutional* democracy into *responsive* democracy.

While the story of how administrative laws protect the interests of particular constituencies against the arbitrary exercise of executive authority is obviously important, no less compelling is the story of how administrative laws came to exist. Ironically, the sponsors of these laws did not intend to prevent executive abuse of authority. On the contrary, these laws, known as APAs (administrative procedure acts), originated in sitting executives' desire to prevent opposing politicians and recalcitrant bureaucrats from undermining policies. But how did these executives end up in this situation? To answer this question, we must begin with the current debate in the literature on democratization to highlight the central role of APAs in addressing questions of accountability in new democracies.

Early theorists of democratization initially assumed that holding elections and changing executives and legislators would result in a shift in state behavior. However, the literature has subsequently recognized that such is not necessarily the case and that new democracies may not be accountable (Geddes 1994; O'Donnell 1999; Przeworski, Stokes, and Manin 1999; Stokes 2001). Multiple factors explain this lack of accountability, including imperfections in the electoral mechanism as a means of controlling politicians. But another problem is that the state apparatus itself is difficult to control. Authoritarian rulers used bureaucracies to pursue their objectives and in doing so created complex institutional structures that were not necessarily brought to heel once elections occurred and new governments were in place.

These institutions might resist change because elected politicians to some extent represent status quo forces (Haggard and Kaufman 1995); because of information asymmetry between elected officials and voters or between bureaucrats and elected officials; or because of cronyism between the bureaucracy and entrenched economic and political forces. Accounting for what happens after a democratic transition requires considering not only the representation of democratic government but also its responsiveness to citizens (O'Donnell 1994).

As a result, the transition to democracy also involves a complex struggle over the state apparatus itself, a struggle involving voters, politicians, bureaucrats, and interests tied to the bureaucratic apparatus. This book studies and explains this process, considering the different ways that politicians try to restructure the state. If politicians simply make the bureaucracy responsive to politicians, they are replaying the original problem; if they make the government more open and accountable to different societal forces, they reduce their own power. Under what conditions will new governments seek to increase bureaucratic accountability?

In the case of Korea, the consolidation literature would presumably attribute the changes to democratic consolidation, whereas the party literature might emphasize a maturation of Korea's party system. But these analyses are insufficient. Neither can explain exactly how Korea achieved greater democratic responsiveness or who benefited or suffered from the process. Such an explanation requires understanding the balance of power and interests of the various actors in government as well as the processes of governance. What changed in Korea were the rules of the game—that is, the administrative laws governing the formulation and implementation of policy.

The Political Origins of Administrative Procedural Reform

Elected officials, even with the aid of political appointees, cannot oversee all of a modern, complex government. Successful management of government requires delegation of some aspects of authority. Yet while delegation can resolve many management problems—for example, allowing the government to broaden its range of activities—it also carries certain inherent risks, most notably the potential for agency slippage. Agency slippage arises when an underling (agent) to whom an elected or appointed official (principal) delegates responsibility has an agenda that conflicts with that of the principal. Not surprisingly, principals want their agents to carry out their wishes rather than pursuing alternative agendas. To mitigate this risk, those delegating authority need tools to prevent their underlings from shirking—that is, failing to do what they are told or what is expected of them.

Given the nature of delegation and its potential problems in democratic governments, a variety of means exist through which principals can seek to control their agents (Alchian and Demsetz 1972; Fama 1980; Kiewiet and McCubbins 1991; Thies 2001). Such means include but are not necessarily limited to (1) choosing loyal agents who share the principal's preferences, (2) writing complete contracts that address all contingencies in the relationship between the principals and their agents, (3) requiring that agents submit proposed actions to the principal for approval, and (4) constraining an agent's ability to act independently (Thies 2001). Although each of these mechanisms appears effective in theory, the first two are often impractical, and the third requires a great deal of the principal's time and effort. The fourth option arguably offers the most cost-effective solution to many potential problems of delegation, and this book focuses on several instances in which new democracies in East Asia have employed this control mechanism, both assessing the effects of pursuing this strategy and exploring the implications of procedural constraints for democratic responsiveness.

Ex Post versus *Ex Ante* Democracy

Democracy can imply that citizens hold leaders accountable after the fact—that is, *ex post*. This is a typical definition of representative democracy. Alternatively or additionally, democracy can entail *ex ante* influence over the policies politicians pursue. In other words, *ex post* democracy implies that leaders choose policies and voters then retain the leaders if the results are pleasing and vote the leaders out of office if the results are not. But citizens have no say over the policies themselves. *Ex ante* democracy implies that citizens can raise or lower the likelihood that politicians will implement particular policies. In this way, *ex post* democratic responsiveness is indirect, arising from politicians' fear of losing power if they deviate too far from citizens' preferences. Any such fears, in turn, depend on citizens' capacity to recognize such deviations, which is not always a simple task. For example, as Schmitter and Karl (1991, 78) summarize, "However central to democracy, elections occur intermittently and only allow citizens to choose between the highly aggregated alternatives offered by political parties."[2] Popkin (2007, 74) observes that *ex ante* checks "would gain the additional benefits of 'insider trading.' People who are privy to what is happening inside parliament can hold politicians accountable for what happens during deliberation, while all others can only pass judgment on the policies after the fact, holding politicians accountable for the final legislation without knowing the alternatives."

In this book, I am primarily interested in what is called notice and comment rule making in the United States. Section 553 of the APA, plus judicial review provisions and subsequent amendments, is the key part of the U.S. law that deals with the policy-making process in federal departments and independent agencies. It concentrates on the making of rules with the force of law, and it requires public notice, a comments process, and a statement of reason accompanying the issuance of the final rule. Judicial review focuses on the agency's conformity with procedural requirements and the consistency of the rule with the underlying substantive statute. The rest of the statute deals with adjudications and formal rule making (a more courtlike process that is quite uncommon). The comparative work focusing on rule making is understudied, but important scholarly research has examined the implications of the absence of procedural constraints on rule making (Bignami 1999; Rose-Ackerman 1995, 2005).

Since the mid-1990s, many new democracies have enacted APAs. As is the case with the U.S. APA, these administrative laws require executive branch agencies to follow specific procedures when writing regulations across all policy areas. When a president or an executive agency wants to change the direction of policy in any area of government, an APA prevents such action simply by decree. Instead, executive agencies must jump through a variety of hoops designed to slow them down, allow the public to see exactly what they are up to, and even invite interested observers to intervene in the process.

For example, APAs in new democracies often require that agencies notify the public, incorporate public comments, and hold public hearings during the policy-making process. APAs empower both individual citizens and organized interest groups to voice their opinions about virtually every government decision. These procedural reforms enfranchise new groups of people and thus increase monitoring, predictability, and control of agency decisions. Enhancing the accountability of government to the people is arguably an important aspect of democratic governance.[3] Henceforth, when I use the term *APA*, I am referring to notice and comment procedures for rule making and judicial review provisions.

If democracy lies on a hypothetical continuum from *ex ante* to *ex post*, APAs offer a means of moving along the continuum toward *ex ante* checks on politicians' activities. In other words, APAs shift the distribution of power and information. In pure *ex post* democracy, citizens can vote yes or no on a policy package only after the fact. *Ex ante* democracy affords citizens the capacity to influence what the package will contain. APAs enhance responsiveness by granting citizens *ex ante* checks on politicians' activities without requiring people to wait for the next election to validate or invalidate policies that have already been implemented.

Generalizing from the U.S. Case

Scholars of delegation have concentrated on the relationship between politicians—usually legislators—and bureaucrats, almost exclusively based on the single case of the United States (Bawn 1995, 1997; Calvert, McCubbins, and Weingast 1989; Epstein and O'Halloran 1999; Lupia and McCubbins 1998; McCubbins, Noll, and Weingast 1987, 1989; McCubbins and Schwartz 1984; McNollgast 1999; Weingast and Moran 1983). These authors generally assume that the interests of the chief executive and the administrative bureaucracy are identical. But this assumption does not necessarily apply in new democracies or across a more general set of countries. More recently, scholars have begun to study delegation beyond the United States (Huber and Shipan 2002; Katz and Mair 1995; Kitschelt and Wilkinson 2006; Moe and Caldwell 1994; Strøm, Müller, and Bergman 2003). Moreover, much of the earlier literature has nominally focused on the control issues that arose as a consequence of the U.S. Congress's delegation to the bureaucracy. However, the logic of interbranch delegation should apply to delegation by the head of the executive branch as well. Indeed, presidents' ability to control the agencies and bureaus nominally under their authority is important for effective democratic governance.

Yet while an APA has been in place in the United States for more than 50 years, not all countries—or even all democracies—have such laws.[4] Popularly elected presidents of South Korea (1994 and 1997) and Taiwan (1999) supported APAs: Why would they do so when APAs are designed to restrict their ability to freely rule the executive branch? Indeed, why did President Kim Young Sam support the same law that appears to have thwarted his administration's Youngwol Dam project? Administrative reform limits the power of the executive. Legislatures might want APAs to enhance control of the executive branch, but it is not clear why presidents would support such measures. Why not just appoint like-minded individuals as heads of agencies and fire them if they do not behave as expected? The problem is that presidents do not always have the constitutional authority or organizational capacity to freely appoint and dismiss.

Resisting or Facilitating Change: Locating APAs within a Broader Framework

Politicians support procedures that increase the power of their supporters and decrease that of their opponents. How best to accomplish this goal depends on both their policy goals and their time horizons. Politicians' policy goals may entail reversing the policies of prior administrations, implementing a new policy course, or preserving existing policies beyond a particular executive's tenure in office. Politicians' time horizons—that is, how long they expect to retain power—can also influence the types of procedures they will support. All else being equal, those with short time horizons are likely to prioritize the sustainability of their policies beyond their tenures in office; those with longer horizons are likely to emphasize the ability to implement policies. Depending on the interaction of these two factors, politicians may prefer a highly responsive bureaucracy capable of reacting quickly to directives or a bureaucracy that resists influence by external actors, including other politicians, citizens, or interest groups. Under what conditions will politicians prefer one or the other outcome? Politicians are likely to favor status-quo-oriented policies—including a relatively insular bureaucracy—in a system of separated powers when, for example, both the president and legislative majority expect to lose the next election. Conversely, they are likely to prefer a more open and responsive bureaucracy when they face intrabranch conflict between the executive and a recalcitrant bureaucracy (see chapter 2).

Politicians view the bureaucracy as an instrument of political power. Those who expect their party to remain in power for a long time will want a strong bureaucracy to push through their programs. Those who expect another party to take power will want a bureaucracy that cannot later be turned against them. So politicians expecting political transitions may sacrifice some short-term power in exchange for insurance that their successors cannot change policies without following time-consuming, public procedures.

Numerous countries around the world have passed APAs as a means of influencing bureaucratic behavior. In this book, I argue that reform-oriented presidents use APAs to force recalcitrant bureaucracies to change policy directions. Further, it follows that entrenched, status-quo-oriented leaders will oppose APAs. Evidence from several East Asian cases, including Korea, Taiwan, and the Philippines, supports this prediction (Baum 2007a). Korea and Taiwan passed their APAs during the tenures of reform-minded presidents (Kim Young Sam and Lee Teng-Hui, respectively) who wanted to change their nations' status quo policies but confronted bureaucracies that resisted reform efforts.

APAs weaken leaders' ability to rule arbitrarily yet may also strengthen new leaders' ability to change policy. In other words, an APA can be an imperfect but best available tool for solving intrabranch delegation problems. Sometimes, as in the Youngwal Dam project, such rules inhibit the president's capacity to implement his policies. Yet such limitations may be an acceptable cost for reining in a recalcitrant bureaucracy. APAs are born of political struggle. Presidents enact APAs to enhance their power vis-à-vis political adversaries, a process that requires enhancing the government's responsiveness to the people and renders governance more predictable, accountable, and transparent. These three factors, in turn, are widely considered to be cornerstones of democracy (Organisation for Economic Co-Operation and Development 2005; Przeworski, Stokes, and Manin 1999). Consequently, while APAs are not necessarily aimed first and foremost at enhancing democratic responsiveness, their enactment may nonetheless do so. Restated in the language of economics, enhanced democratic responsiveness may be a positive externality of APA passage.

Increasing State Accountability through an APA

Procedural openness refers to the structures and guidelines that executive agencies must follow that open the administrative decision-making process to public scrutiny and participation.[5] Most important, codified procedures affect the relationship of individual citizens and organized groups—including those not aligned with the ruling party—to the policy process. In general, APAs establish procedural hurdles that all executive agencies must overcome to implement policy across all regulatory policy areas. At a minimum, an APA requires executive agencies to provide access and information to the public. In this sense, these measures increase the difficulty of changing the policy status quo (Noll 1976, 267; McCubbins, Noll, and Weingast 1987). They do so by requiring agencies to hold public hearings, notify the public of their activities, allow interest groups to comment on all proposed rules, and respond to all relevant interests, not just those favored by the president and his appointees. These procedures hold agencies accountable for how they make their decisions.[6] The key features of rules are that they originate in agencies and articulate law and policy limited by authorizing legislation (Kerwin 1999, 6).

To date, Korea and Taiwan have passed APAs, while the Philippines has not, thereby allowing me to investigate the applicability of my theory in the absence of an APA. More generally, the East Asian cases, with their varying institutional features, are important because the existing theory of APA passage rests solely on the U.S. case. Consistent with this rationale, table 1.1 shows the variation among APAs in the United States, Korea, and Taiwan.

The key elements of rule making are information, participation, and accountability. These elements mean very specific things and, as table 1.1 shows, the APAs of these three countries share some features yet are unique in other areas.[7]

Information

The most basic information requirement is advance public notice of all proposed rules. All three countries share this feature. Taiwan's APA also requires that agencies investigate administrative action appeals and notify all relevant parties about decisions. A freedom of information provision is another major feature of Taiwan's APA, requiring that most agencies disclose information to the public upon request.

Korea's APA also incorporates this principle via the 1996 Law on the

TABLE 1.1. Cross-National Variation in Administrative Procedure Acts

Requirement Category	United States (1946)	Korea (1994–97)[a]	Taiwan (1999)
Information	• Public notice of proposed rules	• Public notice of proposed rules • Consult all relevant ministries • Collect opinions of local government, private interests, and research institutes • Regulatory impact analysis	• Public notice of proposed rules, agency reorganization, hearing • Public access to agency information • Record and notify parties of decision justifications regarding appeals
Participation	• Fixed public comment period for rules • Informal hearing • Tight deadlines or numeric limits for comment period • Formal rule making; parties may present evidence and cross-examine witnesses at trial-type proceedings; record • Publish final rule in *Federal Register* • Published rules must state concise and general statement of basis and purpose	• Fixed public comment period for rules • Informal public hearing • Tight deadlines or numeric limits for comment period, sunset law for regulations	• Tight deadlines or numeric limits • Formal adjudication; parties present evidence, cross-examine witnesses at hearing; record • Public comment period determined by individual ministry
Accountability	• Establishes broad standing, entitling any party "adversely affected or aggrieved by any agency action" to seek judicial review • Reviewing court can intervene only if agency has committed lunacy	• Centralizes final confirmation and inspection of rules to oversight ministry and Regulatory Review Committee	• Leaves final confirmation of rules to individual ministry • Entitles any party whose "rights or legal interests are infringed upon through an unlawful administrative act by a central or local government agency" to "initiate an administrative action . . . in the high administrative court"; delegates review of administrative actions to courts[b]

Source: U.S. Congress 1946; Office of the Prime Minister, Republic of Korea, June 1999; Administrative Litigation Act of Taiwan 1998; Administrative Procedure Act of Taiwan 1999.

[a]The 1994 Korean APA was amended in 1997.

[b]The 1998 Administrative Litigation Act (ALA) authorizes judicial review of administrative actions. According to former legislator John K. C. Huang, the "ALA follows the German Administrative Court Act and is not intended to include TAPA or to be a part thereof from the very beginning" (e-mail exchange with author, March 12, 2001).

Disclosure of Information Held by Public Authorities. Yet Korea's measure focuses more on information that agencies must collect or consider when writing rules. For example, an agency writing a rule must consult with all agencies that the rule could affect. Moreover, agencies must gather opinions from local governments and private interests and conduct a regulatory impact analysis (e.g., cost-benefit assessment) prior to publishing regulations.

Participation

Like the U.S. APA, the Korean and Taiwanese APAs require that agencies solicit "written comments" and allow all interested parties to communicate their views.[8] Taiwan's APA allows formal adjudication, whereby parties have the right to present evidence and cross-examine witnesses at an oral hearing. In contrast, the U.S. APA requires that agencies allow written comments but does not mandate participation in any other form. Still, the U.S. APA allows for forms of rule making other than the informal notice and comment provisions:

> Specifically, if Congress indicated that rule-making was to be conducted "on the record," the procedures that normally apply in adjudication would come into force. In addition, when this type of rule-making is invoked, the standard of review shifts from the permissive "arbitrary and capricious" standard to a considerably more demanding requirement that agencies demonstrate "substantial evidence" for the decisions embodied in the rule. (Kerwin 1999, 57)

While Kerwin's claims may have been true at the time of passage, it is not obvious that in practice, the "arbitrary and capricious" standard is less demanding than the "substantial evidence" standard.[9] Korea's APA requires only informal public hearings (i.e., "legislative hearings") through which agencies collect views from interested parties prior to drafting regulations.

Accountability

Judicial review is the primary mechanism for accountability in the U.S. APA. While the APA establishes a broad definition of standing, entitling any party "adversely affected or aggrieved by any agency action" (U.S. Congress 1946) to seek judicial review, agencies' rule-making decisions can in principle be judged by either substantive or procedural standards. In practice, however, agencies have little difficulty meeting the minimal standards. Nonetheless, since the late 1960s, developments in U.S. administrative law have placed a high burden of justification on agencies. As a result, book-length reports citing documentary evidence typically accompany proposed rules.

According to the Korean APA, the Regulatory Reform Committee, a twenty-member group under presidential authority with the prime minister and a civilian serving as cochairs, is the main vehicle for confirming, monitoring, and evaluating agency rules.[10] The committee reviews all regulations after the various ministries have resolved their differences.

Taiwan's APA designates each ministry to be responsible for confirming, monitoring, and evaluating its rules. There is no centralized monitoring agency. In addition, the 1994 amendments to the Administrative Litigation Law established an administrative court. Taiwan's 1998 Administrative Litigation Act allows judicial review of administrative actions.

Benefits of APAs

What do elected officials gain from adopting these particular procedural requirements? As McCubbins, Noll, and Weingast (1987, 258–59) explain, these requirements help elected officials govern information collection and dissemination by agencies. The political implications are critical for at least five reasons. First, since agencies must announce their intention to examine a policy issue prior to a new decision, they are less able to conceal either information or their activities.

Second, through the notice and comment requirement, agencies must take into account the relevant political interests before making a new decision. In so doing, agencies consider political costs and benefits associated with the range of actions. However, the weight of an interest group's participation will depend on its level of organization. Dispersed groups that do not or cannot participate are less likely to influence or veto agencies' decisions.

Third, since the process is public, agencies and their favorite constituencies are less likely to make backroom decisions that the legislature or the president do not support. Fourth, the sequential nature and slowing down of the decision-making process reduce any strategic advantage agencies might otherwise maintain. Each step of the process gives principals (presidents, their appointees, and legislators) multiple opportunities to respond if an agency deviates from policy preferences.

Finally, the extent of participation by interest groups in the administrative process serves as a gauge of political interest and controversiality (Noll 1971). In essence, arduous procedural requirements generate the most complete information about the most controversial issues. Furthermore, they ensure "warning about the likely decision that, in the absence of political intervention, the agency is most likely to make" (McCubbins, Noll, and Weingast 1987, 259; but see Hamilton and Schroeder 1994).

In short, arcane as they may appear, administrative procedures can determine the winners and losers in a political struggle by stacking the deck in favor of one or another interest. Reform of these procedures through APAs or similar laws represents a shuffling of this deck, thereby changing who is more likely to win and who is more likely to lose as a consequence of governmental policy. To the extent that the new winners are typical citizens and their representatives while the new losers tend to be entrenched interests representing the prior authoritarian regime, APAs can be important tools for enhancing democratic representation.

Outline of Book

In selecting my cases, I include countries with presidential systems that recently transitioned to democracy. My evidence comes from detailed case studies of three presidential democracies in East Asia (Korea, Taiwan, and the Philippines). These countries vary along a variety of pertinent dimensions, such as the presence and extent of intraexecutive branch conflict over policy between chief executives and bureaucrats as well as the executive's authority to hire and fire career bureaucrats. These variations are particularly noteworthy because both Korea and Taiwan have APAs, while the Philippines does not. I thus test both existing theories of APA passage and my alternative theory in cases other than the United States.

For each country, I examine multiple administrations both before and after APA passage. My units of analysis are presidential administrations rather than countries, thereby ensuring that my dependent variable varies not only across countries but also over time. In addition, to test my theory against existing theories, I required data regarding the policy preferences of both politicians and bureaucrats, the nature of the most significant regulatory issues, status quo policies, and expectations about future elections. I collected these data for a subset of relatively new democracies. While enhancing procedural openness is not necessarily the intrinsic motivation for enacting administrative procedure acts, such laws can contribute to democratic responsiveness. For this reason, it is important to understand the political determinants of procedural openness in the contexts of relatively new democracies. I thus devote chapters to each of the three countries, comparing the history of procedural reforms to the predictions of my theory. I devote an additional chapter to the sunset law in Korea, the only one of the three countries that has passed such a measure.

There is no reason to believe that the key political institutional variables that make the possibility of enacting APAs in East Asia more or less likely are unique to Korea, Taiwan, and the Philippines. Many nations, particularly presidential democracies, have APAs—including the United States, Argentina, Chile, and Mexico; all U.S. states also have APAs (see de Figueiredo and Vanden Bergh 2004). My key independent variables—both structural (e.g., presidential democracies) and contextual (e.g., existence or absence of intraexecutive conflict)—thus are not unique to East Asia. At the same time, however, this focus allows me to control for any number of potentially confounding factors across regions and institutional forms, including but not limited to the timing of democratic transition.

In chapter 2, I delineate my theory on when politicians in general and presidents in particular will choose to adopt an APA. I also discuss my research design and case selection. The "lock-in" hypothesis (McNollgast 1999) is one frequently cited explanation for why politicians adopt APAs. It holds that the U.S. APA passed in 1946 because the majority party in the legislature (Democrats) wanted to lock in the policies of the New Deal in the face of an expected Republican anti–New Deal political tide in the late 1940s. Under such circumstances, therefore, Democrats supported an APA to constrain any future Republican president. Whether or not this argument accounts for the U.S. APA, the key question remains whether the theory applies to other cases. There is no reason to presume that the logic of interbranch conflict delegation would not also apply to intrabranch delegation. After all, presidents' ability to control their agents seems equally important to the functioning of a democratic government. In fact, the lock-in hypothesis cannot explain why APAs passed in Korea and Taiwan. Instead, my case studies illustrate that presidents can also use APAs to overcome current control problems.

My "reining-in" theory of administrative procedural reform holds that presidents support APAs to help control their executive branches. This idea of course raises the question of when intrabranch control is likely to pose a significant problem. In fact, the potential for such problems arises because some presidents are constitutionally prohibited from appointing ministers or bureaucrats. Moreover, they must sometimes share political power with coalition partners who do not share all their preferences. The less autonomous a president (in either sense), the greater the risk of agency slippage and the more interested she will be in instituting procedural controls to rein in her agents. Specifically, presidents who must compromise in their cabinet or bureaucratic appointments will support formal procedures as a means of pursuing their policy agendas in the current administration (Baum 2007a). Three circumstances give rise to this condition:

1. when a constitutional requirement for legislative approval constrains the president's ability to appoint cabinet ministers and the legislature has different preferences than the president;
2. when the support coalition that the president must accommodate is internally divided because it is either a coalition with multiple parties or a factionalized ruling party; or
3. when, upon entering office, the president is confronted by bureaucrats who cannot be replaced and whose preferences differ from those of the president.

Chapter 3 presents an in-depth case study of Korea's episodes of APA passage during three periods: the Roh Tae Woo administration (1987–92), the first part of Kim Young Sam's administration (1993–94, when the APA was passed), and the later part of Kim's administration (1995–97, when the law was amended). A careful examination of the executive decision-making process shows the importance of an autonomous civil service for both the timing and substance of Kim's decision to initiate and eventually sign the various acts governing administrative regulations.

In 1993, President Kim took over from a military government that had stacked the bureaucracy with its loyalists. Unlike his predecessor, Kim wanted to change Korea's economic policies. He wanted to increase the government's growth orientation and deregulate the economy to raise the level of domestic market competition. This policy shift threatened the existing political equilibrium among the key players responsible for Korea's successful economic development under military rule. Since these key players' political success depended on maintaining status quo economic policies, Kim confronted a hostile bureaucracy with civil service protection—that is, hostile bureaucrats whom he could not fire. Administrative procedures such as the notice and comment process would limit bureaucrats' ability to undermine Kim's reforms, so he supported an APA. As evidence, I employ archival data, third-party sources, and interviews with presidential advisers, senior career bureaucrats, and politicians gathered and conducted during field research in Korea.

Chapter 4 offers a second case study: Taiwan under the Lee Teng-Hui administrations (1988–96 and 1997–99). Unlike Korea, where the reformist Kim confronted a bureaucracy with conflicting preferences, Lee dominated Taiwan's civil service. However, Lee's control of his party deteriorated as factional disputes increased over time, and he eventually determined that the political survival of the Kuomintang (KMT) depended on major reforms. At this stage, the status-quo-oriented bureaucracy, hitherto a key source of support for Lee and his primary constituencies, became an impediment. Consequently, the immediate benefits of resolving current delegation problems—that is, preserving the KMT's political dominance—outweighed the potential long-term cost of tying his successor's hands.

Specifically, a shift in voter preferences electorally strengthened the KMT's reform wing, creating a new KMT median legislator. The KMT reformers wanted to change the party's image from one of entrenched corruption and of favoritism toward wealthy private interests to one of a "clean government" party. To do so, the party had to rein in the same bureaucracy that had long served as the cornerstone of its power. Under the status quo, bureaucrats' regulatory decisions consistently favored corrupt private interests. This bias both tarnished the party's image with a large segment of the electorate and produced policy outcomes that alienated the nation's fastest-growing electoral demographic: younger voters. This development provided reformers within the KMT with an incentive to manage current delegation to the bureaucracy with strict procedural requirements.

Presidents sometimes face delegation problems within the executive branch that lead to support for APAs, and APAs can move a country from institutional democracy toward responsive democracy. But APAs offer only an imperfect solution, because presidents presumably would prefer to replace disloyal agents with loyal ones. In the Philippines, President Corazon Aquino was able to use the latter strategy, setting her country apart from Korea and Taiwan. Chapter 5 examines the case of the Philippines, which corresponds closely to the typical stylized picture of the executive as a unified hierarchy. Whereas the Korean and Taiwanese presidents could not rely on unconstrained appointment and dismissal powers to control their agents, the Philippine president could.

In 1986, Aquino's democratic administration replaced the authoritarian regime of Ferdinand Marcos. To control the bureaucracy she inherited, Aquino ordered a national purge of all elected and appointed officials and employees and created additional undersecretary positions for her loyalists. Aquino also ordered three major cabinet reshufflings to resolve conflicts with different factions of her coalition. Given her success in resolving her delegation problems through unilateral action, Aquino had no need for a less efficient solution, such as an APA.

Chapters 6 and 7 test two potential implications of my theory, focusing on the supply and demand of policy, respectively. On the supply side, I compare the mix of regulatory policies prior to and following APA enactment to see whether regulations preferred by the beneficiaries of an APA are more likely to emerge and endure following APA passage and whether those preferred by interests associated with the prior regime fare better prior to APA passage. On the demand side, I focus on the APA's effects on citizens. If APAs empower average citizens, this development holds implications for their attitudes toward their democracy and its institutions. In particular, factors that enhance governmental responsiveness to average citizens should enhance public confidence in a given country's democratic institutions in general and (in this instance) in the civil service in particular.

The Korean APA (KAPA) contains major provisions that are clearly inconsistent with the lock-in hypothesis. Most notably, the KAPA contains a sunset provision, according to which all policies and regulations covered under KAPA automatically expire after five years unless they are explicitly renewed. This provision clearly facilitates rather than inhibits changes in policy. This sunset provision prevented professionalized bureaucrats from returning to the regulatory policies that prevailed prior to Kim's administration.

Sunset provisions are a common component of administrative reform outside the Korean case, and they clearly do not lock in a status quo but rather do precisely the opposite. Why would a president support a reform proposal that limits the life of his administration's regulatory rules? In chapter 6, I develop a spatial model to investigate the motivations for and implications of the sunset rule. The model demonstrates how a president can use administrative reform to accelerate policy change rather than to lock in a current policy regime.

To test the model's predictions, I gathered data on the persistence or expiration of all regulations from all ministries in Korea between 1998 and 2005. With this data, I investigate the correlates of regulatory sunset at the intraministerial level. In particular, I investigate whether within each ministry, regulations that do not benefit the president's support coalition are, as the model predicts, more likely to expire than are regulations that benefit the president's support coalition.

If an APA has the intended effect(s), we would expect to see some change in the level of public confidence in the civil service before and after passage. Consequently, the level of public confidence in the civil service is an important indicator of the extent to which an APA has opened up the bureaucracy. Moreover, confidence in the civil service is closely related to faith in a given nation's democracy, suggesting that to the extent that they enhance public confidence in the civil service, APAs may also strengthen public confidence in democracy.

To investigate these implications, chapter 7 presents the results of multiple regression analyses of pre- and post-KAPA changes in public confidence in Korea's democracy in general and its civil service in particular. If my argument is correct, after controlling for a variety of potential alternative causal factors, public trust in the country's democratic institutions—especially the civil service—should be enhanced. I then replicate key aspects of these tests against data on public attitudes toward the civil service in Taiwan and the Philippines.

My primary data are derived from the 1990, 1994, and 2001 waves of the World Values Survey (WVS), the 1996 and 2001 waves of the Korea Barometer Surveys (KBS), and the 2001 and 2002 waves of the East Asia Barometer (EAB). These surveys allow a series of pre- and post-APA comparisons. While the data do not allow a direct test of the effects of APA passage on either procedural transparency or the public's response to enhanced transparency, they reveal a variety of patterns that are precisely what one would anticipate if APAs produced just the sorts of transparency- and participation-enhancing effects that I argue follow from their passage. In other words, while the available data are inadequate to measure directly the effects of APA passage in Korea and Taiwan and nonpassage in the Philippines, the data offer suggestive evidence of a positive relationship between administrative procedural reform and public attitudes toward democratic institutions.

Finally, in chapter 8, I integrate the predictions from the reining-in theory and case evidence to produce a more complete picture of administrative procedural reform in presidential systems. I also discuss my research's implications for how and under what circumstances we should expect to see changes in administrative procedural openness among new democracies. Though not all democracies have implemented administrative procedural reform, and though APAs do not appear to be a necessary feature of democracy, my evidence suggests that enactment of APAs in new democracies appears to enhance democratic responsiveness.

2 | The Logic of Intrabranch Delegation

Over the past two decades, many of the world's fledgling democracies have joined long-standing democracies in implementing administrative procedure laws. Administrative procedural openness is important for democratic consolidation because it reduces arbitrariness and increases predictability in government. It also reduces corruption by increasing bureaucratic transparency and accountability to citizens and elected officials. Administrative procedural reform may not be necessary for responsive democracy but it is nevertheless an important contributing factor. Yet for politicians, especially in the executive branch, achieving these goals comes with a price: it constrains their political power. Thus arises this book's central question: Why would self-interested politicians voluntarily limit their own power?

The literature on delegation in democracies that is not centered on the United States is small, but growing (Baum 2002, 2005, 2007a, 2007b; Eaton 2003; Huber 1998; Huber and Lupia 2001; Moe and Caldwell 1994; Ramseyer and Rosenbluth 1993; Thies 2001). The literature focused on the United States assumes that the executive is unified and hence discounts the possibility of agency problems within the executive branch (Epstein and O'Halloran 1999; Ferejohn and Shipan 1990; Huber and Shipan 2002; an exception is Moe 1985b).[1] Yet not all presidential democracies have unified executives. And even where they do, presidential systems were explicitly designed to limit executive power. While scholars of public administration and the American presidency have long recognized executive delegation problems, they too have focused almost exclusively on the U.S. case (Neustadt 1990; Niskanen 1971; Weber 1968; Wilson

1989). My theory therefore complements both literatures by investigating the problem of executive delegation in recently democratized countries.[2]

Given the complexities of modern government, delegation is inevitable for purposes of division of labor and access to specialized expertise (Kiewiet and McCubbins 1991). Yet when elected politicians delegate policy-making authority to unelected bureaucrats, the possibility arises that bureaucrats will resist the politicians' policy preferences—what is known as agency slippage (Alchian and Demsetz 1972; McCubbins, Noll, and Weingast 1987, 1989).

If, in turn, government is to be truly representative, elected officials must be able to control policy outcomes. Otherwise, a critical aspect of representative democracy is called into question. Because voters in democracies hold elected politicians rather than bureaucrats accountable for policy outcomes, it follows that politicians will have an incentive to ensure that bureaucrats—the implementers of public policy—are responsive to elected officials' policy preferences. An administrative procedure act (APA) is one means of doing so.

Yet an apparent paradox is embedded in the passage of all APAs, particularly in countries with separately elected chief executives. Because administrative reform limits the power of the executive branch, it is clear why the legislature would want an APA in a separation-of-powers system. But absent a credible threat of a veto override, it is not clear why presidents would accept laws designed to restrict their ability to act freely. Under what circumstances will presidents support such laws? To answer this question, I develop a theory of the political determinants of administrative procedural reform.

Identifying the political considerations that motivate politicians to pursue procedural openness can provide insight into the process of making political institutions in new democracies responsive to citizens and in so doing may help explain why so many new democracies have chosen to pursue administrative reform. The more intrabranch conflict presidents face while in office, the more likely they will support an APA. Thus, while previous theories (e.g., McNollgast 1999) view APAs as aimed at protecting current policies favored by legislators by tying the hands of future administrations, presidents can also use APAs to overcome current control problems. Moreover, the more incomplete the president's control over her appointees, the more likely she is to support an APA (Baum 2007a).

The next section discusses several alternative explanations for APA passage as well as whether and when democratically elected presidents will need or want APAs. I then consider why APAs can prove useful to an executive bent on gaining control of an unruly and autonomous bureaucracy. In the course of this discussion, I derive several implications from the theory, which I test in subsequent chapters. I also discuss my research design and my selection of Korea, Taiwan, and the Philippines as case studies.

Explanations for APA Passage

Numerous potentially sufficient conditions could give rise to passage of an APA, among them response to corruption scandals and imitating a seemingly successful foreign example. APAs may even be a logical step in the maturation of a democratic polity. However, I seek not to identify every possible sufficient condition for APA passage but rather to highlight several necessary conditions. Nevertheless, I also assess several potentially sufficient conditions.

Despite its clear advantages for enhancing democratic responsiveness, APA passage is by no means inevitable and is probably not a necessary feature of a democracy. In the United States, for example, the APA passed in 1946, just before the country's 170th birthday. Yet the United States was certainly a democracy prior to 1946. Similarly, many of Europe's oldest democracies lack APAs. The U.S. APA passed following a massive post–New Deal expansion of the federal government; such was not the case for Korea and Taiwan. On the contrary, both countries' APAs passed during deregulation and downsizing of the civil service (Painter 2004, 375). Moreover, the many parliamentary systems that lack APAs—for example, Great Britain, Japan (pre-2005), and Germany—are every bit as complex as the American regulatory state.[3]

Democratization might create a public demand for administrative procedural reform as a consequence of corruption scandals. Many new democracies certainly have significant levels of corruption (Treisman 2000). In these countries, politicians might be pushed toward reform. But this condition by itself does not explain why politicians adopt APAs in some new democracies and not others. For example, the Philippines redemocratized at about the same time that Korea and Taiwan first became democratic, yet the Philippines has not passed an APA.

APAs could simply result from new democracies imitating older, successful democracies. For example, drafters of the Korean and Taiwanese APAs analyzed various administrative procedural laws around the world (Baum 2002). However, both countries had been examining other APAs for many years prior to passing their APAs. While models may well play an important role in providing drafters and politicians with a menu of options from which to choose specific administrative requirements, this explanation does not account for either the motivation of politicians or the timing of APA passage.

The Logic of Intrabranch Delegation

Presidents sometimes have good reasons for supporting APAs, yet it is not clear whether a president will support such a law to help herself govern or to ensure that her policies outlive her administration. Under what conditions do politicians in transitioning democracies adopt procedures that open up the bureaucracy? The type of procedure chosen primarily depends on politicians' goals and time horizons. In the former case, politicians may support administrative procedures for three possible reasons: (1) to reverse policies and policy outcomes put in place previously by politicians with conflicting interests (which I term *pry bars*); (2) to entrench new policies and outcomes, in which case politicians will prioritize speed and flexibility; or (3) to install a back door—that is, to ensure, perhaps by empowering favored interest groups, that these politicians (directly or indirectly) retain the ability to influence government decision making after they leave office.

If political actors' preferences change over time, so too will the nature of their bargain regarding administrative procedures. Time horizons influence politicians' preferences regarding the three potential APA goals. Four potential time horizons exist. First, a politician may be uncertain about the likely outcome of future elections and hence his party's likelihood of retaining power. In this case, the time horizon is unclear. Second, a politician may anticipate retaining power only for the short term (i.e., very temporarily). Third, a politician may anticipate a long-term decline of her party or eventual loss of power (e.g., as a consequence of term limits). Finally, a politician may anticipate the long-term ascendancy or dominance of his party. In the first three cases, politicians will prefer to install a wide-open back door—that is, to put in place a highly responsive bureaucracy (controllable, permeable, or capable of acting quickly). In the final case, however, politicians will prefer to close any potential back doors—that is, to maximize their control over the bureaucracy while minimizing the influence of competing power sources.

All of these cases assume that politicians view the bureaucracy as an instrument of their political power. When they expect to be relatively strong for an extended period, they prefer that this instrument be potent. Otherwise, they prefer a weaker instrument that cannot be turned against them by future leaders. In other words, in the final case, politicians have an incentive to sacrifice some potency in exchange for extending the life of their preferred policies beyond their anticipated tenure in power.

According to McNollgast (1999), for example, APAs serve as tools for political control. Indeed, one of the authors' major theoretical contributions is their recognition that APAs can emerge as a result of conflict between the legislative and executive branches. This finding makes particular sense given the de facto three-party system (Republicans, Democrats, and southern Democrats) in the U.S. Congress from 1937 until 1946 (Cox and McCubbins 1993; Poole and Rosenthal 1997; Rohde 1994). Yet in addition to preventing change—that is, preserving the status quo—APAs can be powerful tools for facilitating change.

APAs facilitate change by setting new rules for determining who can participate and control the policy-making process, typically by reducing bureaucratic discretion. If a ruling party, including the president, is satisfied with the status quo, then it has little incentive to support procedures that will open up the policy-making process to the public. Thus, status-quo-oriented ruling-party politicians will resist administrative procedural reform because the new rules for making policy, if enacted, would force them to pay special attention to previously excluded public interest groups (Baum 2007a). Of course, if the ruling party expects to be out of power, then it will have an incentive to pursue procedures aimed at preserving its access to the bureaucracy.

If politicians intend APAs to facilitate changes in policy direction, then we should observe change-oriented reformers but not entrenched status quo-oriented leaders supporting such laws around the world. In fact, the Korea, Taiwan, and Philippines cases appear consistent with this prediction (Baum 2007a). Korea and Taiwan passed APAs during the tenures of reform-minded presidents (Kim Young Sam and Lee Teng-Hui, respectively) who wanted to change their nations' status quo policies but confronted entrenched bureaucracies that resisted these efforts. Indeed, these reformers definitely did not want to preserve the status quo. President Corazon Aquino of the Philippines also wanted to reverse her nation's policy direction. Yet she was able to do so without an APA.

The key to explaining why presidents do or do not support APAs in new democracies appears to be the degree to which they confront various types of conflict within the executive branch. In other words, the lock-in story does not ring true in these cases because the new presidents' policy preferences differed from those of either members of their own coalitions or bureaucrats left over from previous regimes. In Korea and the Philippines, Presidents Kim and Aquino confronted entrenched bureaucracies dominated by loyalists from prior authoritarian regimes. As reformers, Kim and Aquino sought to change their countries' policy directions but faced major barriers to change from bureaucrats who sought to preserve the status quo. And in Taiwan, Lee decided that the political survival of his party depended on administrative reforms designed to keep the status-quo-oriented bureaucracy in check (Baum 2005).[4] Thus, for these presidents, managing current delegation problems was a higher priority than tying their successors' hands.[5]

Of course, a president who can freely appoint and dismiss ministers and bureaucrats has little need for an APA, as in the Philippines. Aquino managed her delegation problem by distributing patronage jobs to her agents. Thus, even though APAs by definition weaken a leader's ability to rule arbitrarily, presidents are likely to favor APAs when constrained by constitutional requirements or coalitional conflict within the executive branch. In other words, if a president cannot control the bureaucracy by hiring loyalists and firing opponents, an APA can be the second-best tool for solving intrabranch delegation problems. Korea and Taiwan enacted APAs in part as a result of this constraint.

The delegation problems I identify highlight an important issue pertaining to the study of East Asian bureaucracies. Many scholars have argued that strong states with autonomous bureaucracies have played a central role in economic development policy in Asia (Amsden 1989; Haggard 1990; Johnson 1982; but see Kang 2002). Yet my findings indicate that some of these "strong" East Asian bureaucracies are not immutable and are in fact being cracked open.[6]

Motivating Assumption

I begin with the rather modest assumption that presidents care about policy outcomes. Therefore, presidents have incentives to control bureaucrats who oppose their policies. Bureaucratic incentives and preferences, however, are a bit more complex. I assume that under authoritarian rule, the president and his bureaucracy typically share common goals and priorities. As long as the status quo policies that sustained the strong relationship between the president, bureaucracy, and the primary interest group(s) with access to the bureaucracy persist, the president faces no significant control problems.

With democratic transition, bureaucrats can no longer rely on the previous rules of the game to guarantee their long-term goals (promotions and side payments from big business). In democracies, multiple principals, including the public and the legislature, have increased access to the policy-making process and hence influence on bureaucrats.

Because administrative procedural reform involves setting rules that determine who can participate and control the policy-making process, often reducing bureaucratic discretion, politicians and bureaucrats have a special interest in it. Bureaucrats might resist administrative procedural reform because the new rules for making policy require the bureaucrats to pay special attention to public interest groups, traditionally excluded from the previous regime. The drawbacks for bureaucrats are that (1) they have a reduced ability to set their ideal policy along any dimension and (2) they have reduced policy discretion and can no longer count on exclusive control over their favored issue areas. As a result, bureaucrats cannot necessarily depend on side payments from their favorite constituents.

Constitutional Restrictions: Appointment and Dismissal Powers

Shugart and Carey (1992) have found that presidential powers vary across different separation-of-powers constitutions. In particular, the president cannot necessarily perfectly control who can be in her cabinet. While most presidential systems do not require legislative approval of appointees, many nations give the assembly some influence over cabinet formation. Divergent preferences within the executive are more likely to arise and persist in such countries.

For example, since the enactment of the 1987 Korean Constitution, only the prime minister is subject to confirmation by the unicameral assembly. The prime minister then appoints the other cabinet ministers. Neither the prime minister nor any other cabinet minister is subject to the ongoing confidence of the national assembly. Therefore, only the president can dismiss cabinet ministers. As Shugart and Carey (1992, 111) point out, "If presidents are forced by the assembly to compromise considerably in the choice of [the prime minister], then they could endure significant agency loss in the composition of 'their' entire cabinet." The confirmation role of the Korean national assembly vis-à-vis the prime minister could represent a significant threat to the president's policy agenda.

In the Philippines, however, cabinet nominations are subject to approval only by the Congressional Commission on Appointments, consisting of the president of the Senate (who presides), twelve senators, and twelve representatives. Commission members are selected according to the proportional representation of parties in each chamber.[7] The president of the Senate casts a vote on appointments only in the case of a tie (Shugart and Carey 1992, 111). As in Korea, if the president's policy preferences differ from those of the dominant forces in the legislature, she may face cabinet ministers with divergent preferences, leading to the first implication of my theory.

> *Implication 1:* The more the president's ability to appoint and dismiss cabinet ministers is constrained by a constitutional requirement for legislative approval and the greater the divergence between presidential and legislative preferences, the more likely the president will be to support administrative procedural constraints.[8]

Presidential Support Coalition and Heterogeneous Preferences

Presidential power can also vary by the size and cohesiveness of a president's political support/coalition base. Variation in a president's support/executive coalition in the legislature affects her ability to control the executive branch. Shugart and Haggard (2001), for example, argue that policymakers in presidential systems must consider both the separation of powers and the potential for separation of purpose. A case of extreme unity of purpose would arise if the president ruled with a fully disciplined partisan legislative majority. Conversely, separation of purpose increases—"and with it the potential for deadlock, instability and balkanization" (2)—if the president represents a minority party and the legislature is ideologically polarized or if the legislative parties are fragmented and poorly disciplined.

Contrary to claims that presidentialism is not conducive to political cooperation and is therefore "perilous" (Linz 1990), Shugart and Haggard (2001) show that very few presidential cases fall under either of these extremes. For my purposes, their approach to policy-making in presidential systems is useful for understanding variations in presidents' cabinet control.

These variations in presidential power have direct implications for presidents' abilities to control the executive branch. Appointment powers are particularly critical for understanding the level of conflict that arises in the executive branch. If the president is constrained in his appointment powers or his party lacks a legislative majority, he might appoint a multiparty coalition cabinet. Doing so would mean a greater likelihood of conflict arising from the cabinet's heterogeneous makeup. Under these situations, presidents are more likely to seek a second-best control mechanism—such as an APA—to check possibly disloyal agents.

Cabinet Formation in Presidential Democracies

In parliamentary systems, cabinets generally are formed through the selection of partisan ministers. Indeed, previous studies have focused primarily on the bargaining conditions that influence parties' decisions about whether to join a government (Laver and Shepsle 1996; Lijphart 1984; Strøm 1990).

In contrast, scholars of cabinet formation in the United States have focused on patterns of ministerial selection (cabinet secretaries selected based on level of education, gender, ethnicity, regional origin, and professional career) rather than on executive-legislative bargaining (Fenno 1959; Polsby 1983). The most compelling reason for this emphasis is the U.S. two-party system, which means that coalition cabinets are practically nonexistent and that appointments instead go to members of the president's party.[9]

In systems where presidents are restricted to one term, appointing cabinet ministers based solely on symbolic representation of electorally important constituencies (as might be the case in the United States; see Cohen 1988) is less important. Only recently have scholars begun to study cabinet formation across different presidential systems. Amorim Neto, for example, argues that understanding cabinet formation in Latin America requires "the analysis of presidential policy-making strategies [implementing policy goals via statute or decree] and the interaction of ministerial selection patterns with executive-legislative bargaining" (1998, 32; see also Amorim Neto 2006). According to Amorim Neto, if the president primarily favors passing statutes, he will prefer to build a partisan cabinet to solidify legislative support. But if he primarily favors issuing decrees, then he will prefer to pack his cabinet with cronies, technocrats, and others who, for example, bring policy expertise into the cabinet (1998, 43). In reality, cabinets in pure presidential systems reflect varying degrees of partisanship. This variation is a function of the potential deals struck by the president and party leaders and the selection criteria for cabinet ministers.

Intra- and Interparty Conflict

When ministers are selected on a partisan basis, the president must share executive powers with coalition partners from other parties, most likely representing different constituencies and policy preferences. On average, we would expect greater conflict between the president's party and other parties sharing the cabinet, who are likely to oppose at least some of the president's preferred policies. When this situation arises, there is a greater possibility that the president's party will have difficulty implementing its policy agenda because it will have less influence over executive agency activities. Therefore, to reduce cabinet ministers' ability to move policy away from the ideal point (Thies 2001), the president has a greater incentive to favor *ex ante* rather than *ex post* controls. *Ex ante* controls, such as extensive administrative procedures, reduce coalition partners' informational advantage (e.g., hidden information or action). For precisely this reason, the partners in a coalition cabinet would also support an APA.

Similarly, factionalized single-party cabinets can also threaten a president's agenda if substantial disagreement arises over policy between the president's faction and other factions within her party and if the opposing factions are large enough effectively to block the president's program within the executive branch. In short, under factionalized single-party cabinets, the president is more likely to face a ministry whose preferences differ from her own, a situation that gives her an incentive to institutionalize her control *ex ante* via administrative procedures.

For example, suppose a president would like to increase domestic competition in a given industry to improve national economic performance. Suppose also that the status quo policies benefit the opposing factions within the president's party, whose primary support constituencies favor the status quo. These opponents of reform may be employing corrupt practices (e.g., by providing below-market credit allocation to their favorite firms) to limit domestic competition. To reduce their ability to block economic policies, the president may seek to make economic decision making more transparent to the public and allow public participation, thereby exposing the antireformers within her party. Hence, administrative procedures can check opponents within the president's own party. The president may also want to break political stalemates within his party or put pressure on his opponents to get his policies enacted, leading to a second implication of the theory.

> *Implication 2:* Presidents prefer more extensive procedural constraints on bureaucrats when the presidential support coalition is either a multiparty coalition or a factionalized ruling party.

Degree of Civil Service Autonomy

Meritocratic recruitment and promotion of civil servants restrain political patronage. At one end of the continuum, the civil service might be highly professionalized with a merit-based recruitment and promotion system, giving presidents less control over the bureaucracy. Japan, Korea, France, and Germany, among other countries, use the hierarchical Mandarin (or "closed-entry") system for bureaucratic recruitment. Recruitment is highly selective, based on a centralized national civil service entrance examination that applies rigorous standards to screening applicants. Performance after recruitment is maintained through clear objectives and criteria for upward mobility and rewards for meritorious long-term service. In Korea, for example, promotion is based on a formula that combines seniority with merit-based criteria. In contrast, the United States, Australia, New Zealand, and others use open recruitment systems that are decentralized, give managers more autonomy and flexibility in hiring, and are increasingly market-driven. The United States, for example, replaced its centralized competitive entrance examinations with profession-specific exams, permitting entry at any point in the hierarchy without age restrictions (World Bank 1997, 92–94).

At the other end of the continuum, the bureaucracy might be highly politicized, with a personalistic, patronage-based system that gives presidents greater control over their agents. Because promotions are politicized, such civil servants worry more about satisfying their superiors or influential politicians. In the Philippines, for example, political appointments run much deeper than in other East and Southeast Asian countries (including Indonesia, Korea, Malaysia, Singapore, Taiwan, and Thailand). Between 1984 and 1988, political appointments in the Philippines spanned five levels, cabinet secretaries to service directors, whereas the other Asian countries had political appointees only at the top two levels (World Bank 1997, 93).

Government posts in Latin America traditionally have been filled by people who promised the largest contribution to (1) the president's personal welfare (usually members of the presidents' families); (2) consolidation of political support for the presidents or their parties; and (3) administrative effectiveness (probably the most technically qualified applicants) (Geddes 1994, 27). Moreover, Amorim Neto (1998, 11) argues that for Latin American presidents, controlling the executive branch's bureaucracy means resolving conflicts of interest with retainers (long-term public servants with no professional qualifications). Retainers are holdovers from previous administrations appointed by former presidents and opposition political parties and thus represent a great challenge to presidents' ability to govern effectively.

If civil servants are protected under the law, they are more likely to resist complying with elected politicians' policy preferences. Civil servants who know that they cannot be fired for their actions face little risk in resisting preferred presidential policies. Therefore, a president who cannot unilaterally fire civil servants needs alternative mechanisms to constrain their behavior. This leads to a third implication of the theory.

> *Implication 3:* Presidents will prefer more extensive procedural constraints when they are confronted by bureaucrats who cannot be replaced and who do not share the presidents' preferences.[10]

Taken together, these three implications suggest a more complete explanation of presidential incentives and the political conditions under which an APA is a viable solution for principal-agent problems. In sum, presidents are more likely to prefer APAs when they are weak. Whether their powers are constrained by constitutional requirements (appointment and dismissal power of the cabinet), coalitional support with conflicting preferences, or bureaucrats who cannot be fired, APAs can mitigate agency slippage by keeping track of bureaucrats' activities.

Administrative Procedural Reform in Three New Democracies

Research Design

The key variables representing the several explanations for APA enactment are most appropriately evaluated through comparative case studies, rather than large-*N* statistical analysis. Large-*N* analysis would require standardization of the content and meaning of various provisions of APAs across either countries or states within countries. Developing such a standardized, categorical dependent variable to capture the degree of strictness of APAs would be extremely difficult because scholars have not yet studied the content of APAs in sufficient detail to accurately identify all potentially relevant dimensions. Absent such contextual knowledge that could be generalized across cases, it is impractical to categorize APAs according to a standardized scale measuring degree of strictness, the key concept under investigation in this book.

It is possible, of course, to study merely the presence or absence of APAs over time by coding each case (country, region, or state) dichotomously (i.e., either an APA exists in country *y* in year *t* or not). Such a specification would, however, sacrifice the rich content of APAs and hence much that is of interest in investigating them. For example, had I only looked for the existence of APAs, I would not have discovered the sunset review provision that is unique to the Korean APA (the subject of chapter 6). According to the Korean APA, existing regulations can only be extended beyond the statutory five-year limit if bureaucrats submit an extension request one year prior to expiration. Unless the status quo regulation is extended, it expires. In addition, agencies must first notify the public and allow for comments prior to submitting such a request to the Regulatory Reform Committee. Without this finding, I could not have distinguished between the lock-in and reining-in hypotheses.

Specific types of procedures, such as the sunset review process, are important because they have different effects on policy outcomes. The sunset review provision played a significant role in Korea for a reformer president who wanted to remove the status quo policy bias. In other words, the sunset procedure forced the bureaucracy repeatedly to revisit existing regulatory policies.

Also, while APAs in Taiwan and Korea include a public notice and comment provision for all regulations, such a provision is absent in the Philippines. If the president wants to change a status quo policy, given that a notice and comment process is in place, the agency will be unable to offer its ideal proposal (unless it mirrors the preferences of key interest groups). Participating enables those groups—especially previously excluded groups—enfranchised by the president through the notice and comment process to influence policy outcomes so that agency proposals will adhere more closely to the preferences of participating groups than would be the case absent the notice and comment procedure.

Moreover, the U.S. APA, 1987 Philippine Administrative Code, and

1998 Taiwanese Administrative Litigation Act include judicial review of administrative actions. In the United States, judicial review of agency decisions has been a key mechanism for locking in status quo regulatory policies by offsetting agency drift and reinforcing the intent of the previous Congress. In addition to conformity with the legislative intent of the enacting coalition, judges could also consider the letter of the law, as several interviewees confirmed to be the case in Taiwan. This difference is important because it suggests that politicians sometimes allow for judicial review of agency decisions to create another avenue through which existing regulations can be overturned. In other words, judicial review in this case is intended to change rather than reinforce the status quo.

Future research is needed to develop the necessary coding scheme for conducting a large-*N* statistical analysis. Because of the limited number of cases and difficulty of employing econometric techniques in a small-*N* environment, I focus here primarily, albeit not exclusively, on in-depth qualitative case studies. The most notable exception is chapter 7, where I use multiple regression analysis to investigate the effects on public opinion of APA passage in Korea and Taiwan as well as of the absence of an APA in the Philippines.

Case Selection

The remaining chapters of the book present my case studies of Korea, Taiwan, and the Philippines as well as in-depth investigations of specific aspects and implications of administrative reform in Korea and Taiwan and the relative absence thereof in the Philippines. By using individual administrations as my units of observation, I derive multiple observations from each case, providing additional variation in my dependent variable, the extent of codified administrative procedural controls during a particular administration, and thus helping to avoid the worst kinds of selection bias (Geddes 1990). Perhaps most important, my focus on East Asia represents an effort to expand the scholarly debate beyond the U.S. case to a comparative context.

Table 2.1 summarizes the basic institutional structures of Korea, Taiwan, and the Philippines—focusing on the legislative and executive branches, as they are most relevant for the three implications.[11] As the table shows, the president in both countries is elected by a popular vote, holds office for a fixed term, selects and directs part or all of the cabinet, and has some legislative authority. Korea has a unicameral National Assembly, while the Philippines has a bicameral legislature.

Under Taiwan's constitution, the five *yuan* (executive, legislative, judicial, examination, and control) comprise the core institutions of government, sharing constitutional powers among themselves. The president is head of the Executive Yuan but also appoints the premier. Taiwan has a legislative assembly (the Legislative Yuan) as well as a National Assembly. The latter has no legislative power and has been confined to voting on constitutional amendments and holding the power of presidential impeachment (Hicken and Kasuya 2003, 126). The Examination Yuan is responsible for the recruitment and promotion of civil servants. The Control Yuan exercises the powers of consent, impeachment, censure, and auditing.

In chapters 3–5, I operationalize the key conditions for an APA: the presence of "problem ministers" and "problem bureaucrats" with an intervening condition—that is, whether bureaucrats have civil service protec-

TABLE 2.1. Constitutional Features: Korea, Taiwan, and the Philippines

Country	Legislative Branch	Executive Branch
Korea	Prime minister subject to confirmation by unicameral National Assembly	One-term limit for president No vice presidency President appoints prime minister Prime minister appoints and president dismisses cabinet
Taiwan	Unicameral Vote of no confidence requirement is simple majority Recall of president or vice president requires motion of one-fourth and is proposed with concurrence of two-thirds of National Assembly Must pass national referendum by simple majority	Two-term limit for president and vice president President appoints premier without legislative consent President can dissolve the legislature following vote of no confidence
Philippines	Bicameral Two-term limit for senators Cabinet subject to consent of commission on appointments	One-term limit for president Vice president on separate ticket President appoints and dismisses cabinet

Source: Constitutions of Korea, Taiwan, and the Philippines; Hicken and Kasuya 2003.

tion. Table 2.2 shows which of the key conditions for APA passage existed under each of the five administrations in Korea, Taiwan, and the Philippines. The table also compares the actual outcome with the logical prediction if the goal of each president had been to lock in the status quo.

The second condition, problem bureaucrats (with civil service protection), corresponds to APA enactments in Korea (K2) and Taiwan (T2); the Aquino administration in the Philippines did not need an APA because although bureaucrats satisfy both key conditions, they have no civil service protections. Hence, officials sympathetic to the administration could freely be hired. In the other cases, neither of the key conditions was satisfied and no APA passed.

These predictions differ from what would have been predicted if the presidents had been interested in locking in the status quo rather than in reining in the bureaucracy. President Roh Tae Woo, with whom the bureaucracy agreed, would have wanted a lock-in APA if that were its function, but he obtained none. This suggests that APAs are designed to control the current bureaucracy; Kim Young Sam, who wanted to change rather than protect the status quo, needed an APA, whereas his predecessor, Roh, did not. Indeed, members of Kim's government cite limiting bureaucratic discretion as the primary purpose of their APA.

Taiwan's first Lee Teng-Hui administration had all key players in agreement, so a lock-in would have been appropriate, but no APA was forthcoming; instead, Lee concentrated on obtaining an increase in presidential power. During the second Lee administration, however, he and the bureaucrats disagreed, and an APA followed. Lee concluded that increased control was necessary for the KMT's political survival.

TABLE 2.2. Factors Affecting APA Enactment

Presidential Cases	Problem Ministers?	Problem Bureaucrats?	Civil Service Protection?	Did APA Pass?	"Lock-in" Prediction
Korea 1: Roh (1987–92)	No	No	Yes	No	Yes
Korea 2: Kim (1993–97)	No	Yes	Yes	Yes	No
Taiwan 1: Lee (1988–96)	No	No	Yes	No	Yes
Taiwan 2: Lee (1997–99)	No	Yes	Yes	Yes	No
Philippines: Aquino (1986–87)	Yes	Yes	No	No	No

Conclusion

The voluminous literature on delegation and its potential problems in democratic governments has suggested a variety of means through which principals seek to control their agents. Presidents face delegation problems similar to those faced by legislators: the principals cannot trust that their bureaucratic agents will share their preferences or faithfully implement their favored policies. I focus on APAs that establish procedural hurdles that executive agencies must overcome to implement policy. APAs are a particularly important type of control mechanism because they can help legislators delegating to the bureaucracy (interbranch conflict) or presidents delegating to cabinet ministers and bureaucrats (intrabranch conflict). A legislative coalition (including the incumbent president) can use an APA to lock in its preferences for fear of losing control of either the executive or legislative branch in future elections (McNollgast 1999). Alternatively, when presidents are constrained by constitutional requirements or coalitional conflict within the executive branch, they may opt for APAs to solve current delegation problems. Thus, APAs can be designed to change the status quo rather than lock it in.

The cases investigated in subsequent chapters support the reining-in theory. The Korean president initiated and supported an extensive APA when he could not replace bureaucrats whose economic policy preferences conflicted with his own and who acted against his interests. In Taiwan, increased factional conflict within the ruling party led the president to view the status-quo-oriented bureaucracy as an impediment. His desire to redirect the bureaucracy explains the APA's passage. But in the Philippines, despite the fact that the new president confronted a divided cabinet and a bureaucracy full of loyalists from the previous authoritarian regime, she managed delegation by distributing patronage jobs to her agents and hence did not need an extensive APA.

Although not all new democracies have enacted APAs and APAs do not appear to be a necessary feature of democracy, passage of APAs in new democracies can nonetheless have important ramifications for democratic responsiveness. APAs typically open up bureaucratic decision-making processes to the public by enfranchising nongovernmental organizations and other interest groups or by allowing citizens to trigger judicial review of agency decisions. This process enhances the three cornerstones of democracy: transparency, predictability, and accountability. But if political leaders are secure in government, they are less likely to institute fundamental and lasting procedural reforms. In other words, an APA—

and, by extension, the entrenchment of responsive democratic governance—results from political conflict among politicians vying for power. Democratic responsiveness results less from leaders' normative judgments concerning how democracy should be than from political expedience. Regardless of the motivations underlying such measures, however, APA-like procedures represent an important step along the path from institutional to responsive democracy.

3 | Deregulation, Bureaucratic Conflict, and Passage of the South Korean Administrative Procedure Act

The aim of regulatory reform is ambitious: to move Korea from a highly interventionist and authoritarian model of economic development to a market oriented and open model based on values of consumer choice, democracy, and rule of law. The Administrative Procedure Act . . . seeks "to advance a guarantee of fairness, transparency and confidence in administration and to protect the right and interests of citizens . . . by stipulating common matters regarding administrative procedures." Introduction of the Act was . . . against major opposition from the bureaucracy due to concern about the limits on administrative discretion implied by greater transparency and stricter procedures.

—Organisation for Economic Co-Operation and Development 2000

The Organisation for Economic Co-Operation and Development (OECD) viewed the Korean administrative procedure act (APA) as a tool for enhancing transparency and confidence in administration and protecting citizen rights and interests. In essence, the OECD implicitly described APAs as a mechanism for enhancing democratic responsiveness, recognizing that the desire to increase state accountability constitutes one of politicians' principal motivations for restructuring their bureaucracies in ways that enhance the responsiveness of their democratic institutions.

Elected officials in new democracies, including those in East Asia, commonly have difficulty controlling bureaucrats from the previous authoritarian period.[1] So how do newly elected post-democratic-transition presidents ensure that their policies are implemented? One option is to rein in these bureaucrats by empowering the public to participate directly in bureaucratic policy-making.

As I argue in chapter 2, one way to do so is by requiring all executive agencies to follow specific procedures when writing regulations across all policy areas. If McNollgast's theory is generally true, outgoing presidents in other countries should support APAs to "lock in" preferred policies. Yet at least in South Korea (henceforth Korea), such is not the case.[2] The Korea case suggests that rather than seeking to lock in the status quo, presidents may support APAs in new democracies if they confront various types of conflict within the executive branch. In other words, the lock-in story does not ring true in many new democracies because following a democratic transition, new presidents' policy preferences often differ from those of members of their coalition or of bureaucrats left over from the previous regime. When presidents have incomplete control over their appointees, they may seek to manage delegation to cabinet ministers and their underlings by adopting an APA (Baum 2007a). Whether presidents' powers are constrained by constitutional requirements (appointment and dismissal power of the cabinet), coalitional support with heterogeneous preferences, or bureaucrats who cannot be fired, APAs can mitigate agency slippage by keeping track of bureaucrats' activities. In Korea, APA enactment is primarily, albeit not exclusively, attributable to the third condition. In this chapter, I investigate the enactment of APAs in Korea, a textbook case for examining the applicability of both the lock-in argument and my alternative reining-in theory.

Korea's first civilian leader since 1961, President Kim Young Sam (1993–98), assumed office with an ambitious reform agenda. Yet he confronted an executive branch dominated by entrenched and recalcitrant bureaucrats loyal to the previous authoritarian regimes and with a vested interest in the status quo. Institutional and coalitional factors played important roles in both the timing and substance of Kim's decision to pursue the various acts governing administrative regulations. I investigate his incentives not only before and after passage of the 1994 APA but also when the APA was strengthened three years later.

Nevertheless, it is important to avoid overgeneralizing from evidence based on a single country. Hence, following common practice in qualitative case study research (e.g., Achen and Snidal 1989; Drezner 2000; Eckstein 1975), I employ this case study as a "plausibility probe," intended to illustrate some of the key relationships described in the theory as well as to demonstrate the utility of the theory for further empirical testing.

I begin by outlining the events surrounding the enactment of Korea's APAs. I then briefly describe Korean politics under military rule, focusing on the traditional sources of political support for bureaucrats. I subsequently discuss the goals and policy preferences of Korea's politicians and bureaucrats after democratic transition and test the applicability of the theory to the Korean case.

APA Enactment in Korea

My dependent variable is the change in the degree of administrative procedural control during a particular administration in Korea. Such control increased when an APA passed in 1994 and was strengthened in 1997.

Following his inauguration on February 25, 1993, President Kim established several deregulatory committees.[3] Kim also created the Presidential Commission on Administrative Reform (PCAR) which served through the end of his five-year term. On June 11, PCAR promulgated the Special Measure Act for Deregulation of Corporate Activity. The National Assembly then passed the Basic Law on Administrative Regulations and Civil Affairs Act on January 1, 1994 (Korea 1994). The law, subsequently referred to as KAPA I, and the subsequent Prime Minister Order (April 7, 1994) and Presidential Enforcement Decree[4] (PED) (December 31, 1996), which implemented KAPA I, set the guidelines for a new regulatory process that focused on the legal limits of regulation and the *ex ante* screening of all proposed regulations. In May 1994, the Joint Review Council of Administrative Regulation within the Ministry of Government Administration was established to review and resolve regulatory disputes among ministries.

Deregulation efforts accelerated during Kim's third year in office, when he announced globalization (*segyehwa*) efforts (M.-J. Moon and Ingraham 1998). Kim promoted deregulation to liberalize economic activity, to facilitate market competition, and to improve the creativity of industries (B. W. Kim 1991). Toward this end, the government also introduced an ombudsman system by passing the Administrative Regulation and Service Improvement Act. A main goal of the ombudsman system was to discourage new regulations by mandating regulatory impact analyses prior to implementation (Korea, Presidential Commission 1995).

Also on December 31, 1996, Kim promulgated the Korean APA (KAPA II), which applies to all acts that exclude provisions for the procedures of dispositions, notifications, administrative preannouncement of legislation, preannouncement of dispositions, and administrative guidance.

On August 22, 1997, near the end of Kim's term, the National Assembly promulgated another comprehensive act, known as the Basic Act on Administrative Regulations (KAPA III).[5] KAPA III was far more extensive than KAPA I. Its main provisions included (1) a rule that all regulations must be ordained by law; (2) establishment of a civilian-led Regulatory Reform Committee[6] in 1998; (3) adoption of a policy whereby creation of new regulations or strengthening of existing ones required a mandatory regulatory impact analysis, introduction of a registration system, and a sunset law; and (4) establishment of a Comprehensive Regulatory Improvement Plan for existing regulations. Following opposition party leader Kim Dae Jung's victory in the December 1997 presidential election, the National Assembly amended KAPA III on February 28, 1998, with the Framework Act on Administrative Regulations.

The Political Equilibrium under Military Rule

Korea's formal democratic transition from military dictatorship began on June 29, 1987. Roh Tae Woo, a conservative politician handpicked by Korea's military leaders as the presidential candidate of the ruling Democratic Justice Party, announced major democratic reforms.[7] Following these reforms, the National Assembly amended the authoritarian constitution and adopted the new constitutional framework on October 12, 1987. In a national referendum shortly thereafter, 93 percent of voters ratified the new constitution (Diamond and Shin 2000, 6). With over two decades of democratic experience, Korea has now conducted five free and competitive presidential elections, five parliamentary elections, four rounds of nationwide mayoral and gubernatorial elections, and four series of local council and top city and county administrator elections.[8]

Prior to democratization, Korea's executive branch was a unified hierarchy, lacking presidential control problems. Authoritarian presidents and professional bureaucrats had similar preferences regarding policies. Prereform Presidents Park Chung Hee and Chun Doo Hwan routinely rewarded officers from the Kyungsang province, which was a major part of their military selectorate.[9] This strategy led to the rise of personalistic regional parties. Both military regimes also generated support from rural vote machines[10] financed by political contributions from the *chaebol* (multicompany business conglomerates).

Korean parties tend to lack bureaucratic organization but are highly disciplined. Yet because the parties are largely personalistic, their survival depends on their leaders' continued success. Thus, as long as presidents generated support from these rural vote machines, they maintained strong control over their parties.

Until the 1981 legislative election, the president was allowed to choose one-third of the members of the National Assembly, thereby ensuring a working majority for the ruling party. Prior to the lifting of this rule, the major opposition parties repeatedly failed to achieve the one-third share of legislative seats required by law to initiate bills. In the wake of the rule's abandonment prior to the 1981 election, however, the opposition parties surpassed the one-third threshold, becoming for the first time a potent legislative opposition (see table 3.1).[11]

Thus, while the National Assembly possessed some significant constitutional power, it failed to exercise its independent authority prior to 1987 primarily because the electoral system was rigged to guarantee the president's party a legislative majority. Presidents during the time of military rule thus avoided meaningful conflict with the opposition by ensuring that their parties dominated politics.

Unified Executive Hierarchy

Political survival during Park's regime was tied to economic development through export-led growth (Haggard and Kaufman 1995; Wade 1992). With this goal in mind, Park and his successors needed to build a cadre of skilled bureaucrats who could provide information regarding policy formulation as well as have the expertise and competence to execute and implement economic policy decisions. Therefore, in the 1960s, the government began to promote a merit-based system for recruitment of career bureaucrats. By the early 1970s, this system was firmly established. However, even with the new system, a patronage network based on common regional background, family ties, or school affiliations persisted throughout the bureaucracy (Cho 1975).

Under military rule, Korean presidents set the parameters of interactions between government and private industry by employing incentives and sanctions to discipline bureaucrats and big business (Amsden 1989; Campos and Root 1996; Wade 1990). In exchange for private information

TABLE 3.1. National Assembly Seats (% of total), by Party

Election Year	Ruling Party	Major Opposition Parties	Other
1973	121 (62%)	52 (27%)	21 (11%)
1978	119 (58%)	61 (30%)	25 (12%)
1981	151 (55%)	106 (38%)	19 (7%)
1985	148 (54%)	102 (37%)	26 (9%)

and political support—that is, contributions and votes—presidents rewarded big business for good performance with subsidies and access to low-interest credit.

For bureaucrats, the continuity in economic policies during the Park and Chun regimes created stability in long-term policy planning, thereby minimizing fears of unexpected policy reversals. Presidents were confident that the bureaucrats would not stray too far from presidential preferences as long as job security and promotions remained contingent on loyalty. Hence, until the mid-1980s, the key actors—politicians, big business, and bureaucrats—had little incentive to deviate from this mutually beneficial relationship.

Implementing a merit-based appointment system raised the likelihood that bureaucrats would act contrary to the president's preferences. Civil servants who know that they cannot be fired for their actions face little risk in deviating from such policies.

Shift in Economic Policy and the Decline of Executive-Bureaucrat-*Chaebol* Dominance

Prior to the enactment of Korea's APA, a shift in economic policy began to threaten the political equilibrium under military rule. Yet presidential control problems did not immediately surface. To broaden its support base during the 1990s, the government began to shift its emphasis away from heavy industry development by allowing smaller firms to enter the market (Hahm and Plein 1997, 39). This change reduced the government's role in allocating credit to specific firms, which consequently had to resort to stock offerings and borrowing on the open market for capital.

In addition, the government sold off its stake in commercial banks, thereby relinquishing its power to appoint management, control loans, and set policy, including setting interest rates through its control of the Bank of Korea and the Ministry of Finance (Steers, Shin, and Ungson 1989). In short, concessions by the Chun regime to business interests not only reduced the government's role in the banking and finance sectors but also began to threaten a three-decades-old political equilibrium, which was eventually broken when economic liberalization continued in subsequent administrations.

The reforms increased uncertainty regarding the direction of future economic policy. However, this initial shift did not produce sufficient incentive for bureaucrats to resist Chun's policies. The benefits of continuing to play by the old rules still outweighed the costs of doing so. Chun was a dictator, relying on his personal allies in the highest positions of government to ensure implementation of his policies. Other political institutions—the legislature, interest groups (other than big business), and parties—were relatively weak. Bureaucrats never confronted divided loyalties and, most important, still received rewards for loyalty—prestige, job security, promotions, and salary increases.

Democratic Transition and New Rules of the Game: Goals and Policy Preferences of Key Players

With the 1987 democratic transition and subsequent election of Chun's handpicked successor, Roh, a new set of rules emerged. First, a popularly elected president afforded voters the opportunity to reward or punish presidents (or their parties) at the next election based on performance. Second, the president could no longer dissolve the National Assembly. In fact, the legislature was empowered with important functions, including the authority to (1) stop presidential legislation, (2) legislate "over the head" of the presidential veto (override provisions; Korea 1987, Article 53), (3) hold hearings to determine whether presidents (current or former) were guilty of corruption, and (4) veto the president's nominee for prime minister. Third, the president had to share the right to appoint members of the newly established constitutional court with members of the parliament and the chief justice of the supreme court. The constitutional court, in turn, made the final judgment on impeachment issues and dissolution of political parties.[12] In addition, the constitutional court had various instruments that strengthened judicial review.[13]

Players in this new political game had to operate within a political environment that included term limits, increased legislative power, and independent judicial influence. Consequently, the previous principal-agent relationship between presidents and bureaucrats changed: multiple principals—the president, the legislature, the judiciary, and the public—now competed to influence the bureaucracy.

Presidential Preferences

My argument depends on several assumptions concerning presidents' motivations. President Kim faced serious intraexecutive control problems. He was a reformer who confronted not only an entrenched bureaucracy intent on preserving the economic status quo but also substantial disagreement within his party.

Ruling party conflict resulted from repeated splits and mergers. Typically, if a party leader defected to form a coalition with or to try to recruit members from another party, he could count on his supporters to follow him. (Appendix table A1 reveals the frequent party splits and mergers, indicated also by the constant renaming of parties.)

Despite the historical pattern of party splits and mergers, as the party system grew more competitive after 1987, presidents began to prioritize passing and effectively administering their legislative programs. This change in strategy gave them an incentive to control the bureaucrats responsible for implementing their policies.

One instance of a president seeking to influence future electoral outcomes to increase the likelihood that his legislative programs would be implemented arose in 1990, when Roh merged his party with those of Kim Young Sam and Kim Jong Pil. This merger, intended to give Roh a majority in the National Assembly, led to the formation of the Democratic Liberal Party. Similarly, Kim Dae Jung (president from 1998 to 2003) formed an alliance with Kim Jong Pil's[14] party to increase the chances of winning the 1997 presidential election. This alliance led to the 1998 formation of the first coalition government since the democratic transition.

As a consequence of this merger, Kim Young Sam's party included followers of both Roh and Kim Jong Pil. Subsequent Korean presidents have frequently fought with their cabinet ministers over policy issues.[15] As director general (the highest level of the career civil service) Park Se Jin of the Ministry of Legislation observed, "There's always some sort of conflict or disagreement between different ministers. That's why this [regulatory] reform committee exists . . . to resolve their differences in opinion."[16] In addition, when he took office, President Kim Young Sam purged senior military officers closely linked to Chun and Roh (Y. J. Lee 2000, 106). Justifying his decision with charges of corruption and incompetence, Kim discharged, reassigned, or postponed the promotions of generals and colonels who were members of the Hanahoe (Society of One) (Y. J. Lee 2000, 106).[17] As Y. J. Lee (2000, 113–14) observes,

> Whenever he put forward a new reform measure, President Kim had to deal more with the internal dissenters in his political party than with the external opponents. President Kim thus had to walk a

tightrope between implementing reforms and maintaining his reform coalition.

Cabinet Preferences

Since its democratic transition, Korea's cabinets have typically included a single party with multiple factions, many of which did not share the president's preferences.[18] Factionalized single-party cabinets threaten a president's agenda because substantial disagreement may arise over policy between the president's faction and the other factions and because opposing factions may be large enough to block the president's program within the executive branch. Under such circumstances, presidents have an incentive to institutionalize their control, *ex ante*, by supporting administrative procedures.

According to Hahm and Plein (1997, 52), "turf wars" among Korea's cabinet ministries have rapidly increased along with the

> diversity and instability in presidential cabinets; as a result, bureaucrats will likely get mixed signals from their executive principals. . . . This trend is clearly evident . . . where the ruling party has been cobbled together by combining elements of entrenched regime members and established opposition leaders.

In fact, my data indicate that under Kim, 15 out of 80 new ministerial appointments between 1993 and 1996 clearly came from Roh's faction. Most of the other 65 appointments came from President Kim's faction, with only a few from Kim Jong Pil's faction.

Bureaucrats' Preferences

According to three directors general, bureaucrats' power and discretion declined after Kim came into office. For example, director general Hoh Moon of the Ministry of Trade, Industry, and Energy stated,

> Under authoritarian regimes, bureaucrats were able to express opinions, challenge ministers, and develop sound policies. Since Kim, however, bureaucrats are less involved in decision making. . . . Bureaucrats and ministers used to work in a homogeneous environment where there was continuity and stability. Under Kim,

> there have been multiple reorganizations, resulting in greater uncertainty. This has created confusion and discontinuity in policy direction.[19]

The most important changes derived from Kim's goal of deregulation are the effects of the new procedures. For all regulations, bureaucrats were now required to listen to a broader set of interest groups, including those that the authoritarian regimes had excluded. This new approach reduced bureaucrats' capacity to control policy outcomes, meant that they could no longer depend on side payments from their favorite constituents, and gave them an incentive to resist such reforms.[20]

The one-term limit for presidents further exacerbates the potential for conflict between the president and the bureaucracy. Knowing that a president will not be around for the long term, bureaucrats have a greater incentive to resist presidential initiatives (Huber 1998), especially if they disagree on principle (Huber and Lupia 2001).

Roh did not propose radical changes in economic policy. Hence, even though he changed the rules of the game, he did not need to worry about controlling recalcitrant bureaucrats. Kim, in contrast, proposed a major shift in policy direction toward deregulation. Bureaucrats, who benefited from the status quo, resisted his economic reforms.

Analysis and Evidence

Table 3.2, excerpted from table 2.2, indicates the presence or absence of each of the three key conditions examined in this chapter across the three administrations in Korea. The table shows that a divergence of preferences between the president and career civil servants accounts for the enactments of both Korean APAs (see Baum 2007a). In the 1993–94 and 1995–97 periods, procedural control increased with the passage of the APAs. The table also compares the actual outcome with the logical prediction if the goal of each president had been to lock in the status quo.

TABLE 3.2. Factors Affecting APA Enactment in Korea

Presidential Cases	Problem Ministers?	Problem Bureaucrats?	Civil Service Protection?	Did APA Pass?	"Lock-in" Prediction
Roh (1987–92)	No	No	Yes	No	Yes
Kim (1993–94)	No	Yes	Yes	Yes	No
Kim (1995–97)	No	Yes	Yes	Yes	No

Absence of Civil Service Conflict under the Roh Administration (1988–1993)

By the late 1980s, government officials expressed concern about Korea's position in the world market. Manufacturing firms began to lose international competitiveness, and wages were high. Korea found itself squeezed between newly industrializing countries with lower wage rates and more advanced countries at the forefront of capital-intensive knowledge industries (e.g., microcomputers and biotechnology). In response, Roh advocated the development of new export-oriented initiatives aimed at securing Korea's position in the international market (e.g., automotive technology and semiconductor memory products). By the time Roh reached this decision, however, his administration lacked sufficient time to pass new policies through the legislature, let alone implement them (Hahm and Plein 1997, 71). Roh won the presidential election with a plurality, rather than a majority, of votes. He also lacked a working legislative majority until his Democratic Justice Party merged with two opposition parties.

Roh, however, did not confront policy conflict with the bureaucracy. In this regard, the Roh administration resembles the U.S. case. Like Roh, President Harry S. Truman and his bureaucracy appear to have shared a preference for preserving the New Deal. If this analogy is apt, the McNollgast (1999) lock-in hypothesis appears to imply that Roh should have passed an APA. He, too, shared common interests with his bureaucracy and so had little incentive to crack it open. Indeed, while Roh implemented some relatively modest democratic reforms, he had no incentive to fundamentally reform Korea's bureaucratic system. Doing so would have weakened his core political constituencies. In this regard, an APA designed to lock in the status quo (i.e., a strong bureaucracy plus moderate democratic reforms) should have appealed to Roh. After all, he had justifiable concern that his fundamental support constituency could be threatened by wholesale democratic reforms pursued by a future administration. Yet Roh did not pursue an APA.

Contrary to the lock-in hypothesis, the reining-in theory predicts that Roh would lack any motivation to carry out administrative reform because the bureaucrats largely shared his preferences—many were members of his military faction—and were afraid to cross him even when they did not. In short, the APA passed under Kim rather than Roh because the enacting coalition intended to change rather than to lock in the status quo.

Bureaucratic Conflict under the Kim Administration (1993–1998)

Kim's economic policy preferences clearly differed from those of the bureaucrats. He had difficulty implementing his reforms, which threatened the livelihood of those political actors, including bureaucrats, with vested interests in previous programs, as evidenced by Kim's 1993 Five-Year New Economy Plan, which sought to reduce state intervention through deregulation, financial reform, and privatization, and a 1994 initiative targeting internationalization.[21] Under the privatization plan, 68 of 133 public enterprises were selected for sale between 1994 and 1998 (Korea, Economic Planning Board 1994, 190). The plan was only partially implemented, however. *Chaebol* reforms were also incomplete, in part because of the *chaebol's* political and economic clout. In short, the president could set the agenda, but successful implementation required the cooperation of precisely the political actors who were the targets of reform (Y. J. Lee 2000, 108).

Kim's reform plans threatened bureaucrats' traditional sources of political support, which, in turn, threatened the mutual benefits accruing to bureaucrats and business through their long-standing close relationship. Because these bureaucrats' incentives—foremost among them political survival—depended on the status quo, Kim faced substantial intrabranch conflict. As Kim's chief of staff, Park Kwan Yong, stated, "Bureaucrats were definitely a barrier to the president's administrative reform goals."[22] Since regulators tend to resist deregulation (B. W. Kim 1997, 193), it is unsurprising that a significant percentage of public officials (43.2 percent) reported suspecting that the Kim administration opposed their vested rights, while a substantial percentage of bureaucrats (29.7 percent) worried about a loss or reduction in their powers (Korea Economic Research Institute 1996, 3–4). By reforming procedures, Kim was better able to control conservative bureaucrats who were part of the old core of the military ruling party (the Democratic Justice Party).

When he took office, Kim formed several committees: the PCAR, the Economic Administrative Deregulation Committee, and the Committee on Deregulation of Restricted Corporate Activities. However, the first two committees were ad hoc and lacked full political support. In short, no institutional bodies existed within a comprehensive framework to oversee and review deregulation efforts and the drafting of new regulations. Consequently, substantial deregulation in key sectors was stymied, and bureaucrats continued to write new regulations with little scrutiny.

Reining in the Bureaucracy through an APA

How KAPA I and Presidential Decrees Improve Executive Control

Both Kim Young Sam and the legislature had incentives to manage agency drift while in office. They could do so either by limiting bureaucratic discretion or by enfranchising new groups. KAPA I emphasized the latter. The 1996 PED contains the specific provisions outlining the intent of the 1994 KAPA. The most important requirements include public notice and comment for all proposed regulations and a review committee with oversight authorities.

The new procedural requirements help presidents and legislators collect information about agencies' activities. For legislators, making bureaucratic activity transparent to the public also forces bureaucrats to reveal privately held information and provides information about constituents' positions on regulatory issues. Legislators can thus better position themselves to respond to their constituents, thereby increasing the chances of reelection. Along these lines, Rhee Zusun of the Korea Economic Research Institute's Center for Regulation Studies commented,

> Politicians had no reason to oppose [the APA] as there was very little cost for a lot of gain in information as to what bureaucrats were doing. There are many benefits to politicians because of increased transparency and reduced bureaucratic discretion. If you look at the electoral connection, detection and information is broadened and so is control . . . so they have no reason to oppose [it]. Finally, interest group access has definitely increased since the act. The regulators are regulated. This is a significant change from the past.[23]

By making the process entirely public and enfranchising new principals such as environmentalists and other nongovernmental organizations (NGOs), KAPA I forces agencies to consider the relevant political interests before finalizing new rules. The slowing down of the rule-making process gives new interest groups multiple opportunities to notify legislators when agencies propose actions the legislators oppose.

Finally, the provision granting the prime minister authority to order any agency head to amend, reform, or delete its regulations stands out clearly as a tool to improve current executive management, providing a powerful veto to an incumbent administration.

How KAPA II Improves Executive Control

Several of KAPA II's provisions require PEDs, thereby giving the president some discretion over implementation and further showing that presidents sometimes support APAs to manage current delegation problems.

According to the KAPA II legislation, "The purpose of this Act is to attain fairness, transparency, and confidence in administration, and to protect the rights and interest of citizens, encouraging citizens' participation in administration by stipulating the common matters regarding administrative procedures" (Korea 1996, Act No. 5241, Article 1).[24]

KAPA II requires establishment and public notification of disposition standards as well as advance notice to the concerned parties. It also gives parties the option to submit arguments to the agency and mandates the maintenance of a record of formal hearings. To commence a public hearing, agencies must notify the parties at least 14 days before the hearing date and inform the general public through methods such as official gazettes, public bulletins, and daily newspapers.

Although, unlike the U.S. APA, KAPA II does not govern rule making per se, the purpose of procedural requirements, including dispositions and writing legislation, resembles those requirements outlined in the 1996 PED. Thus, the 1996 decree governs rule making.

How KAPA III Prevents Regulatory Capture

In the spring 1996 National Assembly election, Kim's New Korea Party (NKP) won 46 percent of the seats, falling only 11 seats short of majority status. Kim formed a working majority with 8 independents and 3 defecting opposition party members (Koh 1997, 2).

The lock-in hypothesis presumes that politicians anticipate losses in future elections. In fact, according to a national election opinion poll by Gallup Korea and *Chosun Ilbo* conducted in March 1997, between the 1996 National Assembly elections and the December 1997 presidential elections, popular support for the National Congress for New Politics (NCNP), the "second party," was essentially equivalent to that for Kim's party. The NKP led the NCNP by just 16.6 percent to 16.4 percent, a statistical dead heat. Moreover, 57 percent of respondents expressed no opinion at all, suggesting that their votes might swing either way.

Based on these data, Kim most likely recognized that an opposition party candidate could win the next election. At first glance, this situation might suggest that KAPA III was intended to lock in existing policies. Yet the policy preferences of President Kim's primary opponent, the NCNP's Kim Dae Jung, were farther from those of the bureaucracy than were those of Kim Young Sam. Hence, while the predictions of my theory and the McNollgast theory are in this instance observationally equivalent, they derive from substantially different—or, more specifically, additional—motivations. Yet the two theories are distinct in their capacity to explain one aspect of procedural reform: regulatory sunset provisions.

Perhaps the provision that most strongly supports my reining-in argument is the five-year sunset review requirement. According to the Korean APA, for any existing regulations to be extended beyond five years, bureaucrats must submit an extension request one year prior to expiration. In addition, agencies must first notify the public and allow for comments prior to submitting such a request to the Regulatory Reform Committee (RRC).

Of course, this sunset requirement means that future administrations can also undo any administration's regulations after five years. Why would a president who cares about locking in his policies increase his successor's power to undo his regulatory accomplishments? Indeed, the fact that only KAPA III, enacted just before Kim left office, included the sunset provision strongly suggests that its motivation could not have been solely lock-in. After all, sunset laws are explicitly intended to prevent lock-in. If no new deal is struck, the reversion point is deregulation. Thus, this requirement is clearly not a mechanism for locking in the status quo. Rather, it is a tool incumbent presidents use to manage the executive branch by giving them the authority to sign or veto a particular proposal to renew an existing regulation, thereby biasing outcomes away from rather than toward status quo policies.

Kim included this provision to prevent bureaucrats from attempting to return to the previous era's regulatory policies. Under this five-year review cycle, bureaucrats would not be able to revive Roh-era regulation without a public notice and comment period and a justification process under the RRC. This requirement would limit the policy range within which career bureaucrats could write new regulations. Kim apparently saw the still-conservative bureaucrats as a greater threat than the prospect that Kim Dae Jung might win the 1997 election.

In addition, the passage of KAPA I occurred early in Kim's term, thereby further calling into question the applicability of the lock-in hypothesis. This timing leads to the question of why a president with a working legislative majority would subject his own branch to procedural constraints designed to slow down policy implementation and increase governance costs.

When KAPA I was passed, Kim's party controlled 58 percent of the seats in the National Assembly and had no reason to believe that its majority status was threatened. In a Gallup poll conducted several months prior to KAPA I's passage, Kim and his party enjoyed approval ratings of 85 percent and 55 percent, respectively. At that time, the approval rating for the next-most-popular party (the Democratic Party) was 20 percent (Gallup Korea 2007). Therefore, contrary to the conditions of the lock-in theory, it seems improbable that KAPA I was passed because of an expected loss in the next general elections (scheduled for spring 1996).

KAPA III mandates additional procedural requirements. The consensus among the bureaucrats I interviewed was that the new administrative procedures added another layer to regulatory decision making. My interviewees emphasized that the procedural reforms prevented the continuation of policies that served only *chaebol* interests. Bureaucrats would now have to consider new interest groups' views, especially those that had previously been excluded and that had not been associated with the ruling party. According to Choi Byung-Sun of Seoul National University, a key author of KAPA III,

> The primary motivation was to place some kind of an obstacle or break on bureaucrats' discretion and to institute more democratic procedures of the bureaucracy. The entire bureaucracy was strongly opposed to this law because it interfered too heavily with day-to-day activities. The requirements are so counter to current government practices, and it will put a heavy burden on bureaucratic discretion.[25]

Along the same lines, a report by the Office of the Prime Minister to the OECD clearly indicates that procedural reforms faced substantial bureaucratic resistance: "Difficulties of enacting [regulatory review] were . . . opposition and resistance from vested interest groups and ministries concerned about being the losers of reform" (Korea, Office of the Prime Minister 1997, 17). In fact, Hoh Moon stated, "The establishment of the Office of Government Policy Coordination and the RRC have increased the power of the Prime Minister's Office."[26] Hoh added that since both are checking points, the ministries try to persuade their counterparts in these organizations—in particular, the Policy Coordination Office.

Most of my interview subjects referenced the two major requirements under KAPA III: public hearings and notice of draft rules. A member of the RRC, bureaucrats at the Office of Policy Coordination (Office of the Prime Minister) and Ministry of Legislation, and several directors general who advise RRC members also mentioned a third requirement: review by the RRC.[27] The only bureaucrat who expressed support for the new process was director general Park Nam Hoon, from the prime minister's Office of Policy Coordination, which assists the committee. Park commented,

> The 1994 act, 1997 act, and related enforcement decrees were designed to ensure that agencies consider interest group opinions. Without the RRC, bureaucrats cannot be trusted to enforce a new direction in regulatory policy, allowing for flexibility when needed and making sure that the right kinds of regulations are created and modified. Also, ministries in the past did not have to deal with each other. Now they do.[28]

Joh Jung Jay, a member of the Presidential Committee on Regulatory Reform, explained that in addition to overseeing deregulation, the RRC had to "ensure that the lower-level bureaucrats could not deviate and write their own regulations."[29] Thus, to control bureaucrats, all new regulations or revisions of existing regulations must now be justified via mandatory regulatory impact analysis.[30]

Landscape of Nongovernmental Organizations (NGOs)

One method that politicians can use to reduce bureaucratic discretion and that is evident in Korea is to enfranchise new principals. Since democratization, NGOs have proliferated rapidly and have become increasingly active. Civil society and NGOs began to form in 1987—democratic transition opened up "organizational space" for social interests and interest groups (H.-R. Kim 2000). The year 1994 saw the abolition of a 1963 law that had sought to suppress antigovernment activities by requiring civil organizations to register. The 1998 Information Disclosure Law also increased accessibility and allowed citizens and NGOs to sue state bureaucracies that refused data access (H.-R. Kim 2000, 602). Between the 1980s and the 1990s, the number of registered NGOs grew from 773 to 2,114 (see P. S. Kim and Moon 2003; Koo 2002). According to the OECD, Korea now has an estimated 8,000 NGOs (Organisation for Economic Co-Operation and Development 2000). The *Directory of Korean NGOs* (1999) lists 7,600 organizations, a number that jumps to 20,000 when local branches are included; most of these groups formed in the 1990s (Koo 2002). Korean officials argue that by implementing major new legislation such as the KAPAs, which have increased NGOs' input on policy, the government has facilitated this rapid growth in organizations (Organisation for Economic Co-Operation and Development 2000, 53–54).

Among the NGOs that have proliferated in Korea are three particularly large groups: the Citizens' Coalition for Economic Justice, the Korean Federation for the Environment Movement, and the People's Solidarity for Participatory Democracy (now Transparency International Korea, or TI Korea). These NGOs appear to be central to policy-making and reform; because they were linked to the democratization movement, they are seen as both centralized and focused at the national level. This landscape differs from that of Japan, where NGOs are more grassroots based. Smaller NGOs appear to use these larger NGOs as focal points, lobbying with them or under campaigns run by them (P. S. Kim and Moon 2003; S.-J. Lee and Arrington 2008).

NGOs and Presidents

NGOs appear to play a role in consolidation efforts. According to S.-J. Lee and Arrington (2008, 81),

> Since the Kim Young Sam administration, presidents have recruited former democratization activists and NGO leaders into the public service to legitimize major reforms and jointly fight against vested interests or for women's rights.

The authors argue that one of the primary reasons Korea's advocacy NGOs have taken such root and have become particularly politicized is the underinstitutionalization of party politics.

NGOs (at least advocacy/interest group organizations) are seen as a tool for reformers but not as grassroots organizations. "NGOs also risk being co-opted politically or losing public backing when support for an administration wanes" (S.-J. Lee and Arrington 2008, 82).[31] By this logic, incoming presidents benefit most.

Along these lines, President Kim's chief of staff, Park Kwan-Yong, commented, "Labor and environmental groups play a very important role in Korean politics today."[32] Kim Sung Hyun, the press secretary to Representative Kwon Chul-Hyun, added, "During good economic conditions under Kim Young Sam, citizens began to care about the environment. Key groups started to mobilize and become more active."[33] And Lee Chae-Pil, director of Ministry of Labor's Administration Management Division, Planning and Management Office, observed, "Labor groups have become more important players during the 1990s. Industrial safety regulations have been critical in recent years."[34]

The number of NGOs skyrocketed during Kim Dae Jung's administration, which "believed that the activities of civic organizations would aid it in carrying out the political reforms Kim was committed to" (Shin 2003, 699). This belief, coupled with a high level of skepticism/distrust of parties and other more standard institutions, may explain the link between presidents, bureaucracy, and NGOs.

All of the senior policymakers I interviewed agreed that interest groups, especially civil activist groups, are important players in government decision making. No longer can bureaucrats simply ignore them. "Civic interest groups and other NGOs are performing a voluntary watchdog role to raise [the] quality of regulation observance in the field of environment and consumer protection regulation" (Korea, Office of the Prime Minister 1999, 15). In short, civil society groups' access to the bureaucracy has opened up so that participation is greatest and most visible during the public hearing and notification stages.

Conclusion

The passage of the three KAPA measures is consistent with my reining-in explanation and inconsistent with McNollgast's lock-in hypothesis. Korea is an important test because it experienced one episode where a president agreed with the bureaucracy and another in which he did not. It also includes a clear instance (the Roh administration) when an APA should have emerged if lock-in was the driving motivation, yet no such law passed.

Administrative procedural reform did not occur under Roh because the bureaucrats shared his economic policy preferences. So while the lock-in explanation implies that Roh would want an APA, this explanation cannot account for either the timing or substance of Korea's multiple APAs.

In contrast, President Kim sought to change the country's economic policy and thus threatened the traditional sources of political support for bureaucrats. Since their political survival depended on the status quo economic policies, Kim confronted hostile bureaucrats with powerful incentives to resist his agenda. As a result, Kim initiated procedural reforms to help improve current executive management.

What most distinguishes Korea's 1997 KAPA III from the 1946 U.S.

APA is the sunset provision. Kim sought to prevent career bureaucrats from returning to pre-Kim-era policies by imposing a five-year sunset provision for all regulations. But the fact that the sunset provision was included only in KAPA III, just before the end of Kim's administration, strongly suggests that it could not have been intended solely for lock-in. After all, sunset provisions prevent lock-in.

Any democratic chief executive who is facing intrabranch conflict and who cannot freely appoint and dismiss her agents will have an incentive to implement an APA or comparable law. Coalition governments in parliamentary systems sometimes face intrabranch conflict as well (Thies 2001), and some have passed APAs (Baum and Jensen 2009). Finally, APAs enhance transparency, participation, and the accountability of elected officials and bureaucrats, which are cornerstones of democratic institutions. By passing such laws, countries take an important step toward responsive democracy.

4 | Decline of Kuomintang Dominance, Bureaucratic Conflict, and Passage of the Taiwan Administrative Procedure Act

Now under the administrative reform by the KMT, there is a second track for appeals. [Citizens] can start at the Executive Yuan. When people fail there, then they can appeal through the judicial system. In turn, they can face each other and debate between government and people. In other words, we have created a situation where the third party or the judiciary can arbitrate between the people and government.

—Yao Eng-Chi, Vice President, Legislative Yuan, July 15, 2000

Citizens' ability to challenge administrative policies is a crucial aspect of increasing state accountability. Taiwan, like Korea, has instituted such opportunities for its citizens, thereby enhancing the responsiveness of their democratic institutions.

Taiwan began its democratic transition from authoritarian rule on July 15, 1987, when President Chiang Ching-Kuo lifted martial law and other bans on political activity.[1] In January 1988, after Chiang's death, Vice President Lee Teng-Hui assumed the presidency. While consensus existed within the Kuomintang (KMT) Party regarding Lee's succession, the question of whether he should also become the party's chair became a hot political issue.[2] The following July, however, Lee was elected chair at the 13th Party Congress.

In this chapter, I investigate two periods during Lee's presidency, 1988–96 and 1997–99, to examine another case of the passage of an administrative procedural act (APA) in a new East Asian democracy. I again ask why presidents would voluntarily tie their own hands by supporting measures that limit leaders' capacity unilaterally to pass their preferred policies.

Taiwan is a particularly appealing country for this research question, since an APA passed after some unsuccessful attempts and some periods in which passing an APA was not on the agenda of those in power. This case helps to broaden my explanation of why chief executives support administrative procedural reform.

Theoretically, any executive—a president or a cabinet minister, for example—can have control problems within his or her branch. In Taiwan, Lee confronted an entrenched bureaucracy that needed to be redirected toward policies more responsive to the electorate. Within the KMT, reformers wanted to move away from status quo policies whereby bureaucrats' regulatory decisions were biased toward wealthy private interests toward ones that represented the interests of the nation's fastest-growing electoral demographic: younger voters. Managing this bureaucracy with an APA was one solution.

I begin by discussing the origins of Taiwan's APA (TAPA), its legislative history, and its regulatory requirements. I then substantiate my theory by reviewing the institutional and political environment during Lee's two presidential administrations, arguing that TAPA resulted from a combination of intraparty conflict and a recalcitrant yet institutionally protected bureaucracy. As was the case in Korea, TAPA was designed to promote change in the status quo rather than protect it, as the competing lock-in hypothesis (McNollgast 1999) implies.

TAPA's Origins

Legislative History

The impetus for TAPA came from the KMT's nonmainstream faction. In September 1989, Premier Hau Pei-Tsun, a military general under President Lee, created a research panel under the Council of Economic Development to draft TAPA.[3] A grand justice of the Judicial Yuan (branch) chaired the panel with eight legal scholars as drafters. The panel considered APAs from the United States, Germany, and Australia as well as drafts of measures being considered in Japan (Japan 1993, Administrative Procedure Law) and Korea (Korea 1994). The legislative debate and passage of TAPA spanned ten years.

One reason for the delay was that following Premier Hau's departure in February 1993, subsequent premiers were less active in pushing the bill. Hau's immediate successor, Lien Chan, was a member of Lee's faction rather than of the rival faction. In 1993, legislators from the Democratic Progressive Party (DPP) introduced a draft of an APA; the following year, KMT legislators offered an alternative version. The DPP legislator introduced the version proposed by Hau's panel. Both drafts were jointly reviewed by the legislature's Organic Statutes, Interior, and Judicial Committees. In April 1995, the Executive Yuan introduced its draft and sent it to committee. Over the next year and a half, the committee held five hearings, one of which was public.

All hearings were chaired by legislators from the New Party (NP), composed of rightist former KMT members who defected in 1993, and KMT legislators with reputations for not being corrupt. Shortly thereafter, the KMT legislator who introduced the alternative draft invited a legislator from the NP to promote TAPA. After reviewing the various versions, the NP legislator drafted her version and introduced it with another legislator from her party in December 1996. Of the measure's 31 sponsors or cosigners, 10 were NP members, 11 were from the DPP, 8 were from the KMT, and 2 were independents. Notably absent from the list were the local faction members and representatives of big business typically associated with corruption and money politics. The NP legislator commented,

> After I proposed my version, the Executive Yuan tried everything they could to stop the passage of such a law. The Executive Yuan . . . of course, understandably opposed the passage of replacing administrative orders or regulations with formal law. I can understand their situation, but I totally disagree. What I mean is that if I were a bureaucrat, I would want as much discretion as possible and not to be constrained by procedures mandated by law.[4]

After the NP introduced its draft bill, the reformers held five committee hearings, again chaired by NP, DPP, and KMT legislators with clean reputations. In May 1998, the committee passed the bill after nine committee hearings and one public hearing. A typical bill passes the Taiwanese legislature after only one or two committee hearings.

According to several interviewees, the Executive Yuan's opposition to the substance of TAPA afforded the legislature more opportunities to manipulate the legislative process. For example, the NP legislators invited many scholars to participate, thereby increasing the act's legitimacy and broadening support for a more comprehensive TAPA. Prior to the final resolution, legislators conducted a closed session involving interparty negotiations. On January 14, 1999, the legislature as a whole considered the bill and passed the second and third readings without any vote or opposition (China 1999).

The basic provisions include a public notice and comment process for all regulations, public access to agencies' information, notification of all public hearings, and judicial review of administrative actions. These provisions are designed to increase the degree of public information, participation, and accountability of agency decisions. Bureaucrats interested in continuing corrupt practices were the clear losers.

TAPA's Requirements and Their Effects

Table 4.1 lists TAPA's key administrative procedural requirements for all executive branch agencies when promulgating regulations across all policy areas as well as the political impact(s) of each change in the policy process. TAPA includes extensive technical detail. For example, the notice and comment and judicial review provisions are the central requirements of Taiwan's administrative law and are quite detailed. Agencies must notify the public and allow citizens to comment before publishing regulations. Agencies must then respond to every comment, a process that theoretically could take years. Agencies previously wrote regulations without having to jump through a series of procedural hoops; final regulations now can take years to promulgate. In the case of judicial review, members of the public can go to court to try to convince a judge to reverse regulations, another process that can take years to resolve. Unlike the U.S. APA, the judicial review provision is included in the 1998 Administrative Litigation Act (China 1998), which authorizes a separate administrative court to review agency actions.

These arduous procedural requirements enfranchised new groups and thereby increased monitoring, predictability, and control of agency decisions. These effects solved Executive Yuan delegation problems, allowing executives to control agencies' information collection and dissemination. The notice and comment process forces bureaucrats to reveal information, making their activities increasingly observable to the public. Agencies thus must consider the political costs and benefits of their actions. In addition, the public nature of the process decreases the likelihood that decisions made between agencies and their favorite constituencies will conflict with the preferences of the legislature or the president. Finally each step of the process gives executives multiple opportunities to intervene if an agency deviates from preferred policies (McCubbins, Noll, and Weingast 1987, 259). To the extent that executives conflict with their un-

TABLE 4.1. The 1999 Taiwan Administrative Procedure Act

Procedural Requirement	Political Impact
• Requires public notice and comment period for proposed rules and agency reorganizations (Articles 9, 11)	• Since agencies must consider relevant political interests prior to making a new decision, sufficiently organized interest groups are more likely to influence or veto agency's decision.
• Requires agency investigation of evidence and facts regarding appeals. Must record and notify relevant parties of decision justifications (Articles 36–43)	
• Allows public access to agencies' information (except national security matters) (Articles 44–46)	• Procedural requirements have the benefit of causing the most controversial issues to generate the most complete information.
• Agencies must notify or announce to, in a government document (or by any other method), the relevant parties of a public hearing well in advance. Notice should include purpose, names of participants, date and location, and procedure of hearing (Articles 54–56)	• Since process is public, we are less likely to observe decisions made between agencies and their favorite constituencies that conflict with preferences of president and legislature.
• Chairman of public hearing should be chief executive of agency or any other appointee. Procedures allow relevant parties to state opinion; give evidence; and with chairman's permission, ask for testimony by witness, investigator, and relevant parties. Relevant parties can claim dissent to chairman's decision. Chairman can override dissent. Entire process must be recorded (Articles 60–66)	• Slows down agency decision making process and gives principals multiple opportunities to respond if agency deviates from their policy preferences.
• Entitles any party whose "rights or legal interests are infringed upon through an unlawful administrative act by a central or local government agency" to "initiate an administrative action . . . in the high administrative court" (Article 4). Delegates review of administrative actions to courts (Articles 13–18)	

Source: Administrative Litigation Act of Taiwan 1998; Administrative Procedure Act of Taiwan 1999; McCubbins, Noll, and Weingast 1987.

Note: The 1998 Administrative Litigation Act (ALA) authorizes judicial review of administrative actions. According to former legislator John K. C. Huang, the "ALA follows the German Administrative Court Act and is not intended to include TAPA or to be a part thereof from the beginning" (e-mail exchange with author, March 12, 2001).

derlings on issues of public policy, these tools reduce agents' capacity to deviate from principals' policy preferences.

Why Taiwan Passed an APA

In this section, I examine two episodes of administrative procedural codification in the Taiwanese case: the failure to pass an APA during the first Lee administration and the 1999 passage of TAPA. My dependent variable is the change in the degree of administrative procedural control during a particular administration. Institutional and political changes during Lee's second administration provided the impetus for TAPA's passage.

Intraparty Conflict and Defection of the Nonmainstream Faction

President Lee had no control problems with the bureaucracy during the 1988–96 period. Since he did not have to concern himself with managing delegation to like-minded bureaucrats, he lacked an incentive to constrain the bureaucracy through an APA. After all, the KMT had ruled Taiwan since 1949 and controlled all branches of government until the DPP's Chen Shui-Bian won the 2000 presidential election. However, some factional conflict arose within the KMT in the early 1990s. In 1991, for strategic reasons, Lee chose as his premier a prominent general, Hau Pei-Tsun, from the nonmainstream faction. Prior to 1993, the main conflict involved Lee's mainstream faction and the nonmainstream faction of mainlanders representing the party's old guard (T.-J. Cheng and Haggard 2001, 200).

Shortly after the December 1992 elections, "factions within the party used the KMT's poor performance as a base to launch their attacks against the party mainstream" (Hood 1997, 108). Internal party conflict continued:

> By the Spring of 1993, the battle lines of inner-party strife became especially clear, with the creation of the Chinese Democratic Reformers Alliance. Factional splits within the party now threatened the future of the KMT's electoral success. More importantly, nonmainstream factions came to view a KMT loss in upcoming year-end county elections to be in their favor because the mainstream would have to call on the mainlander factions for help. (108)

In August 1993, portions of the nonmainstream faction broke off and formed the New Party (T.-J. Cheng and Haggard 2001, 200; Hood 1997, 144).[5] Moreover, factional differences led to serious rifts with important consequences for party organization.

> Leaders were unable to stop the diminution of power from the center, and the growing influence of local factions. Factional infighting led to multiple party vice chairmen and a more diverse central committee and central standing committee, thus weakening the largely singular role of party chairmen like Chiang Kai-Shek and Chiang Ching-Kuo. By the 15th party congress, even the central committee and central standing committee had lost the importance they held in the past. Power had shifted almost completely to the elected bodies. (Hood 1997, 144)

With the defection, the Legislative Yuan now included legislators from three political parties: the KMT, the DPP, and the New KMT Alliance/NP. After 1995, with the KMT commanding only slightly more than half of the seats in the legislature, party unity became increasingly critical. Otherwise, the party—both mainstream and proreform factions—was vulnerable to a no-confidence vote. Indeed, as T.-J. Cheng and Haggard (2001, 201) point out, Lee had the support of the new KMT legislators from the mainstream faction, but the rise of the opposition and the threat of outright factional defection (which ultimately came to pass) meant that he needed to appease nonmainstream legislators as well.

Institutional Changes and the KMT's Declining Electoral Performance

Table 4.2 summarizes the institutional changes that affected the powers of the legislature and the presidency. These changes altered both the president's and legislators' expectations about the future and thus their incentives. For my purposes, the key change, in terms of weakening the powers of the chief executive, is the lowering of the no-confidence vote threshold from two-thirds to a simple majority.

The KMT's electoral performance also deteriorated between 1975 and 1998. Figure 4.1 shows this pattern for both the KMT's vote and seat shares. In 1995, the KMT's majority reached an all-time low of 52.3 percent (85 seats, a razor-thin 3-seat majority). Though the party recovered somewhat in 1998, capturing a 54.7 percent share (123 seats), under the post-1997 simple majority no-confidence rule, Lee clearly had reason to worry not only that his party might lose its capacity to control the policy agenda but also that he could lose power. In fact, the DPP, which captured 33.2 percent of the popular vote and 32.9 percent of the seats (54), and the NP, which captured 13 percent of the vote and 12.8 percent of the seats (21), began discussing the possibility of a "grand reconciliation." Hence, the KMT justifiably felt intense pressure to reverse its electoral slide (Y.-S. Wu 1998). Indeed, the coalition of legislators pushing for the APA consisted of a group of DPP, NP, and KMT members with reputations for opposing corruption.

TABLE 4.2. Institutional Changes, 1990–2000

Relevant Dates	KMT/ Legislative Branch	Lee Teng-hui/ Executive Branch
June 1990	Long-term parliamentarians' tenure ends as of December 1991; elections of three reorganized representative bodies in 1991 and 1992	
July 1995		Legislative Yuan approves first presidential election on March 23, 1996.
July 1997		Authority is given to appoint the premier without consent of Legislative Yuan.
July 1997	Legislative Yuan's vote of no confidence requirement reduced from two-thirds to 50 percent plus one	Can dissolve Legislative Yuan within 10 days following vote of no confidence
July 1997	Recall of president or vice president requires motion of one-fourth and is proposed with concurrence of two-thirds of National Assembly. Must pass national referendum by 50 percent plus one.	
July 1997		Presidential and vice-presidential terms limited to one consecutive four-term year
July 1997	Effective 2003, National Assembly has authority to confirm presidential appointment of grand justices (single eight-year term)	

Source: Constitution of the Republic of China.

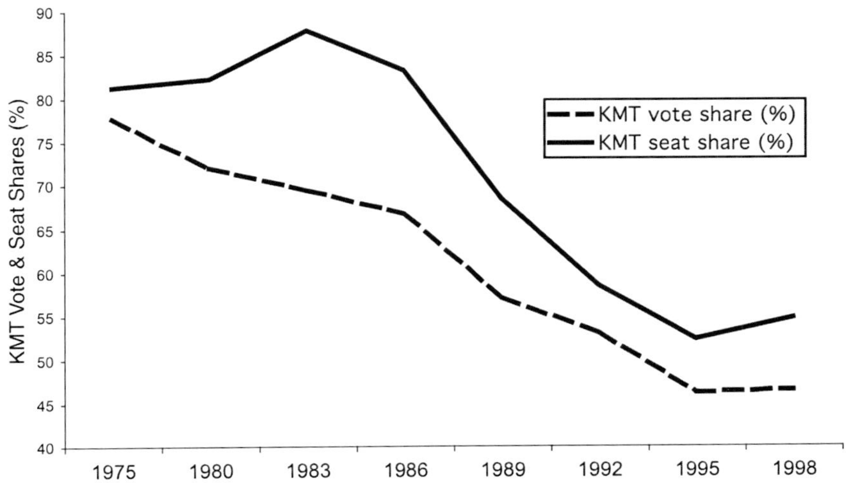

FIG. 4.1. KMT's electoral performance in Taiwan's Legislative Yuan elections. (Data from Central Election Committee [Zhongyang xuanju weiyuanhui], various years; Official Report of the Election [Xuanju gongbao], excerpted from Lin 1996; 1998 data from http://www.agora.stm.it/elections/election/taiwan.htm.)

The 1997 county and city magistratical election results gave the KMT increasing cause for concern about its capacity to retain power. The DPP not only surpassed the KMT vote for the first time, winning 43 percent of the total, but also won 12 districts; the DPP already controlled the Taipei mayorship.[6] Combined, these 13 districts included more than 70 percent of the country's total population (Diamond 2001, 54).

Much of the so-called "black-gold" or corruption money took place at local levels. Consequently, these election results were particularly important. After factoring in the KMT's loss in the 1998 Kaohsiung mayoral race (when the party received 48.13 percent of the votes, compared to the DPP's 48.71 percent), KMT leaders had ample reason to worry that black gold would hamper the party's chances of winning at the national level.

Breaking Corrupt Practices and the Preferences of TAPA's Support Coalition

Anticorruption as an Emerging Priority

With democratic transition and the implementation of popular elections, the political survival of elected officials, including the president, depended on winning popular votes and therefore on satisfying constituent demands. Doing so entailed changing specific status quo policies, especially in those issue areas most salient to the public. And in recent years, inadequate public infrastructure and environmental protections have become among Taiwan's most visible concerns, particularly among younger voters. Voters, in turn, closely associate institutional corruption with these policy areas (H. Chu 2000b; "Soong Laments" 1998) because corruption is increasingly seen as a primary cause of Taiwan's environmental problems and lax enforcement of public health and safety standards in public infrastructure projects (Roberts et al. 2000). In fact, "since 1992, the DPP has sought to make 'money politics' and 'mafia politics' the most salient issue in Taiwan's elections. The muckraking efforts of the opposition lawmakers were assisted by a growing number of independent-minded prosecutors and the market-oriented mass media" (T.-J. Cheng and Chu 2002, 48).

Public opinion data attest to the success of the DPP's efforts. Survey data from 1992–96 show a clear trend toward a worsening KMT image among the general population. For example, when asked whether the KMT "accommodate[s] or fight[s] corruption," the percentage answering "accommodate" increased from 18 percent in 1992 to 42 percent in 1996. When asked whether the KMT "fight[s] or cooperate[s] with special interests," the percentage selecting "cooperate" increased from 21 percent in 1992 to 33 percent in 1995. Finally, when asked whether the KMT "represent[s] rich and powerful or average people," the percentage choosing "rich and powerful" increased from 25 percent in 1992 to 44 percent in 1996.[7]

Overall, public opinion polls show that corruption has become the Taiwanese public's top concern.[8] A poll taken several months before the 2000 presidential election showed that the public perceived the ultimately victorious opposition DPP candidate as having the greatest integrity. Twenty-six percent of respondents named the DPP candidate as having the most integrity, compared to 16 percent who named the People's First Party (PFP) candidate[9] and 11 percent who mentioned the KMT candidate (Clark 2000). Indeed, popular perceptions in Taiwan held that "under the KMT, corruption and cronyism thoroughly infested government at all levels" (Roberts et al. 2000, 1). On this point, President Chen Shui-Bian of the DPP asked the public to "join him in reforming government and ridding it of the 'black-gold,' or corruption money, endemic in [Taiwanese] politics" (H. Chu 2000a, 3). Indeed, Chen's signature campaign and inauguration speech promise was to "eliminate vote-buying and crackdown on 'black-gold' politics" (Chen 2000). Moreover, Taipei mayor Ma Ying-Jeou, a popular KMT figure, commented that "the KMT was in danger of 'bursting like a bubble' and is proposing a string of changes to clean up the party and make it more democratic and accountable" (Hilfe Country Report 2000a, 4).

In turn, according to Taiwan politics expert Shelley Rigger, "The [2000] election turned on the issue of corruption and reform. And apparently Chen had a little more credibility as a reformer than [independent candidate] Soong" (Suh, Reyes, and Cheng 2000, 3). Chin observes even more starkly that "black-gold politics developed into a major problem during the past fifteen years and . . . it might have ended KMT rule in Taiwan during the 2000 presidential election" (2003, 5).

Black-gold politics, including KMT ties to organized crime, thus mattered to the party's reform faction because these policies alienated large numbers of voters, who were increasingly concerned with the consequences of corruption for public policy. This alienation, in turn, represented a tangible threat to the KMT's political dominance. Indeed, younger voters (more than half of the electorate) increasingly demanded improved public infrastructure and greener environmental policies (Chin 2003). Reflecting this perspective, Ray Chen, the chief executive officer of Compal Electronics, commented, "We need the government to create transportation and other infrastructure. . . . We need to make environmental regulations that are strict and clear, with no gray areas" (Chin 2003, 2).

As consumers and environmental advocates began to recognize the public health and safety risks posed by the KMT's corrupt practices, these issues, along with the problem of corruption itself, became highly salient (Frassrand 1998). The KMT routinely won elections when the only noteworthy issue was relations with China. But as these other issues became more and more conspicuous to voters, the KMT's advantage eroded. Political entrepreneurs such as the DPP determined that by identifying themselves as the party of clean government (as well as the party of all the people, a clean environment, high-quality public infrastructure, public safety, and so on), they could use these newly salient issues as a means of challenging KMT dominance (Eyton 1997; Flanigan 1998; Ganz 1999).

These changes explain, at least in part, why Chen Shui-Bian, a former Taipei mayor and the DPP's 2000 presidential candidate, pledged "to end money politics, cozy ties between government and big business and other 'abnormal' practices entrenched after half a century of KMT rule" (Ganz 1999). Chen continued to point to the "KMT's stranglehold on the entire government machinery, underworld ties, one-sided pro-business policies

. . . environmental destruction," adding in classic populist overtones, "Only if the DPP well mobilizes the Taiwan people will we be able to win final victory" (Ganz 1999). Chen's campaign strategy, which included TV commercials "featuring young people in a bid to drum up support among young voters" ("From Poverty to Power" 2000), also demonstrated the increasing importance of younger voters, particularly for proreform candidates.

Hence, the DPP saw the changes in Taiwan's electorate as an opportunity to undermine the KMT. But the DPP faced competition from the KMT reformers who also believed that they could capture young reform-minded voters (Hilfe Country Report 2000a). The KMT had the advantage of the party's brand name (though somewhat tarnished) and could campaign for an end to corrupt practices and thus promote better public health and safety standards and enhanced environmental protection. If the KMT's reform faction could steal these issues from the DPP and change the KMT's image, the party might be able to retain power.

In fact, James Soong, a KMT nonmainstream faction leader who sought but failed to win the party's nomination and then ran as an independent presidential candidate in 2000, pursued precisely this strategy.[10] Along these lines, the *Times* of London thus observed that Soong's "main constituency consists of voters who favor ending corruption but fear that Mr. Chen, the DPP candidate, could provoke a Chinese invasion" ("Taiwan's 50-Year Regime" 2000, 1–2). To accomplish its goal of resuscitating the party's image, the KMT's reformist faction vowed to begin a purge of party elements responsible for corrupt practices. Eric Chu Liluan, a party youth leader and reformist, commented, "This is a turning point for the KMT. We are not stupid. We need the votes—not the money. This reformist faction will strive to be the dominant force in the KMT. We would like the party to be more clean." He added that if the proreform forces gained control of the party, they might return KMT assets to the public (A. T. Cheng 2000, 1, 3). And Lin Feng-Cheng, secretary-general of the KMT Central Committee, commented shortly after assuming office that he sought to transform the party into a "young, localized, pluralistic, grass-roots, volunteer-based and democratic" party, more in tune with the times. He added that the KMT is "sincere in its reforms, and that the thoroughness of the reforms will not disappoint the expectations of the people" ("Lin Feng-Cheng" 2000).

Three high-profile 1996–97 cases that drew public attention to black-gold problems just before the KMT's big loss in the 1997 county and city magistratical elections offer further evidence of the KMT's critical need to respond decisively to the issue of rising crime and money politics. In November 1996, the head of the Taoyuan county government was murdered by gang members who broke into his residence. The motive was reputedly a dispute over fixing land prices. Later that year, Peng Wan-Lu, head of the DPP's women's bureau, was abducted, raped, and murdered in a crime that was widely reported as being politically motivated. At minimum, the connection of a politician with violent crime was bad for the government's image. Finally, in April 1997, the daughter of actress Pai Ping-Ping was abducted and murdered (Chin 2003, 7–8).

Operation Chih-Ping, conducted in 1996, involved a major sweep targeting organized crime members who held elected office. Though not particularly effective, the operation had a high public profile (e.g., media images of crime lords being whisked away by helicopter to the prison on Green Island). By conducting this showy anticrime sweep, the government intended to demonstrate that it was serious about fighting money politics, crime, and corruption (Chin 2003, 7–8).

Courting Younger Voters

Most voters under age 50 were born on the island of Taiwan and hence lack their parents' emotional ties to the mainland (H. Chu 2000a). As one 22-year-old Taiwanese voter said, "Taiwan is independent now in reality. I don't identify myself with mainlanders because I don't have any life experience similar to theirs" (H. Chu 2000b, 1). A 23-year-old voter added, "I think I'm Chinese—but not mainland Chinese. When I travel abroad, I say I'm from Taiwan, not from China" (3).

As self-identified native Taiwanese voters have emerged as a dominant population demographic, politicians in Taiwan have become increasingly concerned with winning those votes. And a growing number of these voters have become fed up with the KMT's corrupt practices (H. Chu 2000a; S. Wu 2000). Younger voters not only recoil from the KMT's perceived cozy relations with organized crime but are increasingly alienated by the policy outcomes such illicit relationships produce (S. Wu 2000). Under the status quo regulatory environment, Taiwan's primary winners were big business and the KMT-dominated bureaucrats who benefited from the distribution of public works contracts. These public works contractors cut corners and built infrastructure projects out of inferior materials that led to crumbling buildings and bridges. Roberts et al. (2000, 5) have summarized the relationship between corruption in Taiwan's contracting industry and rising public safety concerns:

> The construction industry illustrates how corruption also has imperiled public safety. Faulty work was responsible for many of the 2,321 deaths in [the September 1999] earthquake, for example. Investigators allege government inspectors were paid off by contractors to overlook flaws in apartment buildings.

In addition, proenergy industry policies led to relatively unregulated construction of chemical and nuclear power plants. Many of these projects raised serious environmental concerns, which came to a head when a nearly $2 billion chemical plant project was halted in 1997 following accusations of corruption and inadequate environmental protections (Roberts et al. 2000, 5). The corruption problem even extended to the military:

> A three-star general who headed the body responsible for handling military supplies and provisions resigned to accept responsibility for a bribery scandal over the construction of ammunition dumps for the Air Force. Nine other military officers, including a two-star general, have received various penalties for dereliction of duties relating to the case. ("Counting the Cost" 1998)

As a result of this and other similar incidents, the KMT gained a reputation as the party of corruption, money politics, and organized crime (Hilfe Country Report 2000b; "Soong Laments" 1998; Suh, Reyes, and Cheng 2000).

At the same time, as Taiwan grew wealthier, younger voters became increasingly concerned with quality-of-life issues, such as public health and safety and environmental protection ("Soong Laments" 1998). According to DPP leader Lin I-Hsiung, Taiwan's younger voters "want to live on our island, protect the environment and have good relations with the mainland" (Flanigan 1998, 3). No longer focused solely on the issue of national survival, younger voters began to demand more from government than merely national security, and the KMT's corrupt deals put public safety and the environment at risk. In other words, the losers under KMT rule were the consumers and environmental groups excluded under the status quo regulatory decision-making process.

One means by which the KMT could alter its public image to court younger voters would be to appoint younger party members to senior posts. To be effective, such a strategy would need to focus on the mainlander party members who represent the party's old guard. Figure 4.2 presents the trend in average ages of mainlander and native Taiwanese cabi-

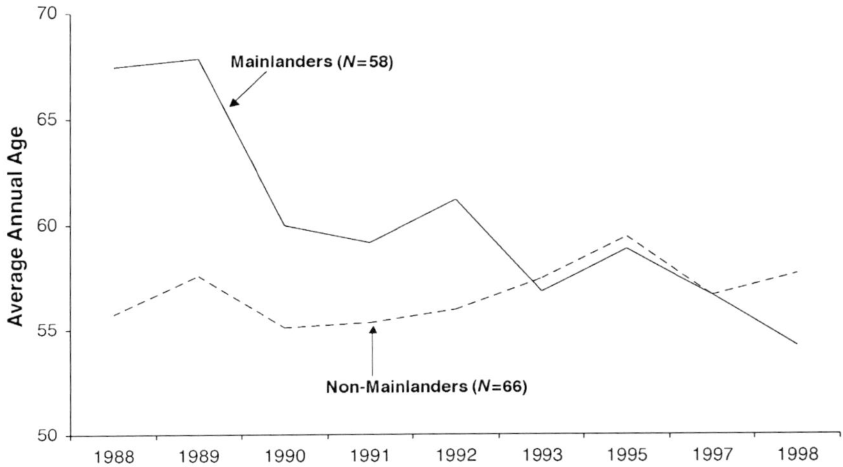

FIG. 4.2. Average age of cabinet ministers, 1988–98.
(Data from Central News Agency 1999; *Who's Who in the Republic of China* 2000; ethnicity data compiled by author from various sources.)

net ministers from 1988 to 1998.[11] In fact, the average age of cabinet ministers belonging to the mainlander ethnic group declined substantially, from 68 in 1988–89 to 58 in 1997–98 period ($p < .01$). Over the same period, the average age of nonmainlander ministers, who tended to be far younger at the outset, hardly changed at all. In the former period, mainlander ministers were, on average, eleven years older than their nonmainstream counterparts (68 versus 57, $p < .01$). By 1997–98, the age gap had disappeared almost entirely (58 versus 57.8). These data suggest that Lee may indeed have sought to present a more youthful face to the electorate, in part by appointing younger mainlander ministers.

Heijin (Black-Gold) Politics and the Bureaucracy

Changing status quo policy outcomes in Taiwan required controlling the bureaucrats. Seeing why requires considering in greater detail the relationship between bureaucratic corruption and public policy. Black-gold politics is the central corruption issue in Taiwan (A. T. Cheng 2000; H. Chu 2000b). In Taiwan, black (*hei*) means the underworld; gold (*jin*) means money or business. "Black-gold politics consisted of the penetration into politics of violent underworld figures and greedy business tycoons and the inevitable subsequent social ills such as vote buying, political violence, insider trading, bid rigging, and official (and unofficial) corruption" (Tsai 1998 quoted in Chin 2003, 5).

The term *black gold* evokes the image of bribery and gangsters associated with the influence of big business in contemporary Taiwanese politics. Under this system, "public works contracts are routinely let out to unqualified but well-connected companies" (Roberts et al. 2000, 3). The result, according to Rigger, is that much of the industry "is controlled by government and gangsters who build buildings out of tin cans" (quoted in Roberts et al. 2000, 3). Moreover, Chin (2003, 128) explains, black-gold politics is a direct consequence of a steadily declining ruling party adopting extreme measures to maintain its hold on power:

> The KMT hoped to counter the growing challenge from the indigenous political party, the DPP, which had been encroaching on its power base by winning a significant number of seats in major elections. While facing this daunting challenge from outside the party, the split between two factions within the KMT, and the subsequent establishment in 1993 of a third party—the New Party—by former KMT members, all the more convinced KMT leaders that their alliance with local factions, business tycoons, and gangsters was [a] necessary evil if they wanted to remain in power.

Black gold is also linked to a $6 billion slush fund from which the KMT reportedly drew money to buy votes (A. T. Cheng 2000). The KMT's possessions, which in 1999 yielded $261 million in net profits from equity investments alone (see table 4.3), consisted mainly of shares in seven major holding companies, listed in table 4.4. The majority of these enterprises

TABLE 4.3. Money Machine: Kuomintang Equity Investments (in U.S. dollars)

Year	Total	Net Profit
1993	$712 million	$173 million
1994	$1.36 billion	$307 million
1995	$1.4 billion	$240 million
1996	$1.6 billion	$286 million
1997	$2.0 billion	$542 million
1998	$2.23 billion	$395 million
1999	$2.29 billion	$261 million

Source: Cheng 2000.
Note: Investments do not include real estate and other fixed assets owned by the party.

TABLE 4.4. Big Seven KMT Holding Companies

Central Investment Co.
Kwang Hua Investment Co.
Central Motion Pictures Corp.
Hua Hsia Investment Co.
China Broadcasting Co.
Central Daily News
China Daily News

Source: Cheng 2000.

were highly profitable and had formerly been owned by the state. "The remaining assets are in the form of stakes in dozens of listed and privately held companies in Taiwan and abroad, including mainland China. Key stakes in these concerns were held by prominent local families, which had grown rich and powerful under the patronage of the KMT regime" (A. T. Cheng 2000, 2).

As table 4.3 shows, the KMT's total assets more than tripled between 1993 and 1999. This increase occurred under the management of Liu Tai-Ying, a close friend of President Lee. During this period, opposition parties as well as the reformist faction within the party criticized the KMT for using those assets more for vote buying than for improving the country. Prior to the 1980s, the KMT had funded infrastructure projects and started key businesses that the private sector would not support. But during the 1980s, when the KMT began to implement political reforms such as multiparty elections, it reportedly began redirecting its resources toward buying votes to ensure that its candidates won at the polls (A. T. Cheng 2000, 2).

Black-gold politics, however, became controversial when the media reported that the KMT used gangsters to buy votes. While the KMT denied these charges, Li Ao, the NP's 2000 presidential candidate, stated, "They would give you money in one hand and tell you to vote for so and so" (quoted in A. T. Cheng 2000, 2). This issue reached a new level of controversy when some of the gangsters decided to stop functioning as intermediaries and instead run for office themselves under the KMT party label. According to Eric Chu Liluan, a KMT reformist legislator and official campaign spokesperson for Lien Chan, the KMT's 2000 presidential candidate, at least 10 percent of the Legislative Yuan and 25 percent of the local assemblies are linked to gangs (ibid., 2). Whether or not corrupt practices truly reached such an extent, at least some relationship certainly existed between the KMT and organized crime, and the public accurately perceived that relationship (H. Chu 2000b; "DPP Launches New Campaign" 2000; Ganz 1999; Healy and Eyton 1998; Hilfe Country Report 2000b; Roberts et al., 2000; S. Wu 2000).

In addition, not all the money for buying votes came from party funds. According to a former legislator, the stain spread when corrupt politicians reached office:

> The party will contribute only in key races, forcing many candidates to pay out of their own pockets. This leads to further corrupt behavior once the politician wins, as they may want to recoup their money by taking cuts in public works projects in their constituen-

> cies. In fact, many such projects are subcontracted out by companies linked to lawmakers. (quoted in A. T. Cheng 2000, 3)

How did black-gold politics affect corrupt behavior in the bureaucracy? If the bureaucracy gives favorable regulatory treatment to companies in which the KMT is a prominent shareholder, the party benefits directly as its net profits rise along with the capital valuation of those companies (a rise in stock prices).

In addition, the bureaucracy is likely to award government contracts for regulatory projects, such as public works, to companies linked to the KMT, thereby further enhancing the profitability of such firms. According to Cal Clark (2000),

> When Lee Teng-hui and his young Turks challenged the KMT old guard, they turned to the support of rich business people and local patronage-oriented political factions. . . . The burgeoning political corruption offended general public sensibilities in three major areas. First, many contracts for public projects became highly politicized. Corrupt legislators would form their own companies to bid on contracts and, in many instances, would form ties to organized crime, who, in turn, would deter bids by legitimate businesses. Needless to say, quality suffered greatly, and public cynicism about government projects rose. Second, several prominent business leaders and conglomerates blatantly used political connections and legislative positions to help their corporations and influence the stock market, leading to a seemingly endless series of major scandals in the early and mid-1990s. Finally, local political factions, which had always been patronage-oriented, became increasingly blatant and tied to organized crime.

The end result was shoddy construction and delays in major public transportation projects such as Taipei's subway line, the world's most expensive at $13 billion and finished two years behind schedule (Roberts et al. 2000). The KMT's dominant faction and the bureaucracy had a powerful incentive to preserve the status quo and oppose policies that would break the existing method of delivering public works.

Managing Coalition Politics

The increasingly youthful legislature became more reform oriented and hence more hostile to Lee's more conservative KMT faction. The provision of the 1997 constitutional reform lowering the no-confidence vote threshold from two-thirds to a simple majority, in turn, may have provided Lee with an additional incentive to support the reformers as well as to buy off the legislature to reduce the likelihood of a no-confidence vote. TAPA's timing certainly offers suggestive albeit by no means definitive evidence that the 1997 amendment influenced Lee's decision to accept administrative reform. Along these lines, Huang Jiashu, a senior analyst at the Taiwan, Hong Kong and Macau Research Center of the People's University in Beijing, commented in 1998, "The KMT is a union of interests. . . . Lee can no longer dictate. He must play coalition politics along with others" (Healy and Eyton 1998, 22).

Yeh Jiunn-Rong of National Taiwan University explains the positions of the young KMT reformists and of the mainstream party members:

> The young KMT reformists believed that by passing an APA, the bureaucracy would open up and effectively enfranchise new groups. But the mainstream KMT members and bureaucrats opposed the rule-making provisions. The KMT wanted things to stay the same. In terms of the decision-making process, the KMT had more discretion under the status quo but had less after the implementation of TAPA. There was no opposition from the DPP or NP on rule-making provisions. Not at all.[12]

Soong implicitly acknowledged the potential problem of bureaucratic opposition to TAPA several months before TAPA's passage: "The country cannot afford to see further internal squabbling over government restructuring. . . . Government restructuring should . . . be carried out in a gradual manner in order to reduce the backlash from public functionaries" ("Soong Laments" 1998).

Managing Intrabranch Delegation with an APA

Why an APA?

In one stroke, the APA broke the status quo deal making between the old wing of the KMT, entrenched bureaucrats, and big businesses (including organized crime bosses). The APA forced bureaucrats to change their behavior by enfranchising consumer and environmental groups in the regulatory decision-making process. The new law also shined light on the government contracting process, making it harder for bureaucrats to cut backroom deals with crime bosses.

The winners were consumers, environmental groups, and export-oriented or internationalist businesses that benefited from an improved climate for foreign investors, who were attracted by Taiwan's cleaner political process. For example, the Evergreen Group, an internationally oriented transportation conglomerate, favored reform, including an APA, because increased governmental transparency would facilitate increased foreign investment, thereby helping group members' bottom lines. Not surprisingly, therefore, the Evergreen Group was "a major financial backer of Chen [Shui-Bian]'s political career" ("DPP Launches New Campaign" 2000, 2). The losers under the APA system were the building contractors and other public works businesses that were cozy with the old-school KMT members.

KMT reformers wanted to control the bureaucracy through an APA to rob the DPP of its primary issue, thereby effectively stealing the rival party's political oxygen. To win support among youthful, proenvironmental voters, for example, the KMT reformists sought to thwart a major nuclear reactor project:

> The most celebrated problem in the late 1990s was an attempt by the opposition and dissenting KMT deputies to block funding for Taiwan's fourth nuclear power plant, located at Kungliao. The project was stalled in parliament in May 1996, just ahead of the official announcement. . . . The episode also illustrated the potency of political and environmental opposition to key projects. (Hilfe Country Report 2000b)

The reformist KMT ministers recognized that unless they undertook far-reaching measures to change the party's image as well as public policy outcomes, the KMT was likely to lose power. Reining in the entire government bureaucracy represented a relatively drastic measure, designed to reform the KMT's image by producing different policy outcomes in a broad range of policy areas, particularly with respect to environmental protection and public infrastructure. The reformists hoped that such changes would undercut the DPP's primary source of political strength. By improving executive control over the bureaucracy, the TAPA helped to accomplish this goal. Because the regulation of public works projects was so poor, voters were concerned about public safety and the quality of the nation's infrastructure. And, like their contemporaries in other advanced industrial countries, young Taiwanese voters were wary of nuclear power and environmental degradation and were generally concerned with improving their quality of life. Essentially, the APA undid the cozy relations between bureaucrats and contractors that had become the source of many of the KMT's political problems.

In sum, the APA provided DPP, NP, and KMT reformists with the necessary tools to reduce corrupt practices among the KMT and the bureaucracy. Such procedures as the public notice and comment process and judicial review of agency decisions enabled citizens to hold bureaucrats accountable for their decisions. Under the notice and comment process, bureaucrats must take into account opinions of new groups previously excluded from the KMT's decision-making process.

Why Lee Supported TAPA

The lock-in argument would predict an APA under Lee's first administration because, with his party's electoral dominance at an all-time low, he faced the possibility of losing Taiwan's first popular election. Under that hypothesis, a vulnerable president should seek to lock in his favored policies through an APA. Yet an APA did not pass.

During Lee's second administration, in contrast, the lock-in argument would not predict an APA because the KMT expected to win the next presidential election, especially after increasing its legislative seat share in 1998. In fact, almost none of the officials I interviewed believed that the KMT would lose the 2000 presidential election.[13] Yet in this instance, an APA passed. These two cases suggest that the lock-in hypothesis cannot explain Taiwan's APA passage. Instead, Lee went along with an APA to keep the KMT from losing more young voters.

None of the scholars, legislators of various parties, and senior bureaucrats I interviewed believed that the KMT sought to use TAPA to lock in the status quo. Quite the contrary, the APA facilitated changes to status quo bureaucratic practices by enfranchising new groups previously excluded from the KMT's decision-making process. Cheng Pao Ching, a legislator and convener of the DPP caucus, explained the measure's benefits:

> Because we do not have a formal lobbying system, we see equal opportunity for all groups now. As a matter of fact, the DPP used to maintain better relations with social groups such as environmental or other weaker groups. In terms of new relationships, I do not see much difficulty for these groups in having access to agency policy-making.

In short, by enfranchising new groups, TAPA's supporters, including President Lee, clearly intended to facilitate the alteration rather than the preservation of the policy status quo.

Conclusion

Taiwan's passage of an APA is thus consistent with the reining-in explanation and inconsistent with the lock-in hypothesis. Democratic transition certainly pushed politicians in the general direction of political reform but does not explain why they specifically supported the passage of an APA.

TAPA passed during Lee's second administration because the KMT reformists wanted to change Taiwan's status quo policies regarding environmental protection and public infrastructure. To do so, they needed to break the corrupt relationship between entrenched bureaucrats and big businesses.

Table 4.5, excerpted from table 2.2, shows which of the key conditions for APA passage existed during each period in Taiwan and provides information regarding whether the president had problems with cabinet ministers or bureaucrats and whether bureaucrats enjoyed civil service protection. The table also compares the actual outcome with the logical prediction if Lee had indeed sought to lock in status quo policies at each point in time.

These data support my argument that Taiwan's APA enactment resulted from the president's concern about reining in bureaucrats who could not be fired. During Lee's first administration, neither of the key conditions was present. So even though the bureaucracy enjoyed civil service protection, Lee did not need to worry about constraining disloyal underlings. In Lee's second administration, however, the KMT reformers sought to reverse the party's declining electoral dominance by competing with the DPP for the increasingly critical bloc of young, native-born voters. Reining in the bureaucracy thus provided a means of preventing the DPP from replacing the KMT as the country's dominant political party rather than a tool for locking in the status quo.

To win these voters, the KMT reformers advocated the same policies that led to the DPP's rise and popularity—clean government, environ-

TABLE 4.5. Factors Affecting APA Enactment in Taiwan

Presidential Cases	Problem Ministers?	Problem Bureaucrats?	Civil Service Protection?	Did APA Pass?	"Lock-in" Prediction
Taiwan 1: Lee (1988–96)	No	No	Yes	No	Yes
Taiwan 2: Lee (1997–99)	No	Yes	Yes	Yes	No

mental protection, and a higher-quality (i.e., safer) public infrastructure. The KMT's new guard sought to remake the party's image. By breaking the ties among bureaucrats, wealthy business interests, and in some instances organized crime bosses, KMT reformers wanted to make government policy more responsive to public health and safety concerns. TAPA forced bureaucrats to change their behavior to take into account the views of younger voters and their representatives (e.g., consumer and environmental groups) prior to implementing policies. President Lee did not necessarily prefer to rein in the bureaucrats, who were his political allies, but did so because he prioritized maintaining KMT power over maintaining the relative free hand that his bureaucratic allies enjoyed. In other words, for electoral reasons, he concluded that bureaucratic discretion was a necessary sacrifice to preserve the KMT's political dominance.

Taiwan is an important case for my theory for two primary reasons. First, Taiwan experienced not only an episode in which a president and the bureaucracy had similar preferences but also one in which the two groups' preferences diverged. Consequently, this case provides variation in the dependent variable. Second, Taiwan's transition to a president-parliamentary system makes it useful for showing how APA enactment can be consistent with a reining-in explanation and inconsistent with the lock-in hypothesis.[14]

My case study of Taiwan, combined with the Korean case study presented in chapter 3, suggests that the source of institutional barriers to policy change can vary across institutional and political settings. Despite institutional variations across both presidential and parliamentary systems, as long as the source of institutional barriers gives rise to intrabranch conflict, similar principal-agent problems may arise and similar solutions may be pursued. APAs can provide politicians in new democracies with one solution to this delegation problem.

By adopting TAPA, politicians in Taiwan initiated a citizen-bureaucrat exchange regarding policy-making. Before any new regulation can be implemented, members of the public now have the right to have their say. This process, if successful, is precisely the sort of mechanism that enhances democratic responsiveness.

5 | Cleaning House: Administrative Procedures and Patronage Politics in the Philippines

> *I believe that I was called to the Presidency to reestablish democracy and secure our freedoms by the separation of the powers that had come into my hands. . . . To that end, I bent all my efforts, convinced that that was what our people wanted first and foremost: a true democracy.*
>
> —Corazon Aquino, March 26, 1987

In chapter 1, I asserted that administrative procedural reform may be an important contributing factor but is not necessarily indispensable for the emergence of responsive democracy. Korea and Taiwan illustrate two cases in which presidents faced delegation problems within the executive branch that caused them to acquiesce to an administrative procedural act (APA). However, APA-like procedural controls offer presidents only a second-best solution, trailing the replacement of recalcitrant agents with loyal ones. In the presence of professionalized civil services, such replacement is usually impossible. But not all civil servants enjoy these protections, and this phenomenon sets the Philippines apart from Korea and Taiwan. The Philippines corresponds most closely to the typical stylized picture of the executive as a unified hierarchy. Whereas the Korean and Taiwanese presidents could not rely on unconstrained appointment and dismissal powers to mitigate agency problems, the Philippine president could.

This stark difference raises an interesting question regarding the relationship between administrative reform and democratic responsiveness. What does the Philippines' lack of a substantive APA imply about the state of democracy in that country? At minimum, it suggests that the Philippines may, in at least some dimensions, be less "democratic" than either Korea or Taiwan.

When Corazon Aquino assumed the Philippine presidency in February 1986, it was far from clear that she would be able to restore democracy to her country. Even with a supportive government, the challenges Aquino faced would have been daunting. But she also confronted a divided cabinet and a bureaucracy loyal to her ousted predecessor, Ferdinand Marcos (Timberman 1991). To succeed, Aquino needed the cooperation of political adversaries within her administration. Thus, when she entered office, her situation in many ways resembled that of Kim Young Sam when he took office in Korea.

Administrative procedures were one potential tool Aquino could use to resolve her delegation problems. Yet my theory predicts that in countries that lack professionalized civil service protection—that is, where leaders can freely appoint and dismiss cabinet ministers and fill bureaucratic posts through patronage—leaders will prefer to use these lower-cost tools rather than pursue an extensive APA. In fact, unlike her Korean and Taiwanese counterparts, Aquino relied on unconstrained appointment and dismissal powers to mitigate her agency problems. Consequently, she did not need the second-best option of an extensive APA.

This chapter begins with a discussion of clientelism and shows how patronage appointments play a dominant role in Philippine politics. The prevalence of patronage (or lack of a professionalized civil service) effectively mitigates agency slippage problems, rendering an extensive APA unnecessary. If a president has exclusive power to appoint and dismiss cabinet members, executives can manage intracoalitional conflict without resorting to an extensive APA.

I focus on the transition from the Marcos administration to that of Aquino. Aquino first sought to control the bureaucracy she inherited by ordering a national purge of all elected and appointed officials and employees and by creating additional undersecretary positions that she filled with her loyalists. Aquino resolved her conflict with different factions within her support coalition by ordering three major reshufflings of the cabinet.

After the purge officially ended on February 25, 1987, and after the new constitution was promulgated, Aquino, as a sole legislator, passed the Administrative Code of 1987 (Philippines 1987a, 1987b), including a short chapter on procedures for rules and regulations. The timing of the code's passage represents important evidence in support of my theory. Consistent with the theory, when Aquino's power to control personnel was threatened, she resorted to some APA-like procedures.

The procedural requirements Aquino implemented are not nearly as comprehensive as those of the Korean, Taiwanese, or U.S. APAs. Nevertheless, the Philippine provisions represent the anticipated degree of administrative procedural codification given the availability of alternative control mechanisms.

Clientelist Politics and Development of the Philippine Bureaucracy

Like their counterparts in many developing countries, Philippine politicians support their parties primarily through patron-client relationships. Clientelist politics—that is, the exchange of goods and services for political support—has dominated Philippine politics for decades. Hutchcroft (1998, 29) highlights one example of how the bureaucrats' loyalties were tied to politicians:

> In 1959, the Palace and Congress worked out the so-called *50-50 agreement,* in which responsibility for filling new bureaucratic posts would be divided equally between the president and the House of Representatives. While bureau directors complained about the requirement that they bring unqualified personnel into their units, they lacked the power to stand up to external pressures.[1]

In addition, as Cariño (1985, 14) notes, "Since the political parties were based on personal factions and could not be differentiated in terms of issues—the supreme issue of independence having already been officially attained—it made sense for politicians to put their protégés into the bureaucracy and for career personnel to attach themselves to political leaders." Patronage politics is especially prominent at the provincial and local levels of government. As Timberman (1991, 228) notes, "Provincial and local politicians are dependent upon the executive branch and Congress to provide funds, projects, and patronage opportunities they need. The president and Congress, in return, are politically dependent upon the local politicians to deliver votes in the next election." Finally, according to Soriano (1986, 1–7), the Philippine bureaucracy "is a sorry scenario of mediocre and poorly paid public servants of the old dispensation being replaced with other patronage appointees of no greater competence or experience in their tasks."

Despite the rampant trading of civil service jobs for political support, the Philippine bureaucracy did not always lack merit-based hiring and promotion or political neutrality. In fact, the United States installed a merit system for a new civil government shortly after lifting martial law in 1902. At the time of independence in 1946, the bureaucracy maintained its commitment to a merit-based promotion system. As is characteristic of modern career civil service systems, political appointments did not penetrate very deep into the executive agencies—only down to the undersecretary level. Temporary appointees, or "casuals," routinely left their positions as new governments were voted into office, and politicians rarely intervened in seniority-based promotion decisions (Francisco 1960 cited in Cariño 1989, 211). This system remained intact until Marcos declared martial law in 1972. The preceding year, Marcos had convened a constitutional convention focused on amending the constitution to allow him to stay in power beyond eight consecutive years. But Marcos halted the convention deliberations when he decided to exercise his national emergency powers and proclaim martial law.

Between 1946 and 1971, although the bureaucracy appeared to be on a path toward the institutionalization of a strong civil service, political parties were a different story. The Nacionalista Party (NP)[2] and the Liberal Party (LP) dominated all political institutions, including fraud-ridden elections. The NP and the LP were ideologically indistinguishable and lacked even significant personality differences.[3] Indeed, party switching was quite frequent. For example, Ramon Magsaysay (president from 1954–57) was secretary of national defense under the Liberal Party but ran for president as a Nacionalista. Marcos (1965–86) served as senate president and was president of the Liberal Party before switching and winning as a Nacionalista (Cariño 1989, 244–45).

Marcos put an end to the clear separation between politicians and career civil servants, changing the bureaucracy in ways that compromised career civil servants' neutrality. After staging a palace coup in 1972, Marcos abolished the legislature, suppressed the media, and imprisoned his political opponents. Over the following eight years, he replaced the existing presidential system with a parliamentary one and subsequently with a quasi-parliamentary system.

Marcos passed a new Civil Service Law (Philippines 1975) that formally strengthened the merit system.[4] But this law was merely a formality. In practice, Marcos weakened the bureaucracy in several important ways, most notably by (1) dismissing civil servants, (2) blurring the distinction between political and administrative officials and positions, and (3) creating the New Society Movement (the Kilusang Bagong Lipunan [KBL]).[5]

Marcos had the power to dismiss civil servants at will. Employees could be dismissed either summarily or through courtesy resignations. Summary dismissals occurred if employees committed serious acts or were deemed undesirable. Specifically, summary dismissals were authorized "(a) when the charge is serious and the evidence of guilt is strong; (b) when the respondent is a recidivist or has been repeatedly charged and there is reasonable ground to believe that he is guilty of the present charge; and (c) when the respondent is notoriously undesirable" (Philippines 1972). Courtesy resignations, in turn, were designed to remove all civil servants in case the individual employee could not be dismissed under the summary dismissal category. As Brillantes (1988, 125) describes, Marcos completely dominated the bureaucracy:

> Marcos could fire any government official at any level, at any time—from department deputy ministers and bureau directors, down to division and section chiefs. It did not matter that they were career executive service officers or civil service eligibles. . . . The so-called neutrality of the bureaucracy was compromised. And, of course, the time-honoured principle of security of tenure for bureaucrats was meaningless under the Marcosian dispensation. . . . The presidency was both effectively de-institutionalized and highly personalized. All officials in government—whether professional or political—owed their political survival to Marcos. Thus, they were accountable only to him and not to the people, who had no means of removing them anyway.

Second, Marcos obscured the distinction between political appointments and administrative positions by appointing his elected legislators as deputy ministers (equivalent to undersecretaries). Conversely, he moved career civil servants into political appointee positions and forced a significant number of technocrats to run for office. As a result, career civil servants increasingly coveted political office.

Third, Marcos ordered both the private and public sectors to participate in the KBL. The administration's party, the KBL encompassed non-partisan officials and employees as well. Marcos used KBL members for political purposes, such as election campaigns, popular mobilization, distorting statistics, and "window-dressing" programs (see Dubsky 1981 for more details).

As intended, the net effect of these bureaucratic changes was to destroy the civil service's neutrality and professionalism. In short, Marcos opened up patronage to such an extent that bureaucrats' incentives became directly tied to the preferences of the president and his advisers.

Appointing Loyal Agents: Redemocratization, De-Marcosification, and Patronage Appointments under Aquino

Under Marcos, politicians unquestionably controlled the bureaucracy. By the time of his 1986 ouster, Marcos had imposed a patronage system on the civil service whereby politicians literally traded votes for public sector jobs. After Aquino came into office, the issue of bureaucratic control resurfaced. According to Overholt (1986, 1163),

> Cory Aquino moved into an organizational vacuum. Her new regime . . . did not have a unified executive leadership or effective institutions, such as a reliable military, a unified national political party, or competent civil administration. It was, in short, the beneficiary of a vacuum, not a functioning machine.

During the 1986 presidential election, Aquino's campaign strategy mostly entailed opposing everything Marcos promised to voters. At one point during the campaign, Marcos responded to polls showing that civil servants were supporting Aquino by issuing a threat: "If you vote for Aquino, you will all lose your jobs." In response, the Aquino campaign immediately refuted this statement in a letter to all civil service employees in which she promised to "uphold the security of tenure of the civil service," adding, "Those of you who have performed your duties competently will be protected" (Cariño 1987, 271).

A detailed discussion of how Aquino came into power is neither within the scope of nor directly pertinent to this chapter. It is, however, useful to briefly review the sequence of events. Violent antiregime demonstrations continued for eighteen months after the August 1983 assassination of Corazon Aquino's husband, opposition politician Benigno Aquino. When a government commission concluded that the armed forces chief of staff, General Fabian Ver, was ultimately responsible for Aquino's death, the public began to support Corazon Aquino for office. Confronted by mounting support for Aquino, Marcos authorized an early presidential election to "restore confidence" in his administration. In the wake of the February 7,

1986, balloting, both candidates claimed victory, but on February 22, Defense Secretary Juan Ponce Enrile and Lieutenant General Fidel V. Ramos (acting chief of staff during Ver's suspension and the leader of an anticorruption campaign within the military) announced their allegiance to Aquino. As a result, the military experienced mass defections, and on February 26, Marcos fled into exile in Hawaii (Banks and Muller 1997, 667).

President Aquino's first challenge was forming a cabinet, a difficult process because her support coalition was fragile. The Aquino-Laurel ticket was referred to as a "shotgun wedding," having formed only after significant bargaining between the two principals and the intervention of Cardinal Jaime Sin (Timberman 1991, 169). Aquino faced potential policy-related conflicts among members of her support coalition:

> The coalition was further divided by the inclusion of three Marcos-era holdovers, Juan Ponce Enrile, Fidel Ramos, and Central Bank Governor Jose Fernandez. Finally, the coalition was weakened by its multi-party composition, with considerable (and eventually irreconcilable) ideological differences among its most prominent members. Consequently, the original Aquino Cabinet consisted of a volatile mix of personalities and political persuasions. . . . This disparate mixture of personalities and political views made disagreements and disunity within the Cabinet inevitable. (Timberman 1991, 169–70)

From the outset, Aquino's administration included officials located across the left-right ideological spectrum. Aquino and local government minister Aquilino Pimentel Jr.'s decision to replace approximately 14,000 local officials sparked the first major controversy within the cabinet. Pimentel sought to purge Marcos loyalists and appoint Aquino's people at the local government level, prior to a constitutional plebiscite or national elections. The KBL opposed the decision, causing further instability within the already fragile coalition government.

The KBL members rightly feared that their replacement in the local-level offices would result in a loss of both political and economic power. After all, national politicians depended on local officials to get out the vote in national elections. Since these local offices were important to all parties, Vice President Laurel and other United Nationalist Democratic Opposition (UNIDO) party stalwarts supported the KBL in criticizing Pimentel's decision. In particular, Laurel believed that too few new appointments were going to UNIDO party members (Timberman 1991, 172). Patronage distribution among the coalition partners thus became the first issue dividing Aquino's cabinet. However, the intracoalition disagreements grew to encompass multiple policy dimensions.

> The Aquino government . . . often seemed paralyzed by indecision and internal disagreements. Tensions mounted between Defense Minister Enrile and liberal Cabinet ministers like Executive Secretary Joker Arroyo over the government's conciliatory policy towards the communist insurgents. Important differences of opinion within the Cabinet also emerged on critical economic issues such as the handling of foreign debt, trade liberalization, and land reform. Additionally, the rift continued to grow between Vice-President Laurel, who sought a larger role for himself and UNIDO, and the members of PDP-Laban, who jealously guarded Aquino's and PDP-Laban's pre-eminence within the coalition. (Timberman 1991, 174)

Aquino devoted the bulk of her attention during the first 18 months of her presidency to managing and consolidating power against the military. Despite continuous rumors of an imminent coup (and an attempt on August 28, 1987), Aquino used her unlimited constitutional power to remove and appoint new cabinet members. In November 1986, the Reform the Armed Forces Movement (RAM) faction led by Enrile challenged Aquino by threatening the "God Save the Queen" coup. In response, Aquino called an emergency cabinet meeting and asked the entire cabinet to resign. Enrile resigned and was immediately replaced by his deputy.

A month later, Aquino identified a political need to placate Enrile's supporters in the military. Consequently, she dismissed cabinet members, including Pimentel and labor minister Agusto Sanchez, whom the military considered leftist and incompetent. Finally, in response to the unsuccessful August 1987 coup, Aquino removed the remaining "controversial" cabinet members and increased the influence of Chief of Staff Ramos and the "constitutionalists" in the armed forces. Three close advisers resigned: Arroyo, Finance Secretary Jaime Ongpin, and presidential speechwriter Teodoro Locsin (Timberman 1991, 179–97). The final shuffle, following the August 28 coup attempt, resulted in a more unified and centrist-conservative cabinet. As a result, the degree of conflict within the Aquino administration declined dramatically.

Although removing recalcitrant cabinet officials was no simple task, requiring a fairly substantial amount of time and effort, this process was expeditious compared to Aquino's efforts to remove obstructionist bureaucrats. A key aspect of Aquino's redemocratization efforts involved "purifying" the bureaucracy. She believed that the civil service had functioned as a partner to Marcos and accordingly had to be returned to the status quo ante, or pre-martial-law political structures. But Aquino confronted a major obstacle in carrying out this goal:

> The first challenge to this shaky coalition was the continued existence of the Marcos political apparatus. Though leaderless, this once-formidable machine still remained intact and possessed the ability, it was feared, to thwart the new government's initiatives. Still in place at the national level were the KBL-controlled Batasang Pambansa, the Marcos-appointed judiciary, many generals who had loyally served Marcos, and a bureaucracy filled with officials who owed their jobs to Marcos or other members of the KBL. Equally disconcerting was the near total control of provincial and local governments by KBL officials. Under the existing election code, these officials' term of office did not expire until June 1986. (Timberman 1991, 170)

Aquino thus sought to reform the bureaucracy to restore its pre-Marcos status as an instrument of democracy. Along these lines, the Presidential Commission on Government Reorganization declared, "We must systematically 'de-Marcosify' Philippine society" (quoted in Cariño 1990, 1). Therefore, the structures and processes that tended to perpetuate the old order had been modified. In light of Aquino's vision of the bureaucracy as a democratic instrument, any bureaucratic values or incentive structures that existed under the Marcos administration were no longer considered legitimate. Therefore, in confronting the bureaucracy with her agenda of altering the way it did business, Aquino employed both personnel and organizational changes as tools of control.

Dismissals of Local Officials

As my theory predicts, Aquino first opted to implement less costly tools such as purges and patronage appointments. She began the purification process with local government officials. Though not all of these elected local officials were Marcos appointees, Pimentel, the secretary of local government, demanded their resignations. In early 1986, appointed officers in charge replaced the local officials. Virtually all local executives and legislators were replaced. The purge continued as the new officers in charge pushed for dismissal of the career civil servants in the local bureaucracies, winning the dismissals of both casuals and permanent employees (Cariño 1989, 217).[6]

The National-Level Purge

Aquino reneged on her campaign promises to civil servants, turning to the Marcos model of summary dismissals. In fact, the transition Freedom Constitution that she promulgated a month after assuming office authorized the government to purge all elected and appointed officials and employees (Philippines 1986b, Article III, Section 2).[7] The new cabinet employed two primary methods of cleaning house: (1) courtesy resignations of all ranking personnel, combined with evaluation and removal of those who did not pass the evaluation; and (2) voluntary leave packages. Despite the broad purge authority granted by the constitution, by the end of 1986 only about 10,000 of the 1,300,000 total civil servants had been removed (Cariño 1989, 218).[8]

Several recurring patterns emerged as the dismissal methods were implemented. First, dismissals were targeted at certain agencies and positions, including, among others, career executive service officers; local government civil servants; and employees of the Ministries of Human Settlements, Local Government, Public Works and Highways, Environment and Natural Resources, and Tourism, as well as the National Food Authority, the Philippine Tourism Authority, and other government corporations. Aquino targeted these agencies because they fell within her administration's general definition of types of agencies requiring intervention—that is, "those rumored to be corrupt and obsequious to their superiors or to the Marcoses" (Cariño 1989, 218).

Second, inconsistencies arose across agencies in the means of selecting those who would be removed. Some agencies, such as the Ministry of Health and the Ministry of Education, Culture, and Sports, chose a very arduous process whereby they reviewed employees' performance records and interviewed colleagues and clients. Other agencies disregarded performance records and applied political loyalty criteria. The Office of the Prime Minister employed perhaps the most extreme approach; employees simply received separation notices effective after one month, "to enable [them] to train" their replacements (Cariño 1989, 219).

Third, the purge prompted civil servants to organize. The large volumes of removals across all agencies gave angry civil servants a common grievance. The administration's mission of restoring democracy, in turn, gave civil servant groups a political justification for organizing and publicly protesting their dismissals. In fact, the protests proved successful, at least in part, prompting the Aquino administration to issue Executive Order 17 (May 28, 1986), which limited the grounds for removal to:

> (1) the existence of a case for summary dismissal pursuant to Section 40 of the Civil Service Law;
> (2) the existence of a probable cause for violation of the Anti-Graft and Corrupt Practices Act as determined by the ministry head concerned;
> (3) gross incompetence or inefficiency in the discharge of functions;
> (4) misuse of public office for partisan political purposes;
> (5) any other analogous ground showing that the incumbent is unfit to remain in the service or that his separation/replacement is in the interest of the service (Philippines 1986a).

Despite the limitations imposed in Executive Order 17, however, civil servants continued to be removed without specific grounds for the action. In addition, because the majority of dismissals were in the form of acceptance of courtesy resignations, employees technically could not appeal their dismissals. A central review committee put forward only 700 civil servant appeal rulings; though most were decided in favor of the employees, the review committee had no power to enforce its rulings (Cariño 1992, 134).

Reorganization and Patronage Appointments

Despite the size of the purge, Aquino's goal of de-Marcosification was not fully realized, as many individuals with close ties to Marcos remained in the bureaucracy. Aquino thus turned to reorganizing the bureaucracy as another means of controlling it. The first year of the reorganization effort took place at the same time as the national purge. Civil servants who could not be removed through summary dismissals found their positions abolished through organizational changes. In the words of Juan Miguel Luz of the Asian Institute of Management, a member of Aquino's presidential management staff,

> There were two aspects to reorganization. Both had to do with political content rather than administrative efficiency. First, one prob-

> lem with Cory [Aquino] coming in was to some extent, at least in the higher levels, abandonment of posts. Also, there was a question about where the loyal people were. Do you retain this person because they were Marcos people or not? So a couple of things had to be established early on. She had to lay claim to what legitimacy they had and what authorities they had with the bureaucracy. Cory was very clear that they didn't want to come in a heavy-handed way; [she] could not have an executive branch that was opposed to her.[9]

Luz further noted that the administration sought to use legal instruments to begin moving people in and out. One such method was bureaucratic reorganization:

> For political reasons, there were at least three departments that had to be cut completely. Ministry of Human Settlements was basically creating a superministry of which they poached on everyone else [e.g., housing, education]. Also, Marcos set up an unbelievable number of government corporations with his people occupying the jobs. The third one was Department of Energy. They wanted to split it up. Unfortunately, this is where the private sector was shortsighted. The oil companies were close to Aquino, who at the time wanted to split it up because it was a competitor, regulator, and supplier with unfair advantage.[10]

Although the Presidential Commission on Governmental Reorganization was authorized to serve as the focal point for executive branch reorganization, the process was complicated by the fact that many agency heads initiated individual reorganization plans. Making matters worse were the frequent cabinet turnovers. According to Cariño (1992, 131),

> Each new appointment generated a new wave of reorganization which sometimes brought back personnel who had been dismissed and threw out those who had earlier been retained. As of December 1991, only two of over 20 heads remained as Aquino's first appointees to Cabinet-level positions; one department has had as many as six secretaries.

Despite the convoluted reorganization process, the cabinet approved the Presidential Commission on Governmental Reorganization's recommendations in the autumn of 1986. By that December, Aquino had signed only

4 of 54 reorganization executive orders; a month later, she had signed 17 additional orders. A year later, only 3 of 18 departments, 1 of 2 constitutional commissions, and 12 of 51 independent or public enterprises had completed the reorganization process. Six agencies, including 2 departments, had been abolished, 66 had their functions transferred to other agencies, and several merged into 15 larger agencies. In addition, Aquino approved major privatization efforts, including the disposition of 86 public enterprises, the abolition of 2, and the retention of 18 (Cariño 1989, 223, 226).

Aquino also controlled the bureaucracy by creating new political appointee positions. For each department, she increased the number of undersecretaries and assistant secretaries. Under Marcos, each department had had a maximum of 2 undersecretaries, a career civil servant and a political deputy minister who was a National Assembly member. By July 1987, the number of undersecretaries across all ministries had increased from 45 to 66, and the number of assistant secretaries had grown from 59 to 70. The majority of departments now had between 3 and 6 undersecretaries (Cariño 1989, 227).

The overall size of the bureaucracy did not decrease under Aquino. Even after the removal of tens of thousands of civil servants, the total number of civil service employees increased, with the highest rate of increase visible in senior-level administrative positions. According to the Philippine Department of Budget and Management (1989), of the 39 agencies that reorganized (with an average completion rate of 88 percent), 48,974 additional positions were created. Along these lines, Cariño (1992, 132) also finds that

> the newly appointed were certainly much more than these since this does not disclose the number of terminations. From [my] detailed check of only eleven agencies and 92 public enterprises (of which two and five were abolished, respectively), a total of 16,341 were separated from the service from March 1986 to June 1987. These included personnel summarily dismissed as well as those who voluntarily resigned or retired. It was difficult to estimate the total number of the purged unless one went from agency to agency.

Without a professionalized civil service and a real merit-based system, Aquino initially did not need the more costly tool of passing and implementing an extensive APA. But when purges proved insufficient to secure her control over bureaucrats, Aquino resorted to the codification of some APA-like rules.

Aquino as Sole Legislator: Passage of the 1987 Administrative Code

Between February 1986 and July 1987, President Aquino was the sole legislator in the Philippines. During this transition period, she could alter any policy simply by issuing a presidential decree.

> During her 478 days of "revolutionary" power she issued 302 decrees. Most of them fell into the category of government "housekeeping," but some others . . . were broad in scope. As the days ticked down to the convening of Congress, the paper flow . . . increased; on the last day before Congress met Aquino signed 42 orders. (*Far Eastern Economic Review* 1988, 215)

During the early years of the Aquino administration, de-Marcosification was a powerful justification for dismissals and reorganizations. Voters had given her a mandate to restore democracy and in particular to redemocratize the bureaucracy. This case demonstrates the inadequacy of the (alternative) possibility that presidents pass APAs simply to present the appearance of reform. Aquino had every incentive to create such an appearance yet eschewed an APA. However, with each round of reorganization plans and as the rate of dismissals increased, de-Marcosification weakened as a rationale for governance. According to the Philippine Department of Budget and Management, the number of civil servants dismissed before and after reorganization increased from 3.7 percent in July 1988 to 8.1 percent in January 1989 (1989). Moreover, Aquino appointed to key positions (including within the cabinet) many prominent individuals identified with Marcos or elected under the administration party. Thus, over the course of the Aquino administration, civil servants appear to have paid a steeper price for de-Marcosification than did some Marcos advisers.

The 1987 Administrative Code authorized many of the Aquino administration's reorganizations. Only the final 8 of the document's 374 pages outline administrative procedures. Such a brief set of provisions is consistent with my theoretical predictions. That is, any functioning bureaucracy should have some minimal set of administrative procedural guidelines—a little red tape is unavoidable. At the same time, since Aquino had alternative tools to control her agents—that is, the power to appoint her loyalists and dismiss those she did not trust—it is unsurprising that the extent of the formal administrative procedural guidelines would be limited. Why would a president unnecessarily impose strict and extensive procedures on her agents and thus increase the likelihood of further delays in the implementation of her programs?

Contents of the 1987 Administrative Code

The procedural requirements for rule making in the Philippines' 1987 Administrative Code are less comprehensive than the corresponding laws in Korea, Taiwan, or the United States. Nevertheless, the substance is important. Overall, the eight pages include provisions for rules and regulations, adjudication and administrative appeal in contested cases, including judicial review. Table 5.1 provides a brief summary of the major requirements of the Administrative Code and the political impact(s) of each change in the policy process.

What sets the Philippine Administrative Code apart from the APAs of Korea, Taiwan, and the United States is the flimsiness of the notice and comment provision. Unlike the other three countries, Philippine agencies can decide whether to allow public comment during the proposed rule-

TABLE 5.1. Philippine Administrative Code of 1987

Procedural Requirement	Political Impact
Rules and Regulations (Book VII, chapter 2) • Agencies have discretion, "as far as practicable," to circulate public notices and receive comments for proposed rules (sec. 9, no. 1). • In fixing rates, no rule or final order is valid unless proposed rates have been published in newspaper at least two weeks prior to first hearing (sec. 9, no. 2). • Requires all agencies to file with University of Philippines Law Center three certified copies of every rule adopted (sec. 3, no. 1) • All agencies must maintain a permanent public register of all rules (sec. 3, no. 3). • Each rule becomes effective 15 days from the date of filing unless a different day is specified by law (sec. 4).	• Might raise probability that interest group vetoes agency's policy for groups sufficiently strong and organized • If controversy increases then more information

• Requires UP Law Center to publish quarterly bulletins setting forth the text of rules filed and keep an updated codification of all rules (sec. 5)	
Adjudication (Book VII, chapter 3)	
• A five-day prior notice and hearing are required in all contested cases (sec. 11, no. 1).	• Avoids ex post conflict; more checks.
• All parties can present evidence and argument on all issues; agencies must keep official record (sec. 11, nos. 2 and 3).	• Slows down agency decision making process
• All parties have right to cross-examine witnesses presented against them and to submit rebuttal evidence (sec. 12, no. 3).	
• All agency decisions in contested cases must be in writing and state clearly and distinctly the facts and the law on which they are based. All agency decisions must be made within 30 days following submission of the contested case (sec. 14).	• Procedural requirements increase information and gives principals opportunities to respond to agency decisions
• Agency decisions are final 15 days after the receipt by the "party adversely affected unless within that period an administration appeal or judicial review, if proper, has been perfected" (sec. 15).	
• Requires all agencies to publish all decisions or final orders in the adjudication of contested cases (sec. 16)	
Administrative Appeal in Contested Cases (book XVII, chapter 4)	
• Allows appeals of final agency decisions to department head, unless otherwise provided by law or executive order (sec. 19)	• Gives principals opportunities to respond to agency decisions if agency deviates from their policy preferences
• Party adversely affected by agency decision must file an appeal within 15 days after receipt of decision (sec. 20).	
• Establishes a broad definition of standing, entitling any party "aggrieved or adversely affected by an agency decision" to seek judicial review (sec. 25, no. 2)	
• Review must be made on basis of record as a whole. "The findings of fact of the agency when supported by substantial evidence shall be final except when specifically provided otherwise by law" (sec. 25, no. 7).	

making stage. Therefore, groups cannot necessarily participate to influence policy outcomes. The fact that the Philippine notice and comment provision is less strict than the Korean, Taiwanese, and U.S. versions means that if the president wants to change the policy status quo, the pertinent agency can offer its ideal proposal.[11] In the absence of a notice and comment process, interest groups lack the means to push an agency away from its ideal proposal.

Two other noteworthy features of the Administrative Code are agency adjudication and appeals in contested cases. The basic requirements of these two features resemble those of the U.S. APA. What Shapiro (1988, 110) has written of the U.S. APA applies equally well to the Philippine Administrative Code:

> Agencies were to act like courts when they conducted adjudication, holding oral hearings with formal presentation of evidence on both sides and cross examination. They were to enter final orders that looked like court decisions. These final orders were to be supported solely on the evidentiary record of the hearing and by findings of fact and law of the sort found in judicial opinions. And a reviewing court was to review this trial-type record carefully. Agencies were not to act like courts in conducting rule makings. . . . There need be no oral hearing, no cross examination, no record, and no findings. And a reviewing court was to intervene only if the agency had committed lunacy.

In sum, with the exception of the rule-making procedures, these requirements are designed to raise the likelihood that well-organized groups will slow down the administrative decision-making process by adding more checks.

But why did Aquino focus more on the adjudication and appeals procedures than on rule making? Allowing public participation during the proposed rule-making stage increases the probability that sufficiently strong interest groups will veto an agency's policy. Since the code did not go into effect until late 1988, after Aquino had already replaced Marcos loyalists with people loyal to her, she had no interest in constraining them with strict rule-making procedures. Doing so would have meant slowing down and adding additional costs to the implementation of her own programs. According to Luz,

> It was purposely left vague so that the executive branch would have sufficient discretion to do what they wanted. The presidential legal counsel was a very high position and was very close to Aquino. [Adolf Azcuna] had more to say than Ramos's or even Estrada's legal counsels. I think that when they [drafted the code], they were contemplating how the executive branch would have sufficient discretion.[12]

In short, whereas *ex ante* public notice and comment procedures would have constrained bureaucratic activities prior to final agency decisions, *ex post* appeals, including judicial review, would allow groups to check agency actions after the agency completed its decision-making process. Although these procedures would slow down policy implementation, the costs to Aquino were reduced because they would only do so *ex post.* Hence, the benefit of enfranchising another principal to guard against agency drift appears to have outweighed the (relatively limited) potential costs of delay. After all, Aquino's national purge of the bureaucracy did not remove every potentially disloyal agent. In particular, the judicial review provision theoretically ensured that interest groups would have access after Aquino was out of office.[13] Furthermore, implementing these administrative procedures just before the end of her sole legislator period offered two major benefits: it obviated the need to compromise with Congress and assured speedy passage and implementation.

Fully understanding the rationale for imposing the 1987 code requires placing the procedures outlined therein—especially the adjudication and judicial review provisions—into a political context. According to Chito Salazar, executive director of the W. Sycip Policy Center, Asian Institute for Management, good laws are often not enforced:

> The bureaucracy is captured, meaning patronage is distributed by politicians in power. There needs to be a check in strong bureaucracies such as the United States but not in the Philippines. The government is captured by the elite; strong ties between wealthy families and politicians with a series of patronage. There are good laws but no rules, so the bureaucracy is completely porous. Laws are ignored. . . . Implementation is not a big thing here—it's a chaotic mess such that it isn't an issue. Here, there is no professional bureaucracy as in Korea, Japan, or Singapore. If you have a bureaucracy that is more established and institutionalized, like Korea, and

> has its own culture, then you might have to set up a legal framework for controlling the bureaucracy. But in the Philippines, where bureaucracy is a manifestation of patronage, then administrative procedures are irrelevant, or there are other ways to control bureaucrats. My sense is there are some, but it doesn't matter.[14]

When asked specifically about the nature of the 1987 Administrative Code, Salazar continued,

> In the Philippines, there is no need to enfranchise new groups. There are strong movements, but they're not big enough to matter for elections right now. Again, the laws are not the key source. You have to see if the laws are implemented and enforced! Many are not implemented ever. The administrative procedures in the code may be in there, but it's a very small section and vague, and they didn't want to tie the hands of their own bureaucrats. There are procedures for implementing laws, but whatever it says, there's a way to get around that such that there is no enforcement or enforcer! I know exactly who to bribe and how much . . . for example, a judge. So that's how it's done.[15]

In sum, Aquino incorporated into the 1987 Administrative Code a short but substantive section regarding administrative procedures for the promulgation of rules. The fact that the code did not require public participation during proposed rule making for all agencies suggests that Aquino had alternative tools to control bureaucrats. But a more critical motivation for preserving this discretion for her agencies was that she and her advisers did not want to tie the hands of their agents and thereby limit their capacity quickly to implement presidential policies. Although the judicial review provision may in theory have served—indeed, may have been intended to serve—Aquino's desire to ensure a check on the bureaucracy after she was out of office, enforcement is a major barrier in the Philippines. As Patricia Sto. Tomas, secretary-general of the Eastern Regional Organization for Public Administration and former chair of the Civil Service Commission, explains, Philippine presidents continue to exercise their power and control by appointing their own agents:

> Enforcement and implementation is very selective in the bureaucracy. In the absence of rules, they can make the rules themselves. . . . Every time the president changes, there are massive changes in

> the political positions, even where the law says that the positions should be occupied by career civil servants. Korea and Taiwan seem to adapt to international economic changes without much discontinuity, but in the Philippines, there is so much discontinuity. The bureaucracy is much more strong and stable in Korea and Taiwan, but in the Philippines, it's not as strong.[16]

Conclusion

My theory predicts that when delegating to agents (i.e., cabinet ministers or bureaucrats), presidents will seek to mitigate any potential agency slippage by building in a check on their agents' discretion. But passing an extensive APA is only one solution—and a costly solution, at that—to this delegation problem. Presidents are likely to support extensive APAs solely when they lack the authority, for either political or constitutional reasons, simply to replace disloyal bureaucrats and either the legislature or some members of the support coalition hold conflicting preferences. Presidents who can freely appoint loyalists to both political and career civil service positions can resolve agency slippage problems without an extensive APA. Bureaucratic positions in systems wherein executive appointment and dismissal powers are unconstrained are neither stable nor permanent. So, in general, presidents can control their agents in the executive branch simply by firing people they do not trust and replacing them with loyalists.

In the Philippines, the degree of administrative procedural codification is less extensive than in Korea or Taiwan. The Philippines is the only presidential system in East Asia that has not passed an extensive APA. During the redemocratization after Marcos's authoritarian rule, President Aquino attempted to rein in the bureaucracy by ordering massive dismissals and creating additional patronage positions.

Aquino also controlled conflict within her divided cabinet by frequently dismissing "controversial" members. She carried out these policies for two key reasons: first, as the sole legislator during her first year in office, she had the power to issue numerous decrees that changed the policy status quo. Second, de-Marcosification was a politically sufficient justification for restoring democratic institutions, especially the bureaucracy. As my theory predicts, she first opted to implement the available less costly tools, such as purges and patronage appointments, and she had a fair amount of success in managing her delegation problems without resorting to an APA, a more costly control tool. But when her unconstrained power was about to expire, she reversed course, suddenly finding it expedient to pass some APA-like procedures as part of the Administrative Code just before the end of her term as sole legislator.

Consistent with my expectations, however, the procedural requirements for promulgating regulations are less comprehensive in the Philippines than in Korea, Taiwan, or the United States. Most important, agencies can determine whether to allow public participation during the proposed rule-making stage. In most cases, agencies bypass public consultation when writing rules and publish them only after deciding on the final version. Interviews with scholars and government officials confirmed that Aquino gave agencies this discretion because she and her advisers did not want to tie their agents' hands and thereby limit their capacity to quickly implement presidential policies.

Unlike the weak notice and comment provision, the adjudication and appeals/judicial review procedures appear on paper to be detailed and hence more potent. Theoretically, one reason for including judicial review is to ensure that when administrative decisions are challenged, judges will consider the legislative intent of the enacting coalition. In this sense, the judicial review provision raised the likelihood that favored groups would retain access after Aquino left office. Of course, while she was in office and in control, such groups would appeal to the agencies rather than to the courts. Hence, the judicial review process did not threaten her authority while in office.

Nonetheless, in practice, administrative procedure laws, including the judicial review provision, are rarely enforced in the Philippines. Numerous interviewees confirmed that the implementation of laws, including administrative procedures, is sporadic at best. Without a professionalized bureaucracy, a way around legal formalities can always be found. Patronage politics remains the norm in the Philippines. So despite the existence of some minimal set of administrative procedural guidelines, the rules are only weakly enforced. One implication is that as long as politicians can depend on patronage distributions for political survival, they are unlikely to employ administrative procedures as a mechanism for controlling the bureaucracy.[17] After all, if one has the power to do so, firing one's enemies and hiring one's friends is much cheaper and more efficient than implementing arduous procedures.

The fact that Philippine presidents are free to appoint their cronies and dismiss any bureaucratic employee makes it quite unlikely that the country's leaders would pursue an extensive APA. One consequence is that citizens will not have the opportunity to participate in the policy-making process and thus directly influence policy outcomes. In other words, the lack of *ex ante* mechanisms such as APAs excludes the public from formal participation in the bureaucracy's policy deliberation process. Thus, until politicians in the Philippines have an electoral incentive to reorient the bureaucracy in a way that will broaden the existing restricted set of interests, state accountability will be limited mostly to *ex post* measures—primarily elections. What does this mean for the state of democracy in the Philippines as compared with Korea and Taiwan? At a minimum, both Korea and Taiwan appear to have moved farther along the path to responsive democracy.

Postscript: Continuation of Patronage Politics: The Ramos, Estrada, and Macapagal-Arroyo Administrations

Patronage has continued to dominate Philippine politics since Aquino's presidency. As a result, Presidents Fidel Ramos (1992–98), Joseph Estrada (1998–2001),[18] and Gloria Macapagal-Arroyo (2001–2010)[19] have managed delegation to their underlings without resorting to amending the administrative procedural provisions of the 1987 Administrative Code. Ruben Torres, secretary of labor under Aquino and executive secretary to Ramos, recalled both the managerial differences between Aquino and Ramos and the lack of legislative activity concerning the Administrative Code:

> Aquino was a macromanager except in areas she cared about. Ramos was a bureaucrat for many decades. He was a micromanager. For example, I would brief him four times a week. Ramos didn't have that much concern about putting in controls on bureaucrats—not really. He wanted to downsize by resorting to attrition. He was not like Aquino and her purges. . . . If Cory waited until the new constitution passed and the new legislature was in place, it would have taken years and years to pass the code. So for expediency purposes, the code was passed as a decree. Without this code, she would've inherited an executive branch that was under a dictatorial law. Subsequently, when the legislature came in, they tried to question the code but have not yet amended it. The code is mostly a guide to bureaucrats. My prediction is that until the legislators see

> that the code affects their electoral outcome, they won't mess with it.[20]

Indeed, no amendments have yet added procedural requirements to the 1987 Administrative Code, nor has an APA passed to date.

Ramos controlled the executive branch using tools other than an APA. Like Aquino, he initiated a purge targeted at the armed forces. As of 1994,

> the Ramos government appears to be enjoying greater success in establishing civilian control over the armed forces than did the Aquino government, a reflection perhaps on Ramos's military credentials. In 1993 Ramos initiated a purge of miscreant elements of the Philippine National Police (PNP), the successor organization to the Philippine Constabulary that Ramos had directed during the martial law period of President Ferdinand Marcos. PNP personnel had been implicated in kidnapping businessmen in recent years. In late April, Ramos announced the forced retirement of 62 senior PNP officers, and expects to dismiss 3,000 or more PNP personnel in the coming months. (Riedinger 1994, 142)

Patronage appointments were commonplace under the Estrada administration and continue to run very deep into the bureaucracy. According to my reining-in theory, if control over the bureaucracy were not a problem for Estrada, policy outcomes should adhere closely to his preferences. In fact, several months into his presidential term, his policies began to favor the upper class—in particular, the Marcos family and its cronies. Estrada appears to have ensured that the bureaucracy implemented his top agenda items:

> Estrada counts among his early achievements a deal he "brokered" between management and labor of the country's flag-carrier Philippine Airlines (PAL), controlled by one of Marcos's alleged cronies. The deal, which included a moratorium on collective bargaining for 10 years without automatic wage increases for inflation, may have been necessary for the continued operation of the airline, but it was hardly a victory for labor. Estrada convinced PAL unions to accept management's terms, promising that union members would not be laid off while he was president. One month later, PAL management began laying off workers, and the Department of La-

> bor and Employment announced that it had no right to interfere in PAL's actions. (Montinola 1999, 70)

Estrada's interventions benefited the Marcos family and its supporters in other ways as well.

> Although Estrada cannot directly influence the constitutionally independent judicial bodies of the Philippines, his statements have created an environment conducive to the dismissal of cases and rehabilitation of the Marcos family and Marcos's most powerful cronies. Since Estrada took office, the Office of the Ombudsman has dismissed eight criminal cases against Marcos's kin and cronies. (Montinola 1999, 70)

A similar process has taken place during Macapagal-Arroyo's presidency. Macapagal-Arroyo came to power in 2001 in a "people power" revolt that toppled Estrada after he was weakened by a flood of corruption allegations and a failed impeachment trial. Macapagal-Arroyo hoped that the 2004 election would legitimize her rule, thereby allowing her to pursue badly needed economic reforms (Spaeth 2005).

In 2004, under pressure to reform the economy, Macapagal-Arroyo abolished 80 offices in the Office of the President. With the ruling coalition controlling both houses of Congress, she requested passage of a law enabling her to do away with excess personnel and dead wood in the government: "I ask Congress to pass a law on government re-engineering with a silver parachute for redundant offices" (Macapagal-Arroyo 2004, 4). Macapagal-Arroyo focused on controlling the size of the government in inefficient areas and then redirecting those resources toward her policy goals, including salary increases for teachers and reassessment of the corporate missions of government-owned and/or -controlled corporations.

In 2006, Macapagal-Arroyo directed budget secretary Rolando Andaya Jr. to clean up the entire government bureaucracy, including government-owned and/or -controlled corporations, and to purge "ghost employees." In a memorandum issued "by authority of the President," executive secretary Eduardo Ermita stressed that the presidential directive was consistent with the "strategic review and on-going rationalization of government agencies . . . pursuant to the government's drive against graft and corrupt practices acts." In addition, the memorandum stated, "Subject to existing laws, rules and regulations, the Secretary of Interior and Local Government is hereby directed to ensure that local government units comply with all laws, rules and regulations in the hiring of their employees including the prohibition against the hiring of 'ghost employees'" (Philippines, Office of the President, 2006, 1).

In short, little has changed since President Aquino left office in terms of the extent to which Philippine presidents depend on patronage for effective management. As long as Presidents Ramos, Estrada, and Macapagal-Arroyo remained capable of controlling their bureaucracies with relatively low-cost tools, such as dismissing their enemies and hiring loyalists, they had little incentive to resort to a more costly APA.

6 | Sunset Laws and the Acceleration of Regulatory Reform in South Korea

Since the passage of the 1946 Administrative Procedure Act (APA) in the United States, scholars have sought to understand the rationale for various procedures that executive agencies must follow. How newly elected presidents go about restructuring their bureaucracies can shape not only the development of democracy in general but also the nature and extent of the state's movement toward greater democratic responsiveness.

This book has focused on the passage of APAs as a comprehensive and widely applicable tool for politicians confronting the challenge of restructuring the state. However, APAs are not monolithic; rather, they consist of multiple, discrete regulatory reforms, each with potentially differing effects. Assessing the validity of my theoretical argument thus requires tracing the effects of specific reforms to see whether the actual mechanisms implemented by APA passage produce the predicted effects with respect to executive control over the bureaucracy. In other words, if my theory is correct, specific reforms should be linked to specific regulatory outcomes.

One potentially important regulatory reform, included in Korea's 1997 APA (KAPA II), is the so-called sunset provision, one of several major provisions in KAPA II that are clearly inconsistent with the lock-in hypothesis (described in chapter 2). According to KAPA II's sunset provision, all policies and regulations covered under the law automatically expire after five years unless they are explicitly renewed. The key question thus becomes whether Korea's sunset provision facilitated reforms in the direction favored by the chief executive who enacted it, Kim Young Sam.

Sunset provisions are a common component of administrative reform outside the Korean case, and they do not lock in a status quo; they do precisely the opposite. Why would a president support a reform proposal that limits the life of his administration's regulatory rules? In this chapter, I develop a spatial model to investigate the motivations for and the implications of the sunset rule. The model demonstrates how administrative reform can be used to promote change rather than to lock in a current policy regime.

To test the model's predictions, I gathered data on the persistence or expiration of all regulations from all ministries in Korea between 1998 and 2005. With this data, I investigate the correlates of regulatory sunset at the intraministerial level. In particular, I consider whether within each ministry, regulations that do not benefit the president's support coalition are, as the model predicts, more likely to expire as a consequence of the sunset provision than are regulations that benefit the president's support coalition.

The chapter opens with a brief political history of the adoption of the sunset provision contained in KAPA II before developing a spatial model of the rule-making process both with and without the sunset rule. Next, I apply the model to the Korean case and present evidence on the use of the sunset procedure and renewal process. I conclude with some general observations regarding the role of sunset provisions and with some specific comments regarding the Korean case.

The Adoption of the Sunset Rule in Korea

As discussed in chapter 3, Korea's state-led economic development strategy, begun in the 1960s, yielded impressive rates of economic growth. The military government implemented this strategy via a regulatory regime that favored the interests of industrial conglomerates (*chaebol*) over those of the middle class (Amsden 1989; Haggard 1990; Haggard and Kaufman 1995; Wade 1990). From the perspective of the prodemocratic reformers who inherited the administrative structures left over from military rule, this strategy resulted in excessive government regulations. In recent years, the Korean government and international groups such as the Organisation for Economic Co-Operation and Development have pointed to excessive government regulation as preventing the market from effectively allocating resources as well as lowering Korea's competitiveness. Also, in a period of accelerating globalization, government regulations emerged as a major cause of trade friction (Korea, Regulatory Reform Committee 2004). In response to these concerns, the Korean government began regulatory reform in the 1990s.

As part of KAPA II, the Kim Young Sam administration supported the sunset rule. KAPA II passed in the National Assembly without any opposition (Chun 1998; J.-S. Lee and Han 1999). The details of the sunset provision are delineated in KAPA II, Article 8, "Specification of Durations and Regulations." Article 8.1 states that if central administrative agencies "intend to establish or strengthen regulations, they shall specify the duration of regulations in relevant acts and subordinate statutes which have no clear reason to continuously exist." Article 8.2 states, "The duration of regulations shall be set within the minimum period to achieve the objectives of regulations, and their periods shall in principle not exceed five years." The law further stipulates that for any regulation to be extended beyond the five-year limit, bureaucrats must submit an extension request one year prior to expiration. Finally, agencies must first notify the public and allow for comments prior to submitting an extension request to the Regulatory Reform Committee. The sunset rule differs significantly from typical administrative processes, whereby regulations remain in effect unless bureaucratic agents or legislators take action to change them. Sunset rules vary in form across different nations. In this chapter, I focus on two variants of the general sunset rule: (1) rules that apply only to executive branch policy decisions (that is, regulations but not legislation) and (2) rules that apply to all regulations across all policy dimensions.

The fact that the sunset rule passed under a one-term president is puzzling. The measure sought primarily to dismantle the military government's regulatory regime. Kim Young Sam made some progress moving regulatory policy away from the pro-*chaebol* status quo without KAPA II. However, he did not complete his goal of effectively "sunsetting" a large group of regulations. The KAPA II sunset provision does not grant the executive branch any new powers. Rather, it takes away the executive's ability to effortlessly maintain existing regulations, bringing us back to the question of why Kim would voluntarily choose to limit the life of his own regulations. Under what conditions will presidents favor a sunset rule?

When Presidents Choose Sunset Laws

Why do sunset rules matter? Wouldn't any president prefer to simply renew regulations that he favors and repeal or amend those that he opposes? In the context of executive branch policy-making, one might anticipate that all decisions will reflect the president's preferences from among the set of legally available choices. It is thus not obvious why the reversion point would matter for executive branch decisions as it might in a legislative process governed by a voting agenda and the need to form majorities.[1] In short, how would a sunset provision inhibit a president from implementing his ideal regulatory policy?

Executives face resource constraints. Writing a regulation that accomplishes its intended goal is costly in terms of time and expertise. The president may be unable to implement his ideal regulatory policy simply because he lacks the necessary bureaucratic personnel or policy-specific expertise. If resource constraints prevent a president from changing policy as much as he would like, then he will have to prioritize regulatory decisions to husband his limited resources. Some regulations that the president would ideally prefer to reform will remain unaltered. Given resource constraints, the reversion point thus becomes critical.

Figure 6.1 illustrates the effect of resource constraints in a spatial model with two policy dimensions (Baum and Bawn 2005). Policy on each dimension is determined by a large number of individual regulations. Repealing or changing any single regulation will move the regulatory status quo Q a small distance along one of the dimensions, to Q′. I do not seek to determine how many individual regulations are needed to move policy a given distance; the answer presumably varies, as some regulations produce large changes to the status quo, while others produce small changes. Rather, I focus on the resources needed to change policy to a given degree. I assume that quantity of resources needed to change policy by a given amount (in any direction) is proportional to the magnitude of the change. Though clearly an oversimplification, this assumption allows me to focus on the key question of interest: how sunset affects the pace of reform.

For the same reason, I also ignore legislative constraints on regulatory decisions. In reality, executive decisions are frequently constrained by legislation, so that only a subset of the policy space depicted in figure 6.1 would be available to the president (Epstein and O'Halloran 1994; McCubbins 1985). Ignoring legislative constraints is analogous to focusing on cases in which both the status quo and the president's ideal point are within the set of legislatively permissible policies.

These simplifying assumptions allow me to depict the set of regulatory policies available to the president with and without a sunset rule. I first consider the "normal" regulatory process, absent a sunset rule. In figure 6.1, the president's ideal level of policy is point P, and the regulatory status quo is Q. An unconstrained president would issue regulations to move policy to his ideal point P. But if resource constraints prevent him from is-

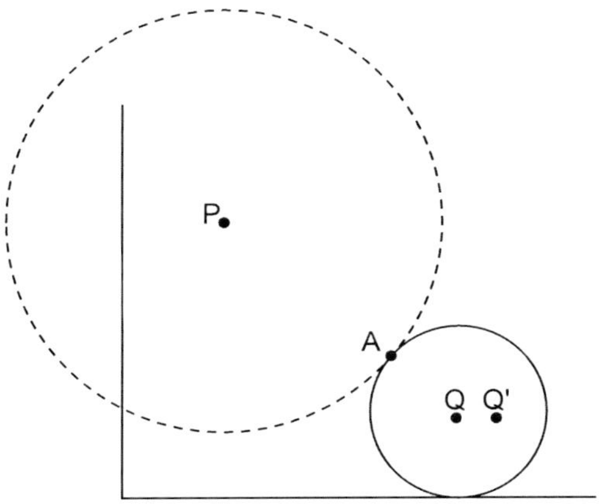

FIG. 6.1. Without sunset, president's choices are constrained to be close to status quo policy, Q. (Best available policy is A.)

suing as many regulations as he would like, he will be able to move policy only some fixed distance (or less) from Q. The set of policies available to the president are shown in the diagram by a circle centered at Q and with a radius given by the level of the constraint (more resources implies a larger radius). The best outcome the president can attain, given this constraint, is point A, where one of his indifference curves (the dotted circle centered at his ideal point P) is tangent to the choice set.

A sunset requirement changes the policy implication of resource constraints. Absent this provision, resource constraints bound deviations from the status quo in executive branch policies. Without sunset, some aspects of the status quo may persist simply because a president opted to concentrate his limited administrative resources elsewhere. In this sense, resource constraints bias regulatory policy toward the status quo.

The sunset provision clearly removes the pro-status-quo bias in regulatory policy. With sunset, action is needed to maintain the status quo. With respect to the impact of resource constraints, the sunset provision arguably biases regulatory outcomes toward the policy corresponding to an absence of regulations. This situation is not, of course, equivalent to the absence of government or even of a regulatory state. Even in the (extremely implausible) case in which the sun was allowed to set on all regulations, a great deal of state activity is legislatively mandated and implemented without regulatory decisions. Nonetheless, it is reasonable to model the sunset reversion point (the policy that would obtain in the absence of any executive branch activity) as implying a relatively low level of government activity on all policy dimensions. I refer to this as the sunset

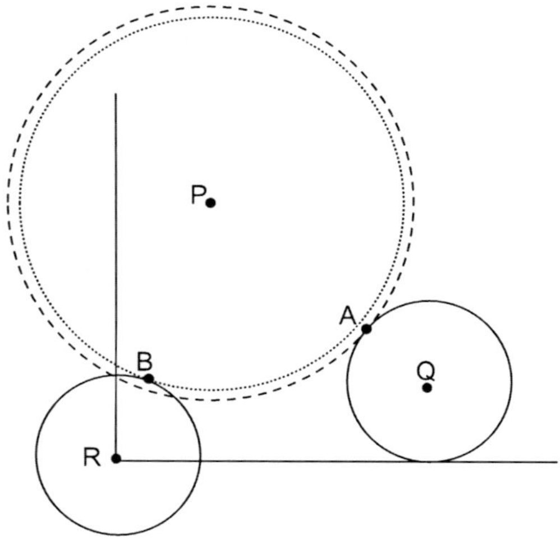

FIG. 6.2. With sunset, president's choices are constrained to be close to sunset reversion policy, R. (Best available policy is now B.)

reversion point and represent it (somewhat arbitrarily) as the origin in the spatial model.

Figure 6.2 depicts one aspect of the bias that can be created by resource constraints under sunset (Baum and Bawn 2005). For comparison, I note the regulatory status quo, Q, and the optimal constrained choice without sunset, A. With sunset, the reversionary point is the origin, R. Resource constraints imply that the president's policy choices must lie in the circle centered at R. As before, the president's best choice is the policy where his choice set is tangent to an indifference curve (in this case, one closer to his ideal point than without sunset). The best choice under sunset is point B, which is closer to the president's ideal point than his best choice without sunset, point A.[2]

Figure 6.2 thus illustrates a case where short-term policy preferences lead a president to prefer a sunset provision. Resource constraints prevent him from promulgating his ideal regulatory policy. So the short-term question becomes whether he is better off deploying his resources incrementally to change the existing status quo or incrementally to build up from the sunset reversion point. In figure 6.2, the president is better off in the short term with sunset. Moreover, if we think of the status quo as reflecting policy before a democratic transition and the president's ideal point as reflecting the preferences of a democratic electorate, the short-term effect of a sunset rule is to accelerate the reform process. Figure 6.2 shows how, given resource constraints, the sunset rule can make policy more responsive to electorally induced preferences.

To the extent that the assumptions underlying the spatial model are valid, several clear empirical predictions follow concerning the patterns we should observe with respect to regulatory sunset. At the most basic level, following enactment of a sunset provision, the number of regulations that expire should increase. After all, this is the central effect of a sunset provision. More important for my argument, if Kim Young Sam supported the sunset provision for the reasons I assert—and assuming that he was not simply wrong regarding its effects—an asymmetry should exist in the rate of regulatory expiration across different areas of government. Regulations favored by the previous, autocratic regime should expire more frequently than regulations favored by the successor, democratic regime. I now turn to an investigation of whether the empirical pattern of regulatory expiration in Korea supports these two predictions.

Regulatory Policy Changes by Kim Young Sam and Kim Dae Jung

Because the sunset law was passed late in Kim Young Sam's term, observing its effects requires looking at both his administration and that of his successor, Kim Dae Jung. Prior to the adoption of the sunset provision, Kim Young Sam issued executive orders that abolished or weakened a significant number of existing regulations. The regulatory reform process appears to have focused immediately on getting rid of rather than setting expiration dates for unnecessary older regulations. J.-S. Lee and Han (1999) studied the overall progress of regulatory reform under Kim Young Sam.[3] They examined the fate of 3,123[4] industry-related regulations (also referred to as "reform cases in economic regulations") that Kim Young Sam inherited from the military regime. They excluded twelve cases as a consequence of "lack of resources for analysis" (24), leaving a total of 3,111 cases. Lee and Han find that 52.7 percent of these regulations were weakened or abolished, while only 2.1 percent were strengthened. The remainder were either left unchanged (4.8 percent) or changed in ways that Lee and Han judged to be primarily procedural (30.2 percent were procedurally simplified, 7.4 percent were made more transparent, and 2.8 percent were transferred to a different administrative unit).

Lee and Han also broke down by ministry the regulations that were weakened, abolished, or procedurally altered and then categorized the extent of the proposed reform action for each completed regulation. In this analysis, the original data include the 4,477 cases of regulatory reform proposed, taken from 11,125 existing regulations. Within this subgroup, the reform process had been finished in 3,918 cases. I present some of the results in table 6.1.

Table 6.1 identifies those ministries (shaded in dark gray) whose existing regulations primarily favored the clientele of the old regime (e.g., agriculture, commerce, finance) and those that primarily favored newly enfranchised groups (shaded in medium gray) (e.g., environment, health and welfare, and labor). Justice and Education (shaded in light gray) are identified as ministries that might favor newly enfranchised groups. Table 6.1 seems to indicate that the Kim Young Sam administration focused primarily on repealing the old regulatory regime, or the "old client" areas.

TABLE 6.1. KYS Regulatory Reform by Ministry

Ministry	% Completed
Foreign Affairs and Trade	90
Finance and Economy	91.6
Justice	79.2
Unification	100
National Defense	80.6
Government Administration and Home Affairs	85.9
Education and Human Resources Development	64
Science and Technology	72
Culture and Tourism	85.7
Agriculture and Forestry	83.2
Maritime Affairs and Fisheries	90.2
Commerce, Industry, and Energy	92.4
Information and Communication	87.3
Environment	75.2
Health and Welfare	80.7
Labor	93.5
Construction and Transportation	87.5
Financial Supervisory Committee	100
Other	75
Total	87.5

Source: Adapted from Lee and Han 1999, 146–47 (table 2).

Note: Figures include regulations weakened, dropped, procedurally reformed. They do not include regulations strengthened (2.1% of total).

Key: = old, = new, = potential new; unshaded rows are unclassified.

Regulatory Reform during Kim Dae Jung's Administration, 1998–2002

Using data provided by Korea's Regulatory Reform Committee (1998–2002), I grouped the regulatory change incidents into two broad categories: new or strengthened regulations and dropped or weakened regulations. I then applied the same categorization of ministries to these data that I applied to Lee and Han's data.[5] That is, I grouped the ministries, to the extent possible, into three categories: unambiguously new guard or social-oriented ministries, ministries that might be new guard or socially oriented, and unambiguously old guard or military-oriented ministries. Ministries that I could not confidently assign to any of these categories appear in white. Figure 6.3 displays the data on Kim Dae Jung's regulatory activity according to this categorization.

Figure 6.3 shows new and strengthened regulations as a proportion of all regulations that were changed (that is, strengthened, weakened, added, or dropped). Three of the four new guard ministries and one of the two possibly new guard ministries have substantially higher proportions of new/strengthened regulations than any of the old guard/military ministries.

The proportions for the four ministries at the top involve very few regulations. The Independent Commission against Corruption and the Gender Equality Ministry had only 3 and 7 total regulations, respectively, applied to them, all of which were either added or strengthened. In contrast, the Ministry of Environment had 614 applicable regulations. Across all ministries, the average is 364 regulations.

The apparent dominance of unclassified ministries near the top of figure 6.3 is thus deceptive. Of those ministries with significant numbers of regulations in play, new guard ministries generally appear substantially more likely to have seen increases in applicable regulations or in the strength of existing regulations.

Overall, I identified four relatively unambiguous new guard ministries, five old guard ministries, and two potentially new guard ministries. Figure 6.3 focuses on proportions at the ministry level. Another way to look at the data is to focus on overall totals by subcategory. At the aggregate level, I expect to observe patterns similar to those suggested in figure 6.3—that is, the largest number of new or strengthened regulations in the new guard/social-oriented ministries and the largest number of weakened or dropped regulations in the old guard/military-oriented ministries. Panel (a) of table 6.2 shows the total number of regulations falling into each category.

The data in panel (a) conform to my understanding of Kim Dae Jung's

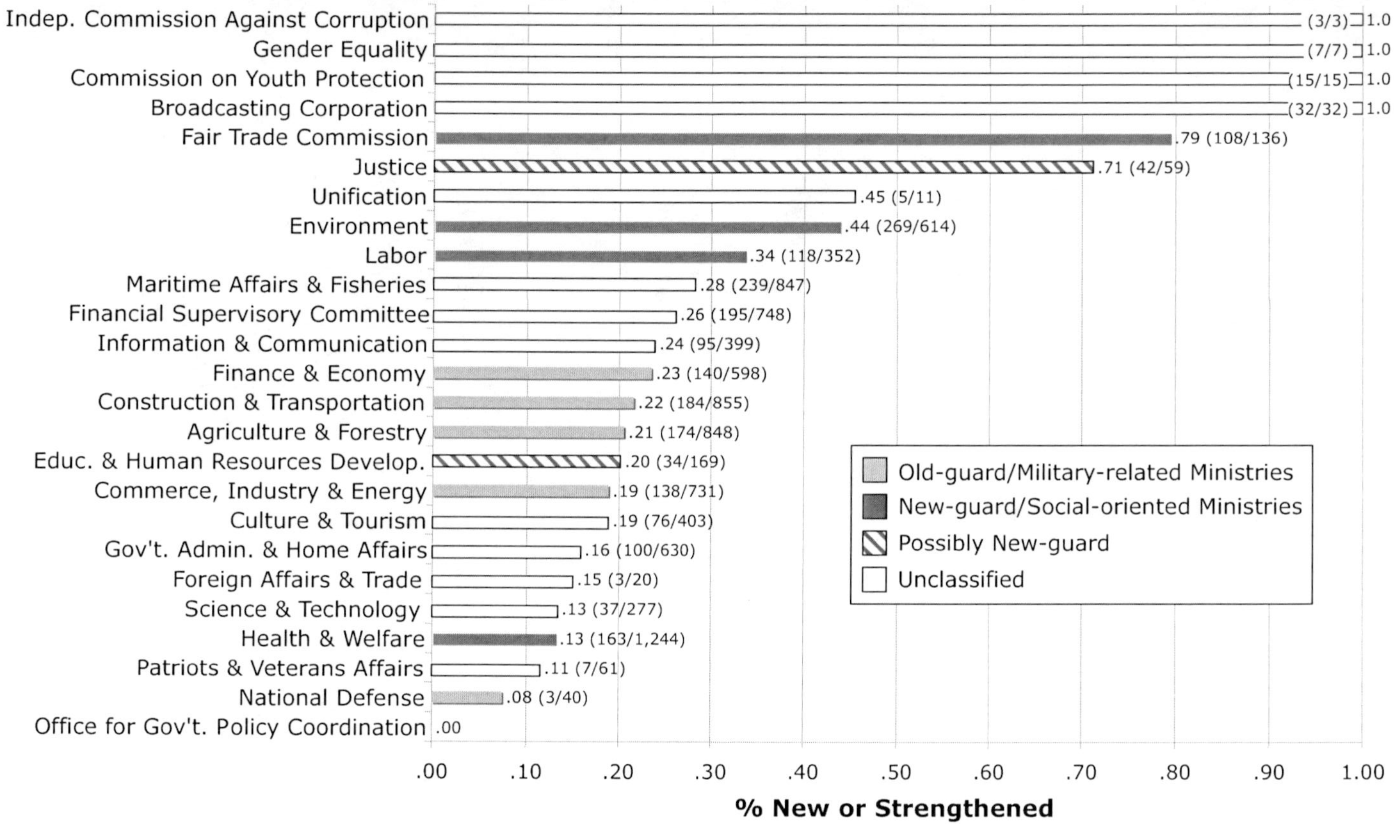

FIG. 6.3. Percentage of all regulatory changes between 1998 and 2002 entailing new or strengthened regulations, by ministry. (Regulatory change is defined as adding new, dropping existing, strengthening, or weakening regulations. Therefore "percentage weakened or dropped" is equal to 1 minus percent strengthened or added. The numbers in parentheses indicate the raw number of regulations for each ministry from which the proportions are derived.)

overall policy preferences. The largest numbers of new and strengthened regulations are indeed located in the new guard ministries, while the largest number of dropped and weakened regulations are located in the old guard ministries. However, because there are five old guard ministries and only four new guard ministries, the number of dropped regulations in the old guard category might be expected to be larger simply because the category contains more regulations. Hence, panel (b) presents the average number of regulations per ministry in each category.

Once again, panel (b) is consistent with my general expectations. The largest average number of new and strengthened regulations remains located among the new guard/social-oriented ministries, while the largest average number of weakened and dropped regulations remains located among the old guard/military-oriented ministries.

Table 6.2 also indicates a high number of dropped regulations in the new guard/social category, a finding that is not consistent with the conventional wisdom. Why were so many regulations dropped in areas such as environment and labor where Kim Dae Jung clearly favored more regulation?[6] While alternative interpretations cannot be ruled out, the large number of dropped regulations in these areas may be a direct result of the sunset provision. Specifically, some of the 345 dropped/weakened regulations in the environment category may have been dropped not because Kim Dae Jung and his administration opposed them but because he did not support them enough to pay the opportunity costs of renewing them. Consistent with this interpretation, Korean bureaucrats and politicians have begun to discuss repealing the sunset provision, at least in some pol-

TABLE 6.2. Regulatory Reform under KDJ

Ministry Type	New/Strengthened Regulations	Dropped/Weakened Regulations
(a) Total Number of Regulations per Ministry, per Category		
New-guard/Social-oriented	**658**	1,688
Possibly new-guard/Social-oriented	76	152
Old-guard/Military-oriented	639	**2,433**
(b) Average Number of Regulations per Ministry, per Category		
New-guard/Social-oriented	**165**	422
Possibly new-guard/Social-oriented	38	76
Old-guard/Military-oriented	128	**487**

Note: Numbers in bold indicate area in which the highest number is expected in each column.

icy areas, precisely because its requirements consume administrative resources that could be deployed to address new regulatory issues.

Conclusion

This chapter focused on the executive's current or short-term control of bureaucratic underlings.[7] The sunset provision can be a valuable tool for presidents to enhance their influence in this regard by breaking the regulatory status quo. The empirical evidence presented in this chapter clearly shows that the sunset provision produced precisely this effect in Korea. Following enactment of the sunset provision, many regulations expired, and a disproportionate number of them affected those ministries most closely affiliated with the previous authoritarian regime.

Nonetheless, viewed in this light, the Korean case may appear somewhat puzzling. Kim Young Sam adopted the sunset rule at the end of his term. Consequently, he could not have done so with the goal of current control, at least not in the sense employed throughout this book.

Consistent with my broader argument, the sunset rule in Korea altered the regulatory status quo favored by the former military regime. Yet the sunset provision did not directly benefit Kim Young Sam while he was in office. So why did he pursue it? The answer most likely lies in the relative preferences of Kim Young Sam and his expected successor, Kim Dae Jung. In short, Kim Young Sam did not want Kim Dae Jung and his more radical policy preferences to stray too far from his own ideal preferences. In other words, while Kim Young Sam clearly favored prodemocratic regulatory reform, he worried that Kim Dae Jung might overreach. Consequently, the sunset provision served two related yet distinct purposes for Kim Young Sam, ensuring that the *ex ante* regulatory status quo could be rapidly changed and that any overly radical regulatory reforms would eventually face sunset. The former goal is more obviously related to my reining-in theory.

The logic underlying Kim Young Sam's decision to support the sunset provision comes into clearer focus in light of its twin purposes. Baum and Bawn (2005) discuss Kim Young Sam's dual motives and their implications, including an extension of the model presented here that accounts for both the short- and longer-term effects of the sunset provision. Even absent this extension regarding the president's motives for passing the sunset provision, however, its effects are clear. Following KAPA II's passage, the pace of regulatory expiration quickened, with the sun setting disproportionately on those regulations that favored the old guard military regime and its clients. In this regard, the data presented in this chapter clearly support both of my predictions.

Newly elected presidents often confront an entrenched bureaucracy invested in the status quo and hence resistant to policy change. This situation can pose problems for presidents who represent different constituencies and interests than do bureaucrats and whose goal is to implement a different set of policies. This presidential dilemma would be even more pressing for a one-term president. In such situations, supporting a sunset provision makes sense. From the president's perspective, the sunset procedure has the clear advantage of quickly changing the direction of policy to respond to a new set of constituencies. The sunset procedure can thus facilitate movement from representative to responsive democracy.

7 | Administrative Reform and Public Attitudes toward Democratic Institutions in South Korea, Taiwan, and the Philippines

Administrative procedure acts (APAs) change the decision-making process within bureaucracies, thereby creating new winners and losers in society. To the extent that average citizens are among the winners, one important indirect effect of APA-like laws seems likely to be enhanced public trust and confidence in the civil service, the part of government primarily responsible for implementing national policy. As discussed in chapter 1, citizens living near Korea's proposed Youngwol Dam, who effectively held veto power over the project, had good reason to feel better about the civil service than did their counterparts at Imha, who were forcibly relocated without consultation or redress.

If an APA has its intended effect(s), therefore, some change in the level of public trust in the civil service would be expected after the measure's passage. The level of public trust and confidence in the civil service thus serves as an important indicator of the extent to which an APA has opened up the bureaucracy. Confidence in the civil service, in turn, is closely related to faith in the nation's democratic institutions more generally. To the extent that they enhance public trust and confidence in the civil service, APAs may also strengthen public confidence in democracy.[1]

To explore this relationship, I turn to regression analysis, investigating trends in Korean, Taiwanese, and Philippine citizens' attitudes regarding their countries' democracies in general and bureaucracies in particular. My data are derived from two waves of the World Values Survey (WVS) conducted in Korea in 1990 and 2001 as well as two waves of the Korea Barometer Surveys (KBS) conducted in 1996 and 2001. The first WVS took place three years after Korea's first democratic election and three years prior to passage of the first of three stages in the Korean APA (KAPA) law, while the second WVS took place three years following implementation of Korea's final major APA stage. The first KBS took place after the passage of the first KAPA, while the second took place in the same year as the second WVS.

Less nuanced data are available for Taiwan prior to and following passage of Taiwan's APA (TAPA) and for the Philippines from the 1994 and 1996 WVS and from the 2001 East Asia Barometer (EAB) surveys. (To facilitate more efficient comparisons across waves and hypothesis tests, I pool the surveys in my statistical analyses, based on the country case.) I conduct additional analyses regarding trends in attitudes toward the civil service in these two countries based on the limited available data from the WVS and EAB data sets.

These data do not allow a direct test of the effects of APA passage on either procedural transparency or public opinion. Consequently, my evidence is suggestive rather than definitive. Nonetheless, comparing public attitudes between these periods reveals a variety of trends that are precisely what one would anticipate if APAs produced just the sorts of transparency-enhancing effects that I have argued follow from their passage. Moreover, employing multiple distinct comparisons across distinct survey instruments and contexts and three different countries enables me to make a stronger, albeit still suggestive, case for my argument than is possible from a single test.

The next section outlines my argument about the relationship between administrative procedural reform and public attitudes toward democratic institutions. From this discussion, I derive a series of testable hypotheses. I then discuss my data and methods before presenting the results of a series of statistical investigations testing my hypotheses. I conclude by considering the broader implications of my findings.

Administrative Reform and Public Attitudes toward Democracy

Passage of APAs can increase access to bureaucratic policy-making for a broader set of interests, including typical citizens and their representatives. All else being equal, this process should raise the level of public confidence in the civil service and perhaps in the nation's democratic institutions. Beyond its direct effects on a state's regulatory process, it is difficult directly to measure an APA's broader effects on democratic politics. However, it is possible to identify secondary implications of the effects of APA passage that are closely related to governmental administrative transparency and, equally important, that are amenable to empirical testing. Such implications can be found in the supply of and demand for policy. On the supply side, one can compare the mix of regulatory policies prior to and following APA enactment to see whether regulations preferred by the beneficiaries of an APA are more likely to emerge and endure following APA passage while those preferred by interests associated with the prior regime fare better prior to APA passage (see chapter 6).

The second approach entails focusing on the demand side—that is, the effects of the APA on consumers. If APAs empower average citizens, this phenomenon has implications for citizens' attitudes toward their democracy and its institutions. In particular, factors that enhance governmental responsiveness to average citizens should enhance public trust and confidence in a given country's democratic institutions, especially in areas such as the civil service, where citizens most directly experience responsiveness.

Of course, citizens in successful democracies with or without APAs do not express universal trust and confidence in their government or in their nation's underlying democratic institutions. Indeed, citizen dissatisfaction with the government and even with democracy is a common feature in many long-standing democracies. But among citizens in democratic states, APAs should be positively associated with confidence in one important democratic institution, the executive bureaucracy.

Most of this chapter explores changes in public confidence in Korea's democracy in general and its civil service in particular from the pre- to post-KAPA periods, followed by a more cursory analysis of Taiwan and the Philippines. After controlling for a variety of potential alternative causal factors, we should observe enhanced public trust in Korea's democratic institutions after KAPA's passage. However, any such increase is unlikely to be universal. After all, like most policy reforms, KAPA produced winners and losers. The primary winners were citizens and groups concerned about consumers in general and social welfare in particular (e.g., health, education, labor standards). Conversely, the primary losers were those who had benefited most under the preceding authoritarian regime, including the military, bureaucrats, and the big business interests (*chaebol*) that had accounted for a large majority of the nation's economic activity. Winners were likely to feel better about the state of the nation in 2001, while the losers were likely to feel better about the nation in 1990 or at least not as much better as the winners in 2001. Since KAPA's most direct effects concerned the activities of the country's bureaucracy, any effects of KAPA on public attitudes are likely to be most immediate and acute with respect to the performance of the bureaucracy. A series of hypotheses follows:

H1 (Pre-KAPA Relative Winners): Prior to KAPA's passage, individuals associated with big business or the military will express greater confidence in Korea's bureaucracy than will individuals involved in groups concerned with consumer/social welfare issues.

H1a (Pre-KAPA Absolute Winners Corollary): Prior to KAPA's passage, greater engagement with big business or the military will be associated with increased confidence in the civil service.

H1b (Pre-KAPA Absolute Losers Corollary): Prior to KAPA's passage, greater engagement with groups concerned about consumer/social welfare issues will be associated with lower confidence in the civil service.

H2 (Post-KAPA Relative Winners): Following KAPA's passage, individuals involved in groups concerned with consumer/social welfare issues will express greater confidence in Korea's bureaucracy than will individuals associated with big business or the military.

H2a (Post-KAPA Absolute Winners Corollary): Following KAPA's passage, the relationships described in H1b with respect to involvement with consumer/social welfare groups will weaken or reverse.

H2b (Post-KAPA Absolute Losers Corollary): Following KAPA's passage, the relationships described in H1a with respect to engagement with big business or the military will weaken or reverse.

These hypotheses are predicated on significant engagement or confidence in a segment of society likely to have been relatively directly affected by KAPA's passage—that is, the individuals most likely to notice the increased transparency and opportunities for participation engendered by KAPA and their effects. This focus makes sense, as these relatively engaged individuals tend to be among society's opinion leaders. While members of the general public presumably also feel the effects of such changes, they are likely to do so more gradually and less acutely, at least over the short to medium term. Consequently, I anticipate weaker effects of KAPA on public attitudes among individuals not involved with or confident in the groups described in H1 and H2 (and their corollaries). An additional hypothesis follows:

> *H3 (Nonactivists):* The relationships described in H1 and H2 will be weaker among individuals with relatively lower levels of engagement with/confidence in the aforementioned organizations or groups than among their more highly involved counterparts.

A (presumably intended) consequence of opening the bureaucracy to public scrutiny is that it becomes an avenue through which the public can both observe governmental functioning and influence policy outcomes. Especially given the stark contrast with an until recently closed bureaucracy, an open bureaucracy is thus likely to emerge as a focal point through which citizens judge government's responsiveness and effectiveness. With a closed bureaucracy, average citizens, who in most cases are not among the bureaucracy's key clientele, are unlikely to trust what they cannot observe. Hence, citizens will tend to employ alternative means of assessing overall governmental performance, including responsiveness to citizens. Bureaucratic responsiveness will simply not be a useful heuristic (Sniderman, Brody, and Tetlock 1991) for helping citizens assess the government. After all, if the bureaucracy is structurally insulated from typical citizens and hence by design unresponsive, they are unlikely to vary in their assessment of it as a function of their general perceptions regarding governmental responsiveness. This idea suggests two additional hypotheses:

> *H4 (Government Responsiveness):* After APAs are implemented, perceptions regarding the degree of responsiveness of the government to citizens will be positively associated with confidence in the civil service. Any such relationship will be weaker prior to passage of such measures.

> *H4a (Non-APA Responsiveness Corollary):* In countries that do not pass APA-like laws (e.g., the Philippines), public trust in the civil service should not tend to increase.

These hypotheses do not specify the direction of causality; perceptions regarding the performance of the civil service clearly may either cause or be caused by (or both) attitudes regarding governmental responsiveness to citizens. But my theory implies that the two trends should covary to a greater extent in 2001 (post-KAPA) than in 1996 (just after KAPA was first enacted).

Of course, attitudes toward the bureaucracy are only consequential for Korea's democracy to the extent that they influence public confidence in it. To the extent that the key assumption underlying this investigation is valid, a direct relationship should exist between attitudes toward the bureaucracy and attitudes toward the country's democratic institutions in general, leading to my final hypothesis:

> *H5 (Democratic Satisfaction):* Confidence in the bureaucracy will be positively associated with satisfaction with the state of democracy in South Korea.

Data and Methods

The WVS and EAB Surveys

Dependent Variables

For my tests of H1 through H3 across all three country cases, the dependent variable is derived from the following question: "I am going to name a number of organizations. For each one, could you tell me how much confidence you have in them? Is it a great deal of confidence, quite a lot of confidence, not very much confidence, or none at all? . . . The civil service?" Statistical testing indicated that it was most appropriate to collapse the four-category indicator into two categories, where 0 = "none at all" or "not very much" and 1 = "quite a lot" or "a great deal."[2] This dichotomous indicator, which, as expected, significantly outperforms the four-category form of the question, has a mean of .75 and a standard deviation of .43. This question is available in one or more survey waves for all three countries.

For my test of H5 in the Korea case, the dependent variable measures the difference between respondents' attitudes regarding the past and current state of the nation. For the retrospective component, I employ the following question: "People have different views about the system for governing the country. Here is a scale for rating how well things are going: 1 means very bad; 10 means very good. Where on this scale would you put the political system as it was ten years ago?" This scale has a mean of 5.12 and a standard deviation of 2.57.

For the contemporaneous component, I employ a four-category scale based on the following question: "On the whole, are you very satisfied, rather satisfied, not very satisfied, or not at all satisfied with the way democracy is developing in our country?" I coded responses as 1 = "not at all satisfied," 2 = "not very satisfied," 3 = "rather satisfied," and 4 = "very satisfied." This indicator has a mean of 2.26 and a standard deviation of .62. These questions were asked only in 2001, however, meaning that I can test H5 only for a single point in time (post-KAPA).

To produce my attitude trend indicator (the dependent variable in my analysis), I subtract the retrospective assessment from the contemporaneous satisfaction variable (with the four-point democratic satisfaction scale normalized to a 1–10 interval). The resulting difference measure has a mean of .61 (representing a slight increase in overall satisfaction) and a standard deviation of 2.49. As a robustness test, I then retest the model using only the democratic satisfaction indicator as my dependent variable with the retrospective evaluation as a control variable.

Independent Variables

For my tests for H1 through H3 (for the Korea case), the key causal variables measure respondents' involvement in a variety of organizations as well as their confidence in the military. To estimate involvement in and concern with social welfare organizations, I create an additive scale based on respondents' self-reported membership in and voluntary activities for groups representing seven types of causes or interests: (1) social welfare services for the elderly; (2) education, arts, music, or cultural activities; (3) labor unions; (4) human rights; (5) environment, ecology, or animal rights; (6) youth work; and (7) women's rights. For each category, I combined two questions: "Please look carefully at the following list of voluntary organizations and activities and say . . . which, if any, do you belong to" and "For which, if any, are you currently doing unpaid voluntary work?" This approach produced a total of 14 discrete questions. In each case, responses are coded 0 = "not mentioned," 1 = "belong" or "doing voluntary work for." The resulting 0–14 scale has a mean of .74 and a standard deviation of 1.42.

The next two key causal variables are intended to capture interests associated with groups that were privileged under the pre-KAPA regime (i.e., business and military interests). The WVS does not ask about respondents' involvement in military-related organizations. Hence, I employ confidence in the military as the best available indicator of support for and/or ties to the military. The precise question wording and coding are identical to that for the civil service except that the specific item under consideration is identified as the armed forces. In this instance, the fully specified form of the variable somewhat outperformed the dichotomous specification employed for the civil service confidence dependent variable. Hence, I do not collapse the military confidence indicator. This variable has a mean of 2.85 and a standard deviation of .82.

Both surveys asked about respondents' membership in and voluntary activities for professional associations.[3] Beginning in roughly 1990, most of Korea's major construction, manufacturing, and retail activities were controlled by the *chaebol,* which were among the bureaucracy's primary clients, making this question a reasonable though imperfect proxy for interests that tended to benefit more from their relationships with the bureaucracy prior to KAPA.[4] This variable (collapsed) has a mean of .13 and a standard deviation of .40. For each of the three key causal variables—military confidence, involvement with consumer/social welfare organizations, and involvement with professional organizations—I also include interactions with a dummy for the 2001 wave of the survey. Finally, for my test of H4, the key causal variable is simply the dependent variable from my prior analyses: the dichotomous indicator of confidence in Korea's civil service.[5]

All models include controls for respondents' age, income, education, marital status, ideology, interest in politics, attitudes toward governments' role in promoting social change, satisfaction with household financial state, patriotism, and confidence in major companies. Tests of H1 through H3 for the Korea case also include controls for membership in and voluntary activities for party groups and a dummy for the 2001 wave. Tests of H4 include a control for respondents' general support for democratic institutions.

Finally, because my Taiwan and Philippines models, which employ the same dependent variable as in the WVS surveys, depend on merging the 1994 and 1996 WVS with the 2001 and 2002 EAB surveys, most of the causal variables described above are unavailable. The exceptions are several demographic indicators (age, education, marital status, interest in politics) and a series of indicators of trust in institutions, including the national government, parliament, courts, police, military, parties, newspapers, and television.[6] Hence, for these analyses, I focus on simple trends and correlations, employing survey years as the key causal variables and controlling for respondent demographic characteristics and trust in various social and political institutions.

The Korea Barometer Surveys (KBS)

The dependent variable for my analysis of the KBS (employed to test H4) is a 0–10 scale based on responses to the following question: "Out of 10 civil servants, how many do you think are corrupt?" Both the 1996 and 2001 KBS include the question.[7] This scale has a mean of 5.74 and a standard deviation of 2.31. My key causal variables include a 2001 wave dummy and a scale measuring the extent to which respondents believe the government is responsive to their concerns. To distinguish between the perceived relationships between governmental responsiveness and civil service corruption in 1996 and 2001 and thereby test H4, I interact the governmental responsiveness scale with the 2001 dummy. This question was available for all three countries.

To account for the possibility that perceptions of civil service corruption might reflect overall satisfaction with the incumbent president or his predecessor or general perceptions regarding political corruption, I include controls for respondents' satisfaction with the current and prior presidents[8] as well as estimates of the prevalence of corruption among politicians, personal preference for democratic governance, and satisfaction with the state of Korea's democracy. I also include several political socioeconomic controls, including interest in politics, degree of trust in other people, gender, education, and homeownership status. (See appendix for wording and coding of control variables.)

Case Selection

In addition to representing the core cases for this book, Korea, Taiwan, and the Philippines represent ideal cases for the present analysis for three reasons. First, they are relatively recent democracies that have conducted multiple democratic elections. Second, while these three countries have clearly passed the initial transition to democracy stage, their locations along the continuum of democratic consolidation remain somewhat unclear. Finally, as previously described, during their first democratic decades Korea and Taiwan implemented APAs, and elections have taken place both before and after passage. While it is important to take care when generalizing from any small set of individual cases, this combination of factors makes Korea and Taiwan ideal case studies for a plausibility probe (Drezner 2000; Eckstein 1975) of the effects of APAs on public attitudes toward democratic institutions.

It is, of course, impossible specifically to account for everything that changed in Korea between 1990 and 2001 or in Taiwan and the Philippines from 1994 or 1996 to 2001 beyond passage and implementation of administrative procedural reforms. A variety of factors doubtless influenced public satisfaction with democracy and perhaps with the bureaucracy. While, at least for Korea, I attempt to explicitly account for many of the most likely suspects (e.g., socioeconomic status, ideology, patriotism, and attitudes regarding Korea's economic, social, and political circumstances), my regression models cannot explicitly account for all such potential influences. Consequently, I include temporal dummies in part to account for the effects of any such exogenous changes not explicitly controlled in my models. In essence, I employ temporal fixed effects, with the 2001 dummy aimed at absorbing the secular effects of time across the two periods in my analyses.

I also include some additional suggestive evidence from Taiwan and the Philippines. To the extent that the predicted patterns arise across all three cases—including the non-APA case, where I would predict an absence of change in public attitudes—it becomes less likely that some single alternative explanation can account for the observed relationships.

Results

My tests of H1 through H3 are based on the WVS data, while my test of H4 is based on the KBS data. I test H5 against both data sets, albeit primarily with the WVS data. Finally, I present the results of my robustness tests, based on trends in Taiwan and the Philippines (H4 and H4a). I begin with my tests of H1 and H2, including their corollary hypotheses. H1 predicts that prior to KAPA's passage, respondents concerned with social welfare or consumer-related issues and organizations are likely to express less confidence in the civil service than are their counterparts associated with business and military interests (the bureaucracy's primary clients prior to KAPA). The corollaries to H1 then predict a positive relationship between business/military associations and confidence in the civil service (H1a) and a negative relationship between consumer/social welfare interests and confidence in the civil service (H1b).

H2 predicts that after KAPA's passage, the relationships will reverse, with respondents concerned with social welfare or consumer-related issues and organizations (interests empowered by KAPA at the expense of the bureaucracy's previously favored clients) expressing greater confidence in the civil service than their counterparts associated with business and military interests.[9] The corollaries to H2 then predict weaker and perhaps even opposing relationships relative to the corollaries to H1, with either a weaker or a negative (positive) relationship between business/military (consumer/social welfare) interests and confidence in the civil service. Table 7.1 presents the results from a logit analysis testing these predictions against the WVS data.

According to these data, involvement with a political party in either 1990 or 2001 has no significant effect on citizens' confidence in one of Korea's most important political institutions, the civil service. This finding suggests that the rising power of political parties[10] vis-à-vis the bureaucracy did not influence citizen attitudes toward the bureaucracy, while involvement with consumer/social welfare groups did influence such attitudes.

For table 7.2, I employed Clarify—statistical simulation software (King, Tomz, and Wittenberg 2000)—to transform the coefficients into expected values of the dependent variable as the key causal variables vary. I also used Clarify to estimate the statistical significance of the changes in the dependent variable associated with variations in the key causal variables, with the other causal variables held constant at their mean values. However, I held involvement in organizations (social/consumer, professional, or party) constant at 0 in various simulations.[11]

Figure 7.1 graphically illustrates the results from table 7.2. Figure 7.1 indicates that in 1990, respondents two standard deviations above the

TABLE 7.1. Logit Analysis of Effects of Group Involvement and Confidence in Military on Confidence in Korean Civil Service (1990 and 2001 waves)

Independent Variables	Coeff. (Std. Err.)
Consumer/Social Welfare Group Involvement	–.152 (.074)*
Professional Association Involvement	.379 (.231)^
Political Party Involvement	.405 (.397)
Confidence in Military	.294 (.100)**
2001 Wave	1.265 (.391)***
Consumer/Social Welfare Group Involvement × 2001 Wave	.230 (.091)**
Professional Association Involvement × 2001 Wave	–.610 (.272)*
Political Party Involvement × 2001 Wave	–.687 (.456)
Confidence in Military × 2001 Wave	–.420 (.129)***
Ideology	–.066 (.023)**
Politics Important	–.046 (.060)
Social Change	–.184 (.101)^
Patriotism	.157 (.071)*
Confidence in Major Companies	.748 (.074)***
Household Finance Satisfaction	.035 (.024)
Age	–.009 (.005)^
Income	.004 (.068)
Education	–.154 (.098)
Married	.171 (.131)
Constant	–1.097 (.590)^
R^2 (N)	.08 (N = 1,964)

$^\wedge p < .10$ $^* p < .05$ $^{**} p < .01$ $^{***} p < .001$

TABLE 7.2. Differences in Confidence in Civil Service among KAPA "Winners" and "Losers," 1990 versus 2001

				Differences			
				(Social Welfare/ Consumer vs. Professional)		(Social Welfare/ Consumer vs. Military)	
	1990	2001	1990 vs. 2001	1990	2001	1990	2001
Highly involved respondents							
Consumer/Social Welfare Groups[a]	.36	.81	.45**				
Professional Associations[a]	.56	.73	.17^				
Confidence in Military[b]	.71	.62	–.09*	–.20*	.08*	–.35**	.19**
Average involvement respondents[c]							
Consumer/Social Welfare Groups	.46	.78	.32**	–.04*	.02^	–.18**	.13**
Professional Associations	.50	.77	.27**				
Confidence in Military	.64	.65	–.01				

^$p < .10$ *$p < .05$ **$p < .01$

[a]"Highly involved" is defined as two standard deviations above the mean.

[b]"Highly involved" is defined as one standard deviation above the mean (which is approximately equivalent to, albeit slightly less than, the maximum value on the confidence in the military scale).

[c]"Average involvement" is defined as the mean level of involvement on a given scale.

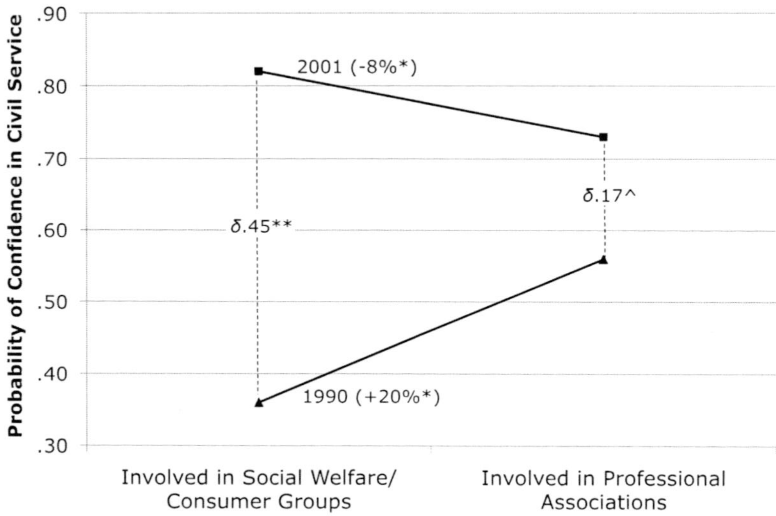

FIG. 7.1. Confidence in civil service among respondents highly involved with social welfare/consumer groups versus professional associations, 1990 versus 2001; $^\wedge p < .10$, $^*p < .05$, $^{**}p < .01$.

mean level of involvement with groups concerned with consumer/social welfare issues—that is, respondents who are relatively more engaged than typical individuals (labeled "highly" involved in table 7.2)—were 20 and 35 percentage points less likely than their counterparts who were highly involved with professional associations and highly confident in the military, respectively, to express confidence in the civil service (.56 versus .36, $p < .05$; .71 versus .36, $p < .01$). These results strongly support H1.

Figure 7.2 focuses on my tests of H2. Here, the patterns observed in 1990 reversed in 2001. In the 2001 wave of the survey, respondents two standard deviations above the mean level of involvement with groups concerned with consumer/social welfare (that is, "highly" involved individuals) were 8 and 19 percentage points more likely than their counterparts who were highly involved with professional associations and highly confident in the military, respectively, to express confidence in the civil service (.81 versus .73, $p < .05$; .81 versus .62, $p < .01$). These results strongly support H2.

Figures 7.3–7.5, also derived from the WVS data, illustrate my tests of

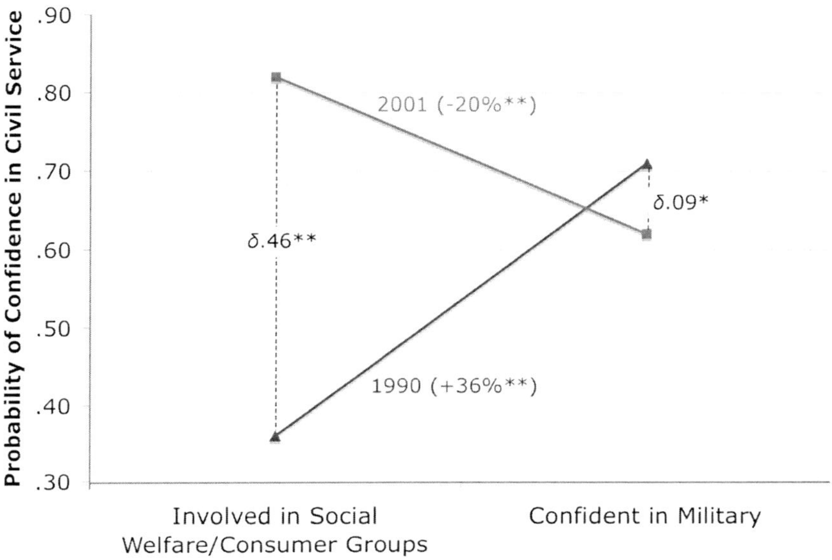

FIG. 7.2. Confidence in civil service among respondents highly involved with social welfare/consumer groups versus highly confident in military, 1990 versus 2001; $^{*}p < .05$, $^{**}p < .01$.

the corollaries to H1 and H2 for consumer/social welfare group involvement, professional association involvement, and confidence in the military, respectively. Figure 7.3 indicates that in 1990, a two-standard-deviation increase from the mean in involvement with consumer/social welfare groups is associated with a statistically significant ($p < .05$) 10 percentage point decline in confidence in the civil service (from .46 to .36).[12] In 2001, the pattern reverses, with the corresponding increase in involvement associated with a statistically significant ($p < .10$) five-point increase in confidence in the civil service (from .77 to .82). These results support H1b and H2a.

With respect to involvement with professional associations, figure 7.4 indicates that in 1990, a two-standard-deviation increase from the mean in involvement is associated with a statistically significant ($p < .10$) nine-point increase in confidence in the civil service (from .49 to .58). In 2001, the pattern again reverses, with increased involvement associated with a statistically significant ($p < .10$) four-point decline in confidence in the civil service (from .77 to .73). These results are consistent with H1a and H2b.

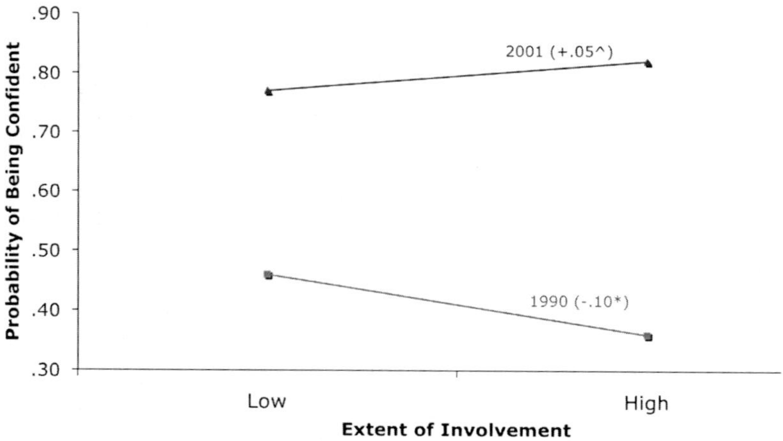

FIG. 7.3. Confidence in civil service as extent of involvement with social welfare/consumer groups varies, 1990 versus 2001; $^{\wedge}p < .10$, $^{*}p < .05$.

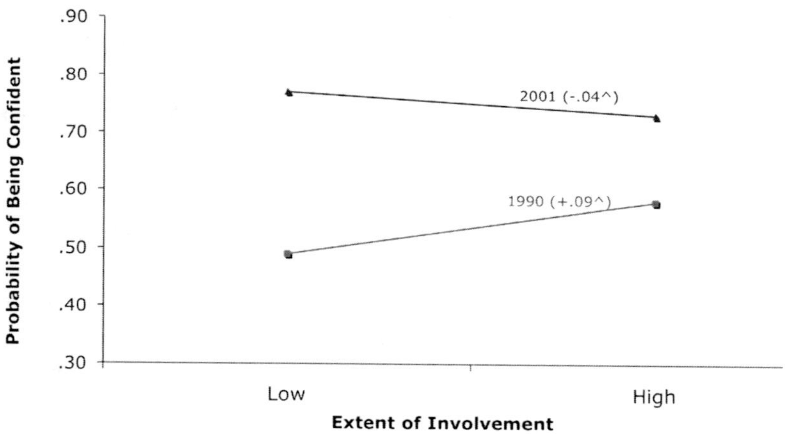

FIG. 7.4. Confidence in civil service as extent of involvement with professional associations varies, 1990 versus 2001; $^{\wedge}p < .10$.

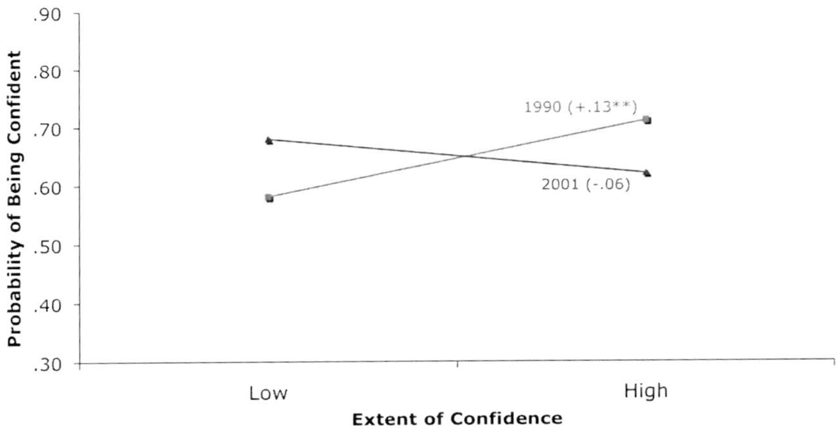

FIG. 7.5. Confidence in civil service as extent of confidence in military varies, 1990 versus 2001; $^{**}p < .01$.

Figure 7.5 shows that in 1990, a two-standard-deviation increase in confidence in the military—from one standard deviation below to one standard deviation above the mean—is associated with a highly significant ($p < .01$) 13 percentage point increase in confidence in the civil service (from .58 to .71). In 2001, increased confidence in the military is associated with a six-point decline in confidence in the civil service (from .68 to .62). In this instance, the negative slope in 2001 does not quite achieve standard levels of statistical significance. However, as predicted, the relationship between confidence in the military and in the civil service moves in opposing directions from 1990 to 2001, and the difference between the slopes of the 1990 and 2001 curves is itself statistically significant. Hence, these results support both H1a and H2b, albeit somewhat less strongly supporting H2b.

To test H3 (employing the WVS data), I replicate the prior analysis, this time setting group involvement to its overall mean levels in the data. Beginning with the 1990 wave, the results summarized in table 7.2 indicate that respondents at the mean level of involvement with groups concerned with consumer/social welfare were 4 and 18 percentage points less likely than their counterparts who were similarly involved with professional associations and located at the mean level of confidence in the military, respectively, to express confidence in the civil service (.46 versus .50, $p < .05$; .46 versus .64, $p < .01$). Though significant in both instances and substantial in magnitude in the latter case, these differences are considerably smaller than those among highly involved respondents (that is, two standard deviations above the mean level of group involvement and one standard deviation above the mean level of confidence in the military), for whom the corresponding differences are five times larger in the former instance and nearly twice as large in the latter. This finding supports H3.

In the 2001 wave, respondents at the mean level of involvement with groups concerned with social welfare were 2 and 13 percentage points more likely than their counterparts who were similarly involved with professional associations and located at the mean level of confidence in the military, respectively, to express confidence in the civil service (rounded to .78 versus .77, $p < .10$; .78 versus .65, $p < .01$). As before, these relationships remain similarly signed and statistically significant as well as substantial in magnitude in the latter instance. However, these differences are again considerably smaller than those among more highly engaged or confident respondents, for whom the differences are about five times larger in the former case and about one-third larger in the latter. These results also strongly support H3.

Table 7.2 as well as figures 7.1 and 7.2 reveals that the largest differences between 1990 and 2001 occur among respondents highly involved with consumer/social welfare groups, with an increase of 45 percentage points in the likelihood of expressing confidence in the civil service ($p < .01$). The corresponding difference among respondents highly involved with professional organizations is a somewhat smaller 17-point increase ($p < .10$). Differences among respondents highly confident in the military are also significant but somewhat smaller in magnitude. In this instance, respondents who expressed high confidence in the military were 9 percentage points more likely to be confident in the civil service ($p < .05$).

These patterns have two likely causes. First, consumer/social welfare interests were largely excluded from the policy process prior to KAPA. Hence, KAPA produced the most profound direct effects for these individuals. In other words, KAPA did not so much freeze out business and military interests as create a new seat at the table for consumer/social welfare interests. To the extent that resources are limited, of course, the former groups were forced to give up some of the benefits they had long enjoyed. However, their losses were likely smaller than the gains secured by newly enfranchised consumer/social welfare interests.

Second, my indicator of consumer/social welfare interests is more direct than either of the other two measures. Professional association involvement presumably includes interests not associated with big business (e.g., medical doctors or dentists), while confidence in the military is a less direct measure of having interests tied to the military than actual membership and participation in military-related organizations. Consequently, the relative magnitudes of the effects appear largely to correspond with variations in the quality of the indicators.

I turn next to H4, which predicts that after KAPA is implemented, citizens will link their confidence in government responsiveness to citizens to their confidence in the civil service. As a consequence, after KAPA, citizens who believe the government is responsive are more likely to express confidence in the bureaucracy than their counterparts who lack this belief. However, when KAPA was first enacted, citizens were less likely to draw strong connections between bureaucratic performance and governmental responsiveness. Table 7.3 presents the results of two ordinary least squares analyses testing this prediction against the KBS data.[13] The first model compares respondents' estimates of bureaucratic corruption—my indicator of confidence in the bureaucracy—while the second adds an interaction between the 2001 dummy and respondent attitudes regarding governmental responsiveness.

TABLE 7.3. OLS Analyses of Effects of Korean Attitudes regarding Governmental Responsiveness to Citizens on Perceived Corruption in the Civil Service, 1996 versus 2001

Independent Variables	Basic Model	Interaction Model
Governmental Responsiveness Scale	.007 (.076)	.007 (.076)
2001 Dummy	–.580 (.101)***	.170 (.310)
2001 Dummy × Governmental Responsiveness Scale	—	–.272 (.113)*
Democratic Satisfaction	–.551 (.290)^	–.513 (.290)^
Politician Corruption Scale	.614 (.023)***	.606 (.023)***
Support for Current President	–.042 (.029)	–.046 (.029)
Support for Prior President	–.062 (.027)*	–.060 (.027)*
Preference for Democracy	.077 (.131)	.113 (.132)
Interest in Politics	–.048 (.058)	–.031 (.058)
Male	–.266 (.090)**	–.280 (.091)**
Trust in Other People	–.177 (.070)**	–.176 (.070)**
Education	.110 (.047)*	.104 (.047)*
Homeowner	–.175 (.094)^	–.185 (.094)*
Constant	2.766 (.385)***	2.764 (.413)***
R^2 (N)	.37 (N = 1,688)	.37 (N = 1,674)

Note: Standard errors in parentheses; — = no data.
^$p < .10$ *$p < .05$ **$p < .01$ ***$p < .001$

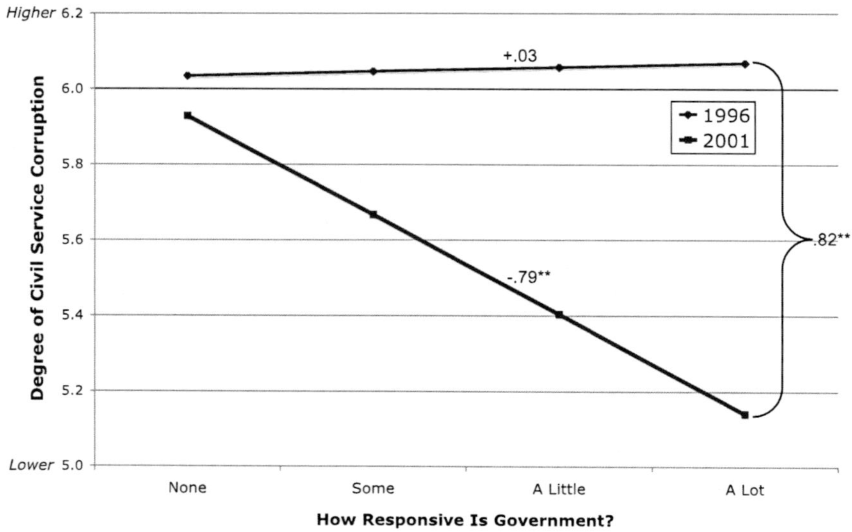

FIG. 7.6. Effect of respondents' self-perceived influence on government on perceptions of civil service corruption, 1996 versus 2001; $^{**}p < .01$.

The results of the first model indicate that on the 10-point corruption scale, respondents' average rating for the civil service declined .58 points, from 6.06 in 1996 to 5.48 in 2001 ($p < .01$), equivalent to .25 standard deviations on the civil service corruption scale. While this finding is broadly consistent with my theory and my prior findings, a more direct test of H4 requires accounting for respondent attitudes regarding governmental responsiveness. Therefore, the second model in table 7.3 interacts the 2001 dummy with the governmental responsiveness scale. Figure 7.6 graphically illustrates the results.

The 1996 curve in figure 7.6 is almost perfectly flat (and insignificant). In 1996, respondents believed, on average, that about 6 in 10 civil servants were corrupt. This belief appears unrelated to broader perceptions regarding citizens' ability to influence their government. In sharp contrast, in 2001, these two factors are strongly inversely related to one another. As perceived citizen influence on the government increases from none to a lot, the average civil service corruption rating declines by nearly .8 points ($p < .01$), from 5.93 to 5.14, a drop of .35 standard deviations on the civil service corruption scale. The difference among respondents who believed that citizens had no influence over the government was small and insignificant. However, among those who believed that citizens had a lot of influence, the .82-point gap is highly significant ($p < .01$), with respondents in 2001 appearing to base their opinions regarding the extent of bureaucratic corruption in significant measure on their perceptions regarding governmental responsiveness to citizens. Most of the overall decline in perceptions of civil service corruption apparently occurred among respondents who viewed the government as responsive to citizens.

These relationships emerge despite an array of controls intended to account for many of the most likely alternative causal factors, including support for the current president (Kim Dae Jung in 2001, Kim Young Sam in 1996) and the prior president (Kim Young Sam in 2001 and Roh Tae Woo in 1996), satisfaction with Korea's democracy, perceptions of corruption among politicians, general trust in other people, interest in politics, belief in democracy, and socioeconomic status. Consequently, my results clearly support H4.

I test H5 against both data sets. Beginning with the WVS data, table 7.4 presents the results of one ordinary least squares and one ordered logit

TABLE 7.4. OLS and Ordered Logit Analyses of Effects of Confidence in the Civil Service on Satisfaction with Korea's Democracy (2001 wave)

Independent Variables	Democratic Satisfaction Trend	Democratic Satisfaction
Confidence in Civil Service	.621 (.184)***	.394 (.162)*
Support for Democracy	–.024 (.096)	.155 (.043)***
Rate Political System 10 Years Ago	—	.028 (.080)
Confidence in Military	–.089 (.121)	.111 (.106)
Ideology	–.043 (.044)	–.044 (.038)
Politics Important	.235 (.102)*	.118 (.086)
Social Change	.113 (.167)	–.228 (.146)
Patriotism	.107 (.122)	.454 (.110)***
Confidence in Major Companies	–.176 (.132)	.202 (.120)^
Household Finance Satisfaction	–.061 (.041)	.044 (.037)
Age	.008 (.009)	.006 (.008)
Income	.020 (.108)	.130 (.094)
Education	–.396 (.166)*	–.438 (.145)**
Married	–.159 (.223)	–.202 (.203)
Constant 1	1.072 (.951)	–.299 (.831)
Constant 2	—	3.093 (.840)
Constant 3	—	7.089 (.904)
R^2 (N)	.04 (N = 845)	.06 (N = 845)

Note: Standard errors in parentheses; — = no data.
^$p < .10$, *$p < .05$, **$p < .01$, ***$p < .001$

model testing H5. The former employs the satisfaction trend indicator as the dependent variable, while the latter employs only contemporaneous (circa 2001) satisfaction with Korea's democracy. Once again, I transform the results into expected values of the dependent variable as the key causal variable varies.

Model 1 indicates that respondents who express confidence in Korea's civil service are .62 points more satisfied with the state of Korea's democracy in 2001 than was the case in 1990 (from +.16 to +.78, $p < .01$), an increase of about .25 standard deviation on the satisfaction trend scale. The simulation results from Model 2 are summarized in table 7.5 and graphically illustrated in figure 7.7.

In the 2001 wave, respondents who were confident in Korea's civil service were more likely to be satisfied with the state of Korea's democracy. Specifically, those who reported confidence in Korea's bureaucracy were 2.8 (from .089 to .062) and 5.4 (from .652 to .598) percentage points less likely to report being "not at all" or "not very" satisfied with the state of Korea's democracy as well as 7.9 (from .252 to .331) and .3 (from .007 to .010) points more likely to report being "rather" or "very" satisfied. Each of these differences is statistically significant ($p < .05$).

Turning to the KBS data, I included respondent satisfaction in democracy as a causal variable in both models from table 7.3. The results indicate that an increase of 1 point on the 10-point democratic satisfaction scale is associated with decreases of .51 and .55 points on the civil service corruption scales for models with and without the citizen influence interaction, respectively ($p < .10$). These differences represent .22 and .24 standard deviation declines in perceptions of civil service corruption, respectively. A maximum increase in democratic satisfaction is associated with a decline in perceived civil service corruption of 5.0 and 5.5 points on the civil service corruption scales, representing 2.2 and 2.4 standard deviation declines in perceived corruption, respectively. While it is entirely possible

TABLE 7.5. Probability of Being Satisfied with Korea's Democracy in 2001, as Confidence in Civil Service Varies (WVS)

Democratic Satisfaction	Not Confident in Civil Service	Confident in Civil Service	Difference
1 (minimum)	.089	.062	−.028*
2	.652	.598	−.054*
3	.252	.331	+.079*
4 (maximum)	.007	.010	+.003*

*$p < .05$

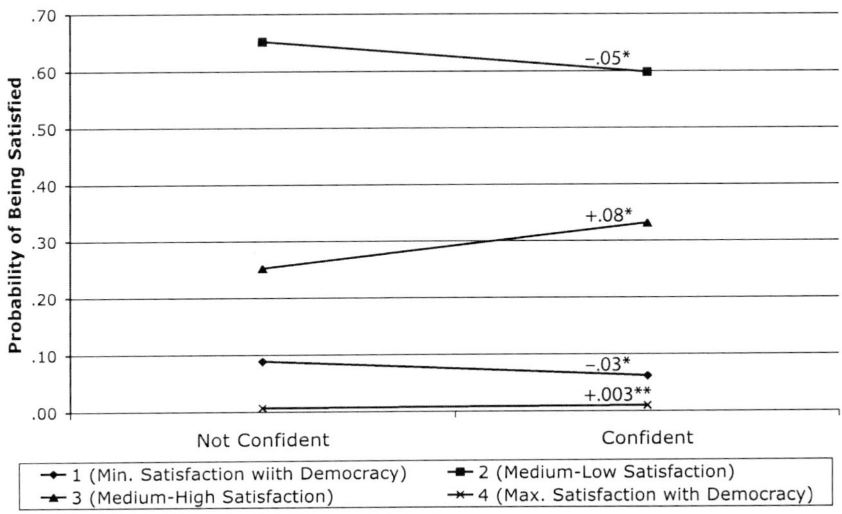

FIG. 7.7. Probability of being satisfied with Korea's democracy as confidence in civil service varies, 2001; $*p < .05$, $**p < .01$.

that perceptions regarding civil service corruption are a cause rather than or in addition to an effect of democratic satisfaction, the two clearly are closely related. Taken together, the results from the WVS (tables 7.4 and 7.5 and figure 7.7) and the KBS (table 7.3) thus offer clear support for H5.

Finally, I use data on Taiwan and the Philippines to test H4 and H4a, respectively. Because I lack appropriate controls for replicating the complete analysis I conducted for Korea, I instead focus on simple over-time comparisons. To test these predictions, I compare public trust in the civil service in 1994 and 2001 for Taiwan and 1996, 2001, and 2002 for the Philippines. H4 would anticipate that citizens in Taiwan should express greater confidence in their civil service after TAPA's implementation than previously. Conversely, H4a would predict no over-time changes in Philippine citizens' confidence in the civil service. I test these predictions using multiple regression and a simple correlation analysis. The latter approach is intended to determine whether, as H4 implies, Taiwanese citizens are more likely to assess the civil service independently of their trust of other institutions, while, as H4a implies, citizens in the Philippines remain similarly likely, over time, to relate their attitudes toward the civil service to their attitudes toward other social and political institutions. Beginning with the regression analysis, table 7.6 presents the results of logit analyses testing H4 and H4a. In figure 7.8, I again employ Clarify to transform the logit coefficients into probabilities of expressing different degrees of confidence in Taiwan's civil service.

Between 1994 and 2001, the probability that citizens would express "quite a lot" or "a great deal" of confidence in the civil service increased by 16 percentage points (from .52 to .68, $p < .01$). This result is consistent with H4. While a simple secular trend represents at best suggestive evidence, these patterns emerge net of trust in a variety of other public and private institutions, including the national government, parliament, political parties, the military, the police, the courts, and the press (print and broadcast).

To the extent that attitudes toward the civil service depend on civil service accountability and transparency, we would expect no comparable trend in the Philippines. The second logit analysis in table 7.6 confirms this prediction: no significant differences existed among attitudes toward the Philippine civil service in 1996, 2001, and 2002.

For the second investigation, I conduct a simple correlation analysis for the various institutional trust indicators. If the APA indeed increased the likelihood that citizens would evaluate the civil service's performance

TABLE 7.6. Logit Analyses of Trends in Trust in Civil Service (WVS and EAB)

	Taiwan	Philippines
2001	.645 (.128)***	.114 (.105)
2002	—	.006 (.103)
Trust TV	.204 (.125)^	.265 (.073)***
Political Interest	.153 (.074)*	–.046 (.046)
Male	.002 (.118)	–.087 (.084)
Age	.014 (.006)*	–.001 (.003)
Married	.068 (.147)	–.008 (.095)
Trust Courts	.049 (.114)	—
Trust National Government	.418 (.120)***	.347 (.068)***
Trust Parties	.316 (.132)*	.251 (.074)***
Trust Parliament	.262 (.114)*	.832 (.076)***
Trust Military	.727 (.107)***	.365 (.062)***
Trust Police	.723 (.111)***	.282 (.065)***
Education	.029 (.055)	.133 (.036)***
Trust Newspapers	.321 (.124)**	.047 (.074)
Constant	–8.486 (.621)***	–5.676 (.359)***
Pseudo R^2 (N)	.20 (N = 1,656)	.23 (N = 3,422)

Note: Standard errors in parentheses; — = no data.
^$p < .10$ *$p < .05$ **$p < .01$ ***$p < .001$

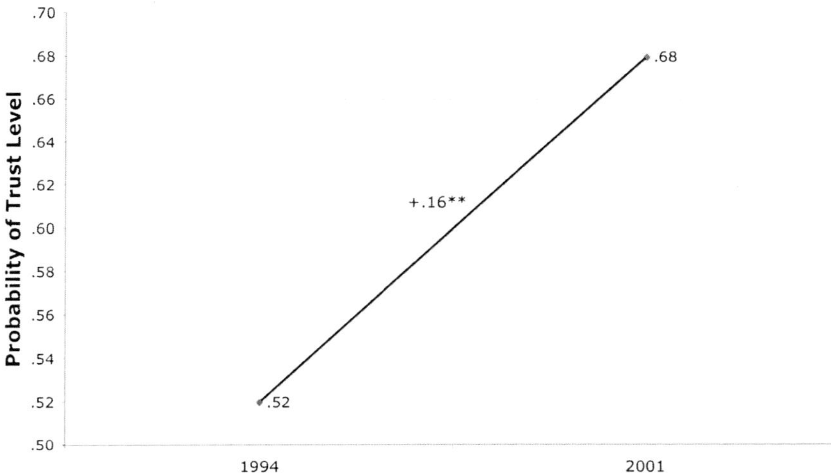

FIG. 7.8. Probability of trusting Taiwan's civil service "quite a lot" or "a great deal," 1994 versus 2001; $^{**}p < .01$.

independent of their evaluations of the executive, legislative, or judicial branches of government or of the political system in general, then higher correlations should exist between trust in the civil service and trust in other institutions prior to TAPA's passage. Conversely, similar correlations should exist in the Philippines across all three periods. Once again, the results support both predictions, as table 7.7 shows.

In Taiwan, the 1994 correlations between trust in the civil service and other institutions ranged from a low of .36 for newspapers to a high of .53 for the national government. The overall average across the eight institutions was .44. In 2001, the correlations ranged from a low of .13 for newspapers to a high of .35 for the military, with an overall average of .24, just over half the previous rate. These results are consistent with my expectations.

For the Philippines, the correlations ranged from .25 to .54 in 1996, from .28 to .53 in 2001, and from .33 to .44 in 2002. The averages across the seven available institutions were .36, .36, and .39 for 1996, 2001, and 2002, respectively. These relatively minor differences are precisely what one would anticipate given the absence of change in the civil service. As a final test, I replicated this correlation analysis for Korea. My theory suggests that the pattern for Korea should more closely approximate that observed for Taiwan than for the Philippines, and the results confirm this hypothesis. The average correlations between trust in the civil service and five other institutions available in both surveys (military, press, business, police, and the legislature) were nearly twice as strong in 2001 as in 1990 (.36 versus .19).[14] While these broad trends are at most suggestive evidence, they are nonetheless uniformly consistent with H4 and H4a. Moreover, the fact that the results for Taiwan and Korea but not for the Philippines move in the predicted directions suggests that global or regional secular trends (economic, political, and so forth) cannot account for the observed patterns.

Potential Alternative Explanations

My statistical investigations do not constitute direct evidence that APA passage has contributed to public confidence in Korea's or Taiwan's democratic institutions. Numerous secular trends and alternative causal factors doubtless influenced citizens' satisfaction with Korea's democracy as well as confidence in the bureaucracy in both countries. In the case of Korea, such factors include the passage of the Korean Freedom of Information Act in 1996, the currency crisis of 1997, former president Roh Tae Woo's 1996 conviction for corruption and involvement in a 1979 coup, and the election of Kim Dae Jung, a prodemocracy activist and former political prisoner, to the presidency in 1997. However, my analyses control for many of the likely attitudinal effects of these and other high-profile events. In the Taiwan and Philippines cases, I control for trust in a wide

TABLE 7.7. Correlations between Trust in Civil Service and Trust in Other Social and Political Institutions

	Taiwan		Philippines		
	1994	2001	1996	2001	2002
Trust Courts	.42	.22	—	—	—
Trust National Government	.53	.24	.37	.37	.44
Trust Parties	.42	.25	.42	.35	.38
Trust Parliament	.50	.23	.54	.53	.44
Trust Military	.39	.35	.37	.28	.44
Trust Police	.50	.34	.32	.40	.39
Trust Newspapers	.36	.13	.27	.29	.33
Trust Television	.40	.17	.25	.30	.35
Averages	.44	.24	.36	.36	.40

Note: — = no data.

range of social and political institutions. Moreover, in Korea I find opposing trends among individuals involved with interest groups likely to have either benefited or suffered from KAPA as well as weaker relationships among respondents less involved with the groups most directly affected by the KAPA reforms. An overall secular increase in confidence in the civil service or with Korea's democracy cannot account for such trends, regardless of their causes.

To isolate as much as possible the effects of association with different interest groups, independent of secular trends, I focused my core hypothesis tests in the WVS analysis (for the Korea case) on relative levels across group associations (e.g., from consumer/social welfare to professional) and degrees of group involvement (low versus high) within survey waves (1990 or 2001) rather than within group associations (e.g., consumer/social welfare or professional) or degrees of involvement across waves. Consequently, while far from definitive, my results are highly suggestive. Finally, the fact that trends and correlation patterns in both Taiwan and the Philippines are consistent with my hypotheses given the presence or absence of an APA makes it somewhat less likely that some third omitted factor can account for all of the observed patterns in the data.

Conclusion

Given the proliferation of APA-like laws among new democracies around the world, determining whether and how they influence public attitudes toward democratic institutions represents an important step in the process of investigating the effects of such measures on democratic politics.

My hypothesis tests in the Korea case revealed precisely the types of patterns, across both space and time, that one would anticipate if the three KAPA laws enhanced the public's trust and confidence in the nation's democratic institutions, most notably the civil service. The WVS respondents most closely associated with the winners under KAPA (mass consumer and social welfare groups) were more likely to express confidence in Korea's civil service in 2001 than in 1990, while those more closely associated with the losers (big business and the military) did the opposite. Similarly, in the KBS data, respondents drew a much closer connection in 2001 than in 1996 between perceptions of civil service corruption and of citizens' capacity to influence their government. Three years after KAPA III, citizens indeed appear to have begun judging the democratic responsiveness of government in part based on assessments of the civil service.

Both data sets demonstrated such attitudes to be strongly related to satisfaction with Korea's democracy, measured both at the absolute level (that is, solely in 2001) and relative to 10 years earlier. Additional tests employing data from Taiwan and the Philippines further supported my hypotheses, reducing the likelihood that some other factor might account for the reported relationships. Although this chapter tests my argument only indirectly, the relationships described here are precisely what one would anticipate finding if KAPA and TAPA had their intended political and policy effects.

My findings strongly suggest that administrative procedural reform should be offered a seat at the table of research on democratic governance, alongside "free and fair" elections. Although they are arguably a necessary element of democracy, elections alone do not appear to be sufficient (Ackerman 2004, 448; Przeworski, Stokes, and Manin 1999), as national elections demonstrated in Afghanistan in 2004, Iraq in 2005, and even Korea between 1956 and 1971.[15] International observers declared the elections in these countries relatively "free and fair" (more than many observers had anticipated), yet by almost any reasonable criterion, among those countries, only Korea has to date successfully established or consolidated democracy. While administrative procedural reforms alone are almost certainly not sufficient for establishing democratic legitimacy, my results suggest that in combination with other factors—presumably including elections—such reforms may make a significant contribution in the movement from institutional to responsive democracy.

8 | Transparency, Participation, and Democratic Responsiveness

Although the twentieth century witnessed the birth of more than 85 democracies, the extent of democratic consolidation across these countries varies greatly (Geddes 1999; Huntington 1991). The U.S. Department of State expresses its commitment to democracy "until all the citizens of the world have the fundamental right to choose those who govern them through an ongoing civil process that includes free, fair, and transparent elections" (U.S. Department of State, "Democracy"). This includes a belief that public officials in a representative democracy hold office in the name of the people and remain accountable to the people for their actions.

By this definition, securing citizens' rights to free and fair elections is only a partial first step along the path toward true democracy. A critical link in the chain of democratic accountability occurs when elected officials delegate sweeping policy-making authority to unelected bureaucrats. After all, as the U.S. government's definition of democracy implies, accountability in governance is a cornerstone of stable democracy. Yet elected officials may be unable to control these bureaucrats and citizens may have difficulty holding these policymakers accountable. This situation is especially troublesome given the extraordinary breadth and depth of the responsibilities that elected policymakers routinely delegate to administrative agencies in modern nation-states, including, in the U.S. case, authority to interpret health, safety, environmental and economic regulations as well as to allocate public investments.

One solution to this delegation dilemma is to empower the public directly to participate in bureaucratic policy-making. In this book, I have sought to explain the recent development of administrative procedural reform in new democracies in the hopes of expanding on existing theories of why politicians adopt procedures that open up the administrative state.

To increase accountability, some countries require that bureaucratic agencies provide the public with information on their past performance (e.g., public disclosure) and direct opportunities to participate in future bureaucratic policy-making (e.g., notice, public hearing, and comment procedures). They also bestow on civil society the right to monitor bureaucratic compliance with legislative directives (e.g., citizen lawsuits and judicial review). Other democracies, however, appear to exclude civil society from direct participation in bureaucratic policy-making.

It is, of course, understandable why legislatures would support administrative procedure laws designed to limit and monitor executive branch power. However, it is less obvious why chief executives would go along with laws that would reduce their underlings' discretion and limit their own power to act freely. To resolve this seeming paradox, I developed a "reining-in" theory of control. My theory identified a key causal variable that appears capable of resolving the paradox: executive branch members with conflicting policy preferences.

My investigation into the conditions under which politicians support administrative procedure acts (APAs) centered on how understanding the effects of institutional variation in presidential democracies on principal-agent relationships can help explain recent enactment of APAs. According to my reining-in theory, a president's ability to appoint and dismiss his bureaucratic agents affects the degree to which conflict arises within his branch. If a president can freely appoint and dismiss loyalists and enemies, he can solve current delegation problems without resorting to alternative mechanisms. However, a president who faces intrabranch conflict over policy issues and who is constrained by constitutional appointment rules will solve his delegation problems by resorting to a second-best solution. The resulting enactment of APAs or APA-like laws represents a new equilibrium outcome from this interaction between a president and his agents. While some scholars have argued that APAs are a tool for preserving the status quo, I find that APAs can help presidents *change* it.

Having developed the theory in chapter 2, the evidence presented in chapters 3 through 5 supported my various predictions. Chapter 3 presented a case study of South Korea's first civilian government under President Kim Young Sam. Archival data, secondary sources, and interviews with key presidential advisers, senior career bureaucrats, and politicians revealed the existence of a professionalized civil service with policy preferences that conflicted with those of the president. This motivated him to initiate an APA. Indeed, the South Korean case showed that when Kim wanted to change the status quo by deregulating the economy, he confronted resistance from bureaucrats whose incentives and professional survival were vested in the status quo. Thus, Kim's ability to control these bureaucrats during his administration was enhanced through strict procedures designed to keep tabs on bureaucratic activities. In addition, the sunset review provision in the Korean APA supported my argument that when presidents seek to change the nation's policy direction, they choose specific procedures that require their agents to revisit the status quo.

In chapter 4, through my investigation of the development and passage of Taiwan's APA, I found that President Lee's control of his party deteriorated as factional disputes within his own party increased over time. Lee ultimately concluded that the KMT's political survival depended on major reforms. Consequently, the status-quo-oriented bureaucracy—hitherto an important source of support for Lee and his key constituencies—became an impediment. Lee supported Taiwan's APA in order to reduce the bureaucracy's capacity to impede reform.

Finally, my case study of the Philippines showed that when incomplete presidential appointment powers are *not* a problem, an extensive APA is unlikely to emerge. Specifically, I presented evidence in chapter 5 that showed when presidents have unconstrained appointment and dismissal powers of the cabinet and access to patronage in the bureaucracy—as was the case with Philippines President Corazon Aquino—they are able to control their agents without resorting to the more costly solution of an APA.

Having addressed the causes of administrative procedural reform, the next two chapters turned to the consequences. I conceptually divided the consequences into the supply and demand for policy. Beginning with the supply side, the sunset law is a prime example of a procedural requirement designed to change the regulatory status quo. KAPA contains a five-year sunset provision, according to which all policies and regulations automatically expire unless they are specifically renewed. In chapter 6, I developed a spatial model to determine why a president would include a sunset provision in an administrative procedural reform law, such as KAPA, given that such a reform unambiguously limits the life of his own administration's regulatory rules. The model demonstrates that, under some circumstances, a sunset law can be a valuable tool for presidents wanting to manage their influence over the bureaucracy by breaking the regulatory status quo. The empirical evidence presented in this chapter showed that the sunset provision had precisely this effect in South Korea. Indeed, as a direct consequence of sunset implementation, many regulations expired. A disproportionate number of these affected those ministries most closely affiliated with the previous, authoritarian regime.

Turning to the demand side, in chapter 7 I sought to link administrative procedural reform to public confidence in democratic institutions. More precisely, I investigated whether citizens' perceptions of their nations' democratic responsiveness in general, and of the bureaucracy in particular, varied systematically with the presence (South Korea, Taiwan) or absence (Philippines) of APAs. My argument in this chapter followed from a simple hypothesis. That is, if APAs increase governmental responsiveness to average citizens, then they should enhance citizens' confidence in their nation's democratic institutions, particularly their civil service.

I tested this hypothesis by investigating trends, pre- and post-APA passage, in the attitudes of citizens in South Korea, Taiwan, and the Philippines regarding their countries' democracies in general, and bureaucracies in particular. I found support for all of my hypotheses, both cross-sectionally and over time. My evidence suggests that citizens' trust and confidence in their nations' democratic institutions was indeed positively associated with APA passage. In South Korea and Taiwan, which passed APAs in the mid- to late-1990s, trust in democratic institutions subsequently increased; in the Philippines, where no APA passed, no such trend emerged. Moreover, these trends were not undifferentiated. For instance, survey respondents most closely associated with the "winners" under KAPA (in South Korea, for which the most complete data were available) were more likely to express confidence in South Korea's civil service in 2001 (post-KAPA), relative to 1990 (pre-KAPA), while those more closely associated with the "losers" (i.e., interests tied to the previous, authoritarian regime) were more likely to do so in 1990 (pre-KAPA), relative to 2001 (post-KAPA). Attitudes toward the bureaucracy, in turn, were powerful predictors of satisfaction with South Korea's democracy, measured both at the absolute level (that is, solely in 2001), and relative to attitudes toward the state of the nation 10 years prior.

I devote the remainder of this concluding chapter to further addressing the implications of my theory for democratic responsiveness in South Korea and other developing democracies. Before turning to these issues, however, I first discuss the implications of the theory for public policy outcomes as well as for other presidential systems and parliamentary governments.

Types of APAs

My reining-in theory holds important implications for predicting public policy outcomes. The relatively wide degree of variation in the specific types of administrative procedures raises the question of why politicians adopt differing procedures in different countries at different times. Based on the results of my spatial model of the sunset procedure in chapter 6, I believe that politicians choose specific types of procedures depending on whether their primary goal in pursuing administrative reform is either preserving the status quo or changing it to speed up various reforms. My findings suggest that the reining-in theory sheds additional light on the motivations of the politicians who supported the U.S. APA (Baum 2007c) and thus that the theory applies beyond the East Asian presidential democracies investigated here.

In addition, these specific procedures suggest that bureaucracies are likely to grow increasingly responsive to interest groups, particularly when the costs of failing to respond are sufficiently high. Paradoxically, however, this trend may also result in bureaucracies that become less responsive to at least some of society's pressing needs. After all, these procedures are designed to build in checks and to slow down the agency decision-making process. For example, the notice and comment process can delay the implementation of new environmental or consumer health and safety regulations. Indeed, in the United States, the proposed rule-making and final rule-making stages for some regulations have taken many years to resolve. For regulations involving controversial issues—with conflicting groups or agencies on opposing sides—the implementation of final rules can be delayed for many additional years.

APAs are thus to some extent a double-edged sword: on the one hand, they enhance bureaucratic accountability to the public; on the other, they reduce the government's responsiveness to particular societal needs, even when such needs are pressing.

APAs across Presidential and Parliamentary Systems

Scholarly attention to APA passage has focused almost exclusively on the U.S. Congress. Hence, this book fills a gap in the literature. However, there is no inherent reason to believe that the logic of my argument would not also apply to parliamentary systems and chief executives in general. Though a few scholars have studied delegation in parliamentary democracies (e.g., Huber and Lupia 2001; Ramseyer and Rosenbluth 1993; Strøm 2000; Thies 2001), none have identified the conditions under which politicians in parliamentary democracies adopt APAs.[1] Therefore, a next logical step would be to investigate the constitutional and coalitional differences across presidential and parliamentary systems and in other regions with the goal of determining the relative importance of such differences in influencing whether and in what form countries pass APAs. For example, if my theory is correct, multiparty coalition governments should be more likely than single-party governments to adopt APAs or similar laws (Baum and Jensen 2009).

One approach would be to determine which forms of democracy most readily adopt statutory directives for bureaucrats that enable public participation in bureaucratic policy-making. The alternative forms of democracy would include single- and multiparty parliamentary systems as well as weak, strong, and multiparty presidential systems.

The key to such a study would be focusing on the behavior of elected principals whose ability to control delegated authority varies across political systems. For example, in a single-party parliamentary system, the prime minister has a weak incentive to force her bureaucrats to share information or extend participatory rights. In weak presidential systems, where multiple principals compete for both information and control, principals have a much stronger incentive to force their common agent (the bureaucratic policymaker) to be more transparent and responsive. In either of these cases, the counterintuitive theoretical implication is that opportunities for public participation increase as a result of competition among elected principals for control of delegated authority.

Moving toward Responsive Democracy

Finally, my theory also holds potentially important implications for democratic responsiveness. What changes in administrative procedural openness should we anticipate or desire in new democracies? Not all new democracies have implemented administrative procedural reform, and APAs do not appear to be a necessary feature of democracy. Yet my findings suggest that enactment of APAs in new democracies facilitates movement from *ex post* toward *ex ante* democracy, a process that can make the state more responsive to its citizens. By making government decision making more transparent and giving citizens a voice in the policy implementation process, procedural openness reduces governmental arbitrariness while increasing citizens' ability to influence policy outcomes.

But my findings also suggest that if political leaders are secure in government, they are less likely to institute fundamental and lasting procedural reforms. In other words, real (i.e., potent) APAs are born of political conflict. Absent such conflict, leaders are content to govern through informal rules. If this statement holds true for all or most new democracies, then my study further suggests that governments in those countries without real APAs are likely to be less directly accountable to citizens and hence, in at least this one sense, less "democratic." Moreover, as chapter 7 demonstrates, open government enhances public confidence, both in the government itself and in democracy more generally. This finding suggests a direction for future research. Do democracies—particularly presidential democracies—with real APAs govern more effectively than those lacking such laws?

Why do some democracies have APAs while others do not? One possible answer is that there are substitutes for APAs. Since an APA is essentially a check on partners in the ruling coalition or on unelected bureaucrats whose pursuit of politicians' preferred policies elected officials would like to monitor, one can imagine other types of institutional checks designed to hold these officials accountable. For example, some multiparty coalition governments use junior minister posts to monitor their coalition partners. By agreeing to assign a junior minister post to a representative of a party different from that of the senior minister, each member of the coalition has a built-in check (Thies 2001).

Another institutional feature of a democracy that might influence the passage of an APA is federalism. A highly decentralized system whereby the states or provinces hold substantial autonomy in policy-making may mitigate the need for a centralized APA. However, if so, the United States appears to be an exception, as it has a strong national-level APA that operates in parallel with a series of separate APAs implemented by all U.S. states (see de Figueiredo and Vanden Bergh 2004). Despite this apparent exception, I believe this issue warrants further research.

As Jürgen Habermas and many other democratic theorists have long argued, a critical link exists between democratic legitimacy and the legal institutionalization of procedures. According to Habermas (1996, 151), "Democratic procedure should ground the legitimacy of law." Moreover, "the legitimacy of law by means of procedures and communicative presuppositions . . . once they are legally institutionalized, ground the supposition that the processes of making and applying law lead to rational outcomes" (414). Indeed, Habermas sees procedural transparency as the cornerstone of legal legitimacy: "The law receives its full normative sense neither through its legal *form* per se, nor through an a priori moral *content*, but through a procedure of lawmaking that begets legitimacy" (135). He further observes, quoting Maus, "The justice of a law is guaranteed by the particular procedure by which it comes about" (189).

In other words, transparency and participation—among the primary effects of an APA—essentially define institutional democracy. In most cases, it is too early to know with certainty whether statutory transparency and participation (via an APA) have contributed to the success of new democracies. However, if public trust is a valid gauge of citizen satisfaction with democracy and thus a useful indicator of the state of democracy within a given nation, I have found at least suggestive evidence that citizens in Korea and Taiwan—especially those not closely affiliated with the previous authoritarian regimes—appear to hold greater trust in their democracy in the post-APA period. Just as elections are an important pillar of democratic accountability, statutory transparency and participation procedures are important for the maturation of new democracies. Nonetheless, only time will tell whether and to what extent APAs ultimately facilitate the transition from *ex post* institutional democracy to *ex ante* responsive democracy in developing democracies around the world.

Appendix

TABLE A1. History of Political Parties in Korea (1948–2008)

Year	Ruling Party	Ruling Party Leader	Opposition Party	Opposition Party Leader
1948	Liberal Party	Rhee Syngman	Democratic Party	Yun Po Sun
1960[a]	Democratic Party	Yun Po Sun	n.a.	n.a.
1963	Democratic Republican Party	Park Chung Hee	People's Party	Yun Po Sun
1967–78	Democratic Republican Party	Park Chung Hee	New Democratic Party	Yun Po Sun
1979	Democratic Republican Party	Kim Jong Pil	New Democratic Party	Kim Dae Jung and Kim Young Sam
1980[b]	Democratic Republican Party	Chun Doo Hwan	n.a.	n.a.
1981	Democratic Justice Party	Chun Doo Hwan	Democratic Korea Party	Kim Dae Jung and Kim Young Sam
1985	Democratic Justice Party	Chun Doo Hwan	New Korea Democratic Party	Kim Dae Jung and Kim Young Sam
1987	Democratic Justice Party	Roh Tae Woo	Reunification Democratic Party	Kim Young Sam
			Party for Peace and Democracy	Kim Dae Jung
			New Democratic Republican Party	Kim Jong Pil

1992	Democratic Liberal Party[c]	Kim Young Sam	Democratic Party	Kim Dae Jung[d] and Lee Ki Taek
1996	New Korea Party[e]	Kim Young Sam	National Council for New Politics	Kim Dae Jung
1997	National Congress for New Politics[f]	Kim Dae Jung	Hannara or Grand National Party[g]	Lee Hoi Chang
2002	Millennium Democratic Party[h]	Roh Moo-hyun	Hannara or Grand National Party	Lee Hoi Chang
2004	Uri or Our Party[i]	Roh Moo-hyun	Hannara or Grand National Party	Lee Hoi Chang
2008	Hannara or Grand National Party	Lee Myung-bak	Democratic Party[j]	Chung Sye-kyun

Source: http://www.iworld.net/Korea/politics/f166.html. Table compiled by author.

Note: n.a. = not applicable.

[a]Indirect presidential election by the National Assembly.

[b]There was no direct election, and opposition parties were prohibited.

[c]Represents merger of the ruling Democratic Justice Party, the Reunification Democratic Party, and New Democratic Republican Party in 1990.

[d]After the December presidential elections, he retired from politics. Shortly thereafter, he returned to politics by forming a new party—the National Council for New Politics.

[e]Formerly the Democratic Liberal Party.

[f]Formed a coalition with United Liberal Democrats.

[g]Formerly part of the New Korea Party.

[h]Merged with the United New Democratic Party in 2008 to form the United Democratic Party.

[i]Formerly part of the Millennium Democratic Party.

[j]Represents merger of the Uri Party and United New Democratic Party in 2007.

LIST OF AUTHOR INTERVIEWS

Korea

All interviews were conducted in Seoul, Korea, between August 9–27, 1999, and June 22–30, 2000.

Dr. Choi Byung-Sun, Seoul National University, key author of 1997 Basic Law for Administrative Regulatory Reform
Dr. Hahm Sung Deuk, Korea University
Mr. Hoh Moon, director general, Ministry of Trade, Industry, and Energy
Dr. Im Hyuk Baeg, Korea University
Dr. Joh Jung Jay, member, Presidential Committee on Regulatory Reform
Dr. Kim Byung Kook, Korea University
Mr. Kim Duk-Oo, director, Ministry of Environment
Dr. Kim Keeseok, Ajou University
Mr. Kim Seung Hee, deputy director, Ministry of Environment, Water Management Policy Division
Dr. Kim Suk Joon, Ewha Women's University
Mr. Kim Sung Hyun, staff member, Office of Kwon Chul-Hyun, National Assembly representative
Mr. Lee Chae-Pil, director, Ministry of Labor, Administration Management Division
Mr. Lee Wang-Oo, director general, Ministry of Construction and Transportation, Water Resources Bureau
Dr. Lee Young Jo, Kyung Hee University
Dr. Lee Kyung Shik, former deputy prime minister/Economic Planning Board minister, former governor of the Bank of Korea
Ms. Lim Ji-Ae, manager of political affairs, Korean Federation for Environmental Movement
Mr. Park Kwon Yong, former chief of staff to President Kim Young Sam, National Assembly representative
Mr. Park Nam Hoon, director general, Office for Government Policy Coordination, Office of the Prime Minister
Mr. Park Se Jin, director general for Legislation Planning, Ministry of Legislation
Dr. Rhee Zusun, Korea Economic Research Institute
Mr. Shin In Jae, deputy director, Ministry of Labor, Management Office

Taiwan

All interviews were conducted in Taipei, Taiwan, July 2–19, 2000.

Ms. Chen Mei Ling, director, Ministry of Justice
Mr. Cheng Pao Ching, convener of Democratic Progressive Party Caucus, Legislative Yuan
Ms. Hsieh Chi Ta, New Party legislator, Legislative Yuan
Mr. Huang John K.C., former legislator, Legislative Yuan
Mr. Kuo Chen-Lung, deputy editor in chief, *China Times*

Dr. Lo Chih-Cheng, chair, Research and Planning Board, Ministry of Foreign Affairs
Dr. Tang Dennis T. C., senior fellow, Academia Sinica/professor of law, National Taiwan University
Mr. Yao Eng-Chi, vice president, Legislative Yuan
Mr. Wu Hsiang-Jung, Democratic Progressive Party staff member, Legislative Yuan
Dr. Yeh Jiunn-Rong, professor of law, National Taiwan University

Philippines

All interviews were conducted in Manila, Philippines, July 20–28, 2000.

Ms. Carmencita T. Abella, president Ramon Magsaysay Award Foundation
Ms. Cecile S. Abella, executive director, Land Transportation Franchising and Regulatory Board
Dr. Alex Brillantes, University of the Philippines, National College of Public Administration and Governance
Dr. Ledivina Cariño, dean, University of the Philippines, National College of Public Administration and Governance
Ms. Milette De Vera, attorney, Office of Legal Affairs, Civil Service Commission
Ms. Pura Vita F. Guia-Pedrosa, chief, Review and Assessment Section (Environmental Impact Assessment Division), Environmental Management Bureau, Department of Environment and Natural Resources
Dr. Juan Miguel M. Luz, Asian Institute of Management, former presidential management staff under President Corazon Aquino
Dr. Alex Magno, president, Foundation for Economic Freedom, former adviser to President Fidel Ramos
Mr. Lorenzo Navarro Jr., director, Office of the National Administrative Register, University of the Philippines Law Complex
Dr. Romulo L. Neri, director general, Congressional Planning and Budget Department, House of Representatives and Asian Institute of Management
Ms. May Reyna, assistant director, Office for Recruitment, Examination, and Placement, Civil Service Commission
Dr. Chito B. Salazar, executive director, W. Sycip Policy Center, Asian Institute of Management
Ms. Patricia A. Sto. Tomas, secretary-general, Eastern Regional Organization for Public Administration, former chair of Civil Service Commission
Mr. Ruben Torres, senior partner, Torres, Trajano, and Associates, former secretary of labor

INDEPENDENT VARIABLE DEFINITIONS (CHAPTER 7)

A. World Values Survey

Age. Measures respondents' age, in years (mean [μ] = 38.4, standard deviation [σ] = 12.7)

Income. Question: "Here is a scale of incomes. We would like to know in what group your household is in, counting all wages, salaries, pensions, and other incomes that come in. Just give the letter of the group your household falls into, before taxes and other deductions." Normalized recoding: 1 = low, 2 = medium, 3 = high; μ = 1.92, σ = .82.

Education. Three-category scale, based on highest educational level attained. Normalized recoding: 1 = lower, 2 = middle, 3 = upper; μ = 2.32, σ = .62.

Marital Status. Dummy variable, coded 1 if respondent reports being married or "living together as married," 0 otherwise. μ = .67, = σ .47.

Ideology. Ten-point scale, derived from the following question: "In political matters, people talk of 'the left' and 'the right.' How would you place your views on this scale, generally speaking?" Coded: 1 = maximum left, 10 = maximum right; μ = 5.60, σ = 2.24.

Importance of Politics. "For each of the following aspects, indicate how important it is in your life. Would you say it is very important, rather important, not very important, or not at all important . . . Politics?" Coded: 1 = not at all important, 2 = not very important, 3 = rather important, 4 = very important; μ = 2.77, σ = .86.

Social Change. Three-point scale, based on the following question: "On this card are three basic kinds of attitudes concerning the society we live in. Please choose the one that best describes your own opinion." Coded: 1 = "Society must be radically changed," 2 = "Society must be gradually improved by reforms," 3 = "Society must be valiantly defended"; μ = 1.89, σ = .51.

Household Finance Satisfaction. Ten-point scale derived from the following question: "How satisfied are you with the financial situation of your household? If 1 means you are completely dissatisfied on this scale and 10 means you are completely satisfied, where would you put your satisfaction with your household's financial situation?" μ = 5.68, σ = 2.07.

Patriotism. "How proud are you to be Korean?" Coded: 1 = not at all proud, 2 = not very proud, 3 = quite proud, 4 = very proud; μ = 3.17, σ = .71.

Confidence in Major Companies. "I am going to name a number of organizations. For each one, could you tell me how much confidence you have in them: is it a great deal of confidence, quite a lot of confidence, not very much confidence or none at all . . . Major companies?" Coded: 1 = none at all, 2 = not very much, 3 = quite a lot, 4 = a great deal; μ = 2.37, σ = .76.

Party Group Involvement. Scale derived from two questions: (1) "Please look carefully at the following list of voluntary organizations and activities and say . . . which, if any, do you belong to" and (2) ". . . and for which, if any, are you currently doing unpaid voluntary work." Coded: 0 = "not mentioned," 1 = "belong." The two questions are added together, producing a 0–2 scale, with a mean of .05 and a standard deviation of .27.

2001 Wave. Dummy variable coded 1 for the 2001 survey wave and 0 otherwise.

Support for Democracy. Scale based on two questions: (1) "I'm going to describe various types of political systems and ask what you think about each as a way of governing this country. For each one, would you say it is a very good, fairly good, fairly bad, or very bad way of governing this country?" Coded: 1 = very bad, 2 = fairly bad, 3 = fairly good, 4 = very good; $\mu = 3.16$, $\sigma = .77$. (2) "I'm going to read off some things that people sometimes say about a democratic political system. Could you please tell me if you agree strongly, agree, disagree, or disagree strongly, after I read each one of them. . . . Democracy may have problems but it's better than any other form of government." Coded: 1 = disagree strongly, 2 = disagree, 3 = agree, 4 = agree strongly; $\mu = 3.16$, $\sigma = .62$. I added the two questions together to form a 2–8 scale, where 8 represents maximum support for democracy, with a mean of 6.33 and a standard deviation of 1.09.

B. Korea Barometer Survey

Governmental Responsiveness Scale. 1996: "How much influence do you think you have on what the government does these days? Or do you think you have no influence at all?" 2001: "How much influence do you think the votes of people like yourself have on the way our country is governed?" Coded: 1 = none, 2 = a little, 3 = some, 4 = a lot; $\mu = 2.48$, $\sigma = .83$.

2001 Dummy. Dummy variable coded 1 for 2001; $\mu = .50$, $\sigma = .50$.

Democratic Satisfaction. 1996: "Please tell me how much you are satisfied or dissatisfied with the way democracy works in our country at the present time." 2001: "On the whole, how much are you satisfied or dissatisfied with the way democracy works in our country? . . . where would you place the current practice of democratic politics?" For both scales, 1 = most dissatisfied, 10 = most satisfied; $\mu = .51$, $\sigma = .18$.

Politician Corruption Scale. 1996: "Out of 10 current politicians in our country, how many do you think are corrupt these days?" 2001: "Out of 10 elected politicians, how many do you feel are corrupt?" $\mu = 7.03$, $\sigma = 2.13$.

Support for Current/Past President. 1996: "[P]lease indicate the degree to which you are satisfied or dissatisfied with each government listed: (a) Roh Tae Woo government? (b) Kim Young Sam government?" 2001: "(a) On the whole, how satisfied or dissatisfied are you with the way the Kim Dae Jung government handles problems facing our society? (b) Where on this scale would you place the Kim Young Sam government?" (For both questions, 1 = most dissatisfied and 10 = most satisfied.) Current president = Kim Young Sam in 1996 and Kim Dae Jung in 2001; past president = Roh Tae Woo in 1996 and Kim Young Sam in 2001. Current president: $\mu = 5.29$, $\sigma = 1.81$; past president: $\mu = 3.47$, $\sigma = 1.81$.

Interest in Politics. 1996: "How interested are you in politics these days?" Coded: 1 = not at all, 2 = not much, 3 = some, 4 = a lot. 2001: "Now I have a few questions about politics and public affairs. How much are you interested in politics?" Coded: 1 = not at all interested, 2 = not very interested, 3 = somewhat interested, 4 = very interested; $\mu = 2.56$, $\sigma = .88$.

Trust in Other People. 1996: "Generally speaking, how much can you trust the majority of the people in our country?" Coded: 1 = trust a lot, 2 = trust somewhat, 3 = do not trust much, 4 = do not trust at all. 2001: "Generally speaking, how much do you think most people can be trusted?" Coded: 1 = a lot, 2 = somewhat, 3 = a little, 4 = not at all; $\mu = 2.55$, $\sigma = .67$.

Education. 1996: "How far did you go in school?" Coded: 1 = no formal education, 2 =

primary school, 3 = middle school, 4 = high school, 5 = college, 6 = graduate school and higher. 2001: "How much education have you had?" Coded: 1 = no schooling, 2 = primary school, 3 = middle school, 4 = high school, 5 = college, 6 = graduate school or higher; $\mu = 3.87$, $\sigma = 1.13$.

Home Owner. "Do you own a house or an apartment?" Coded: 1 = yes (outright or with mortgage), 0 = no; $\mu = .67$, trust = .47.

C. East Asia Barometer Survey

Trust. "I'm going to name a number of institutions. For each one, please tell me how much trust you have in them. Is it a great deal of trust (4), quite a lot of trust (3), not very much trust (2), or none at all (1)?: The courts (Taiwan only), the national government, political parties, parliament, the civil service, the military, the police, newspapers, television." Identical question asked in 1994 and 1996 World Values Survey and 2001 and 2002 East Asia Barometer.

Age. Measures respondents' age, in years; $\mu = 39.9$, $\sigma = 14.7$.

Education. "How much education have you had?" Coded: 0 = no schooling, 1 = primary school, 2 = high school incomplete, 3 = high school, 4 = college incomplete, 5 = college complete, 6 = graduate school or higher; $\mu = 3.13$, $\sigma = 1.25$.

Marital Status. Dummy variable, coded 1 if respondent reports being married, 0 otherwise; $\mu = .72$, $\sigma = .45$.

Male. Dummy variable, coded 1 for men and 0 for women; $\mu = .50$, $\sigma = .50$.

Notes

CHAPTER 1

1. Interview by author, Seoul, South Korea, August 19, 1999.

2. Though arguably the most comprehensive and hence consequential such mechanism, administrative reform is not necessarily the only means of pursuing *ex ante* checks on politicians' actions. Dunn (2005, 176), for example, proposes referenda as a means of moving toward *ex ante* democracy: "Modern democracy, it seems, is principally the citizens very intermittently choosing under highly constrained circumstances. . . . There are many obvious ways in which modern citizens have no need whatever to accept this bargain. . . . Referenda do indeed play a role in the national politics of some states, both over key issues of inclusion or exclusion, and over especially contentious decisions, sometimes including constitutional amendments."

3. One of the most popular proaccountability reforms in recent years has been the creation of independent proaccountability agencies (Ackerman 2003), which are autonomous public institutions responsible for holding government accountable in specific issue areas. Examples include corruption control bodies, independent electoral institutes, auditing agencies, human rights ombudsmen, and public prosecutors. Since the mid-1990s, the creation of such institutions has exploded in the developing world (Ackerman 2005). More than 80 countries currently have national ombudsmen, while only a dozen had one only 20 years ago (Bennett 1997). However, this book focuses on restructuring information flows and structure and process, of which administrative procedures are one important example.

4. To my knowledge, the following countries have adopted APAs or similar laws: Argentina, Australia, Austria, Bolivia, Brazil, Chile, the Czech Republic, Denmark, Estonia, Finland, Georgia, Germany, Greece, Iceland, Japan, Mexico, the Netherlands, Poland, Slovenia, Sweden, Switzerland, and Venezuela.

5. Elected policymakers delegate a startling amount of authority to bureaucratic policymakers to interpret health, safety, environmental, and economic regulations (i.e., the Environmental Protection Agency, the Occupational Health and Safety Administra-

tion, the Food and Drug Administration, the Federal Communications Commission, the Federal Trade Commission, the Securities and Exchange Commission) as well as to allocate public investments (i.e., the Department of Transportation, the U.S. Army Corps, the Federal Aviation Administration, the Department of Energy). Yet other democracies appear to exclude civil society from directly participating in bureaucratic policy-making. Anecdotal evidence from mature democracies suggests that single-party parliamentary systems choose not to adopt many of these statutory requirements that enable public participation in bureaucratic policy-making. Strøm (2000) argues that informational inefficiencies may result. In contrast, weak presidential systems (e.g., the United States) appear replete with all of these statutory incentives.

6. Administrative procedures can encompass a variety of requirements, such as meeting with advisory committees and reporting activities to the legislature. This book focuses on the procedural requirements for promulgating regulations.

7. Along these lines, scholars should not conclude that all APAs or APA-like laws necessarily allow public participation in rule making or do so equally.

8. The Korean notice and comment requirements for rule making go beyond the U.S. requirements by extending the notice requirements to proposed legislation (Korea 1997).

9. I thank Susan Rose-Ackerman for bringing this point to my attention.

10. Thirteen civilian members include university presidents, professors, economists, and business professionals. Seven government members represent various cabinet ministers.

CHAPTER 2

1. For a related study on how ministerial instability affects bureaucratic behavior in parliamentary delegations, see Huber and Lupia 2001.

2. The principal-agent framework is an effective analogy for explaining why some presidents adopt APAs but cannot explain all the possible reasons why presidents support APAs. However, it is extremely useful in part due to its simplicity—it is essentially a two-person game between a president (principal) and a bureaucrat (agent). By applying this framework to the politics of APA passage, I elucidate a necessary—albeit not necessarily sufficient—explanation for why presidents adopt APAs. In other words, I provide not a theory explaining choices of institutional design but rather a set of conditions likely to lead democratic executives to want APAs. My theory suggests that to varying degrees, presidents can choose between direct tools (e.g., patronage) with less costs or indirect tools (e.g., an APA) with greater costs.

3. Japan passed an administrative procedural law in 1993 (Law 88), but it does not include provisions for rule making or extensive judicial review. It was amended in 2005, requiring public notice and comment procedures (Articles 38–45). West Germany also passed an APA in the 1970s, but it too did not cover rule making or judicial review.

4. In Taiwan, administrative reform, like so much else, is permeated by ethnic politics; the bureaucracy is dominated by mainland Chinese, while the Taiwanese reformers (including both ethnic Taiwanese and the descendants of mainlanders) have sought to reduce bureaucratic autonomy with the implementation of APA reforms.

5. My theory may appear implicitly to assume that presidents choose APAs in part because they enfranchise "the people" and so are likely to be popular. However, this idea makes sense only if a president cares about the previously excluded interest groups that an APA enfranchises. Indeed, such groups may represent a broader spectrum of voters. Consequently, an APA might appear to be popular even if presidents do not seek to enhance their popularity by empowering the people.

6. Some evidence that APAs influence bureaucratic behavior is apparent in Korea, where, according to the Ministry of Legislation (*Legislative Reform* 2000), 58 percent of Korean regulations were abolished or amended through 2000. Since 1998, the Ministry of Health and Welfare had the highest rate of dropped regulations (more than 800), including those that had expired or been abolished. The Ministry of Agriculture and Forestry, the Ministry of Commerce, Industry and Energy, and the Ministry of Construction and Transportation have had approximately 400 dropped regulations during the same period (Korea, Regulatory Reform Committee, 1998–2005). In short, the APA has led directly to changes or deletions of more than half of all Korea's regulations. My interview subjects confirmed that comments by private parties in response to a ministry's public notice of a proposed rule—some of which I reviewed—are considered in the final rule-making phase. (See appendix for a comprehensive list of subjects interviewed for this project.) Furthermore, use of the civil complaint system has been overwhelming, with 164 million complaints filed in the first eight months of 2000 ("South Korean Government" 2000).

7. See Philippines 1987b (Article 6, Section 18; Article 7, Section 16 of the Philippine Constitution).

8. Though, for convenience, each of my implications refers specifically to presidents, my theory and its implications potentially apply to all chief executives and/or their cabinet ministers in their relations with the bureaucracy and/or each other.

9. In fact, between 1933 and 1984, only 5.8 percent and 10.2 percent of the cabinet secretaries appointed by Democratic and Republican presidents, respectively, were not members of the president's party (Cohen 1988, 92).

10. One might argue that a president who cannot fire unresponsive bureaucrats might still be able to assign them to outposts where they can do less harm. However, this tactic is of limited value, as it is impractical to reassign large numbers of bureaucrats (beyond political appointees).

11. Both Korea and the Philippines have three branches of government (executive, legislative, and judicial).

CHAPTER 3

1. This problem may have been exacerbated in light of the 1997 economic crisis that swept through much of Asia.

2. Elsewhere (Baum 2005), I argue that Taiwan's APA was also designed to promote rather than prevent change in the status quo.

3. The committees include the Administrative Innovation Commission, the Committee for Deregulation of Economic Administration, under the Economic Planning

Board (currently the Board of Finance and Economy), and the Industrial Regulation Review Committee (B. W. Kim 1997).

4. This type of decree does not change the legislative status quo, as in some Latin American countries, and resembles an executive order by U.S. presidents.

5. On June 23, 2005, the Special Committee on Regulatory Reform announced a general plan for amendments to bolster the effectiveness of KAPA I and to encourage industry and economic development. (J. Y. Kim 2005).

6. The committee is composed of the prime minister and a private individual as joint chairs, private sector representatives, and some public officials. Its primary functions include screening, checking, and evaluating each ministry's regulatory reform effort.

7. The Declaration of Democratic Reform included (1) a constitutional amendment for direct presidential election; (2) revision of the presidential election law to ensure freedom of candidacy and fair competition; (3) amnesty for longtime democratic dissident Kim Dae Jung and other political prisoners, allowing them to resume political activities; (4) protection of human dignity and promotion of basic rights, including an extension of right to habeas corpus; (5) restoration of freedom of the press by abolishing the repressive Basic Press Law; and (6) educational autonomy and local self-government through the popular election of local assemblies and executive heads of local governments (Diamond and Shin 2000).

8. Local-level reforms did not occur until 1995. On June 27 of that year, local elections were held for 6 metropolitan mayors, 9 provincial governors, 230 heads of smaller administrative districts, and approximately 5,416 council members (*Korea Herald*, June 28, 1995).

9. I adopt the same definition as Roeder (1993) and Shirk (1993) when they argue that authoritarian policymakers are reciprocally accountable to a selectorate, a group that can pose a credible threat of removing the policymakers from power.

10. The rural vote machine began under the Park regime. Park's vote machine used selective incentives (e.g., provision of fertilizer and credit allocation) to monopolize and extract rent from the agricultural sector while distributing selective incentives through a local village notables network (*yuji*) to maintain support. The Chun regime continued and maintained this system of political support.

11. In the 1981 and 1985 National Assembly elections, one-third of the assembly seats were allocated by a highly disproportional proportional representation system. Genuine opposition parties were allowed to compete in 1985 but not in 1981.

12. See West and Yoon (1992, 85–88) for a discussion of the legal requirements for the exercise of constitutional court jurisdiction over these two categories.

13. In recent years, the constitutional court and supreme court have battled over jurisdiction. The constitutional court influences supreme court constitutional interpretations when it can issue a prior decision on the statute underlying administrative action (Ginsburg 2003, 240).

14. In the spring of 1995, factional disputes within the Democratic Liberal Party led to the defection of the ruling party's chairman, Kim Jong Pil, and former prime minister Ro Jae Bong. In the same year, Kim formed his own party, the United Liberal Democrats, advocating the interests of the middle class and rural population. Shortly thereafter, his new party merged with a rightist splinter group to gain control of 50 legislative seats (Koh 1997).

15. Interview by author, Seoul, Korea, August 1999.

16. Ibid., August 24, 1999.

17. The Hanahoe was an unofficial fraternity of military officers organized by Chun Doo Hwan and had been a major pillar of authoritarian rule before 1993.

18. The period 1998–2003 is the sole exception.

19. Interview by author, Seoul, Korea, August 9, 2000.

20. For studies on political and bureaucratic corruption, see Golden 2003; Lancaster and Montinola 1997; Montinola and Jackman 2002; Rose-Ackerman 1999.

21. Interview by author, Seoul, Korea, August 1999.

22. Ibid., August 18, 1999.

23. Ibid., June 28, 2000.

24. KAPA II applies to any acts lacking provisions regarding procedures of dispositions, notifications, administrative preannouncement of legislation, and dispositions and administrative guidance (Korea 1996, Act 5241, Article 3).

25. Interview by author, Seoul, Korea, June 26, 2000.

26. Ibid., August 9, 1999. Under the constitution, the prime minister is appointed by the president with the consent of the National Assembly and has the primary responsibility to "assist the President and direct the executive ministries" (Korea 1987, Articles 86–87).

27. The RRC's Regulatory Improvement Plan must be approved by the cabinet and president, announced to the public, and implemented.

28. Interview by author, Seoul, Korea, August 24, 1999.

29. Ibid., August 17, 1999.

30. The regulatory impact analysis requires a justification, explanation of alternative measures, and cost-benefit analysis.

31. In 1999, NGOs received funding by submitting proposals. Although the three big government-patronized organizations still received the lion's share of government funds for NGOs, that funding dropped (H.-R. Kim 2000). Government support to nonprofit civic organizations was around 10–15 billion KRW (Korean Won) (Lowry 2008). NGO income usually comes from membership fees (41.2 percent), government supports (14.8 percent), selling products or services (12.8 percent), enterprises' donations (8.5 percent), public funding (6.8 percent), and other (15.9 percent) (cited in Lowry 2008). For an alternative funding distribution, see S.-J. Lee and Arrington 2008.

32. Interview by author, Seoul, Korea, August 18, 1999.

33. Ibid., August 20, 1999.

34. Ibid., August 19, 1999.

CHAPTER 4

1. Taiwan's democratic transition lasted about six and a half years, until December 1994, when elections for the mayoral posts in Taipei and Kaohsiung and for the new governorship of Taiwan province were finally held. Some scholars date the beginning of Taiwan's transition to September 1986, when the opposition Democratic Progressive Party was born. And the March 1996 presidential election is sometimes considered as the end date of Taiwan's transition.

2. Chiang had been inaugurated for a second six-year term in May 1984. Because

Lee was the first ethnic Taiwanese technocrat to serve as president, the KMT hard-liners were reluctant to install him as party chair. The assembly reelected Lee in March 1990, and he was popularly reelected in March 1996.

3. In 1974, the Committee of Research, Development and Assessment of the Executive Yuan (branch) appointed Professor Lin Chi-Tung of National Taiwan University to chair a committee charged with conducting a comparative study of APAs in the United States, Japan (1964 draft), Germany (1966 draft), Austria, Italy (draft), and Spain (see Huang 1999, 49–51). Although this academic study did not materialize into law at the time, it became TAPA's theoretical foundation.

4. Interview by author, Taipei, Taiwan, July 17, 2000.

5. The NP also supported strong business ties with mainland China to facilitate reunification and rejected a proindependence policy.

6. ROC Election Study Center, National Chengchi University. Results of recent elections available at http://www2.nccu.edu.tw/.

7. Based on 1991–96 survey results from Fu Hu and Yun-han Chu at National Taiwan University.

8. Not surprisingly, the other primary public concern registered in most opinion polls is the question of reunification with China.

9. On July 16, 1999, James Soong, a rebel Nationalist ruling party leader, declared his candidacy for the 2000 presidential elections (Rebel Leader 1999). Soong was expelled from the KMT in November 1999 (*EIU Country Profile: Taiwan* 1999–2000, 7) and formed the PFP.

10. Ironically, however, Soong rose to become a formidable contender during the 2000 presidential election precisely because he used the Taiwan governorship and the fiscal and financial resources under the control of his office to nurture an extensive network with local factions, most of them key players in black-gold politics.

11. I code as mainlanders nine cabinet ministers who claim they are from Fu-Chien province. While these individuals consider themselves mainlanders, other Taiwanese view them as natives of Taiwan. I have elected to classify these ministers according to their self-identification since that is the most pertinent issue for my purposes. Recoding these individuals as native Taiwanese had no material effect on the results.

12. Interview by author, Taipei, Taiwan, July 17, 2000.

13. Ibid., July 2000.

14. I consider Taiwan a president-parliamentary system after the 1997 constitutional amendments. A president-parliamentary system is defined as follows: (1) the president is popularly elected; (2) the president appoints and dismisses cabinet ministers; (3) cabinet ministers are subject to parliamentary confidence; and (4) the president has the power to dissolve parliament, legislative powers, or both (Shugart and Carey 1992, 24).

CHAPTER 5

1. Hutchcroft (1998, 29) finds that in one study, interviews with bureau directors revealed the centrality of patronage in the Philippine bureaucracy: "I have no real control over a man who owes his loyalty to a congressman. . . . [D]iscipline breaks down now. The man who gets his first job through a congressman will also try to get a pro-

motion the same way. Most of those we have to accommodate aren't even eligible." See also Francisco and De Guzman 1963, 109, 112, 116.

2. Founded in 1907, the NP represents the right wing of the Philippines' oldest party. In 1946, the Liberals, organized by slightly left-of-center factions, split from the Nacionalistas.

3. One major difference between the two parties concerned economic policy. The Nacionalistas tended to side with powerful sugar interests, which resisted foreign investment in Philippine enterprises, while most Liberals supported a more flexible foreign capital policy (Banks and Muller 1997, 669).

4. The Philippine Civil Service Law resembled the U.S. Pendleton Act of 1883 (Ledivina Cariño, interview by author, Manila, Philippines, July 24, 2000). The Pendleton Act created the federal Civil Service Commission and authorized the recruitment of individuals to fill the "classified service" positions by competitive examination (Key 1942, 390).

5. In early 1978, the KBL was organized as Marcos's personal vehicle. The party was credited with winning 151 of 165 elected seats in the April 1978 interim National Assembly election and 88 percent of the presidential vote in June 1981. And in May 1984, the KBL obtained 108 of 183 elected National Assembly seats despite losing in virtually all of the country's regions (Banks and Muller 1997, 669).

6. It appears that not all of these jobs were patronage appointments. In 1971, after the last local elections before martial law, the scheduled 1975 expiration of their terms was delayed to 1980. With few exceptions, most employees in 1986 had been in place for 15 years (Cariño 1989, 246).

7. The provision states, "All elective and appointive officials and employees under the 1973 Constitution shall continue in office until otherwise provided by proclamation or executive order or upon the appointment and qualification of their successors, if such is made within a period of one year from February 25, 1986."

8. This purge removed more civil servants than any of the other purges. For example, between 1972 and 1975, Marcos removed only an estimated 3,000–5,000 civil servants (Cariño 1989, 218). However, during the martial law period, the size of the bureaucracy more than doubled, growing from 569,443 in 1973 to 1,300,000 in 1985 (223).

9. Interview by author, Manila, Philippines, July 25, 2000.

10. Ibid.

11. An exception is rate fixing (e.g., taxi fares). Here, agencies such as the Land Transportation Franchising and Regulatory Board of the Department of Transportation and Communications are required to publish proposed rates and hold public hearings.

12. Interview by author, Manila, Philippines, July 25, 2000.

13. This logic differs from the interpretation of judicial review in Taiwan's APA. One interpretation holds that judicial review of agency decisions is designed to reinforce the intent of the enacting legislature (McCubbins, Noll, and Weingast 1987). But in Taiwan, the legal doctrine for judges is to consider the letter of law, rather than the legislative intent, meaning that judicial review can be another way to overturn existing regulations.

14. Interview by author, Manila, Philippines, July 25, 2000.

15. Ibid.

16. Ibid., July 26, 2000.

17. For an extensive analysis of the Philippine bureaucracy and executive-legislative relations, particularly in the 1990s, see Eaton 2002.

18. In January 2001, Estrada was forced from office by mass protests and accusations of corruption. His vice president, Macapagal-Arroyo, came to power when his top generals defected to her camp. Arroyo's government arrested Estrada in April 2001, charging him with plundering more than $80 million from the state (Paddock 2001).

19. She was elected to a six-year term on May 10, 2004.

20. Interview by author, Manila, Philippines, July 25, 2000.

CHAPTER 6

1. On the importance of the reversion point in decisions made by majority rule voting, see Romer and Rosenthal 1978; Shepsle 1979; Shepsle and Weingast 1981.

2. This example presumes that the cost of renewing an existing regulation is about the same as promulgating a new one, as indicated by the fact that the choice set with sunset (centered at B) has the same radius as the choice set without sunset (centered at A). Such would not always be the case. The relative costs of renewing old regulations versus promulgating new ones are determined in part by administrative procedures (the details of the sunset provision and the "normal" regulatory process by which new regulations are promulgated). These costs are also affected by the technical uncertainty.

3. J.-S. Lee and Han (1999) do not cite exact data sources, although their bibliography indicates that their data most likely come from official government publications.

4. This number is a subset of the 3,918 completed reform cases in table 6.1. The number represents both economic and administrative regulations.

5. The statistical results in this section represent the period from August 1998 through December 2002. Presidents in Korea are usually elected in November of one year and take office the following February. Hence, although Kim Dae Jung's presidency officially ended in February 2003, 2002 was chosen as a cutoff point both for the sake of simplicity and because January and February are commonly considered transition months for the new president.

6. The highest number of dropped/weakened regulations occurs in the Ministry of Health and Welfare, but much of this phenomenon is attributable to passage of the National Livelihood Protection Law in 1999. Until that time, Korea lacked a full-scale welfare act guaranteeing basic minimum living standards for all citizens. The 1999 law not only guarantees minimum standards of living for lower-income citizens but also supports future employment and provides productive social welfare services (Ministry of Health and Welfare National Livelihood Protection Program home page, http://english.mohw.go.kr/front_eng/main.jsp). The Kim Dae Jung administration considered this law a major achievement. It is possible that the high number of dropped health regulations in this area results primarily from the National Livelihood Protection Law and is not affected by sunset.

7. Elsewhere (Baum and Bawn 2005), I consider the longer-term implications of the sunset provision.

CHAPTER 7

1. But see Batto 2005 regarding potential for a survey data analysis on the adverse consequences of "too much" trust in government.

2. For this and all subsequent questions, except where otherwise indicated, responses of "Don't know" and refusals to answer are coded as missing.

3. Given the availability of what I consider a somewhat more direct measure of engagement with business interests, I employ confidence in major companies as a control variable rather than as the key causal variable in this analysis.

4. Even in 2001, it is reasonable to presume that professional associations are more likely than social welfare organizations to represent the interests of the country's entrenched economic elites.

5. Professional group membership correlates with social/welfare group membership and confidence in the military at about .30 and –.06, respectively, while social/welfare group membership correlates with confidence in the military at about –.04.

6. An additional control for income was available in the survey. However, as a consequence of missing data, including this control substantially reduces the number of observations. Since this variable does not materially affect the results on the key variables, I do not include it in the reported models.

7. The 2001 KVS substitutes *feel* in place of *think*.

8. Support for the president (current or past) is unavailable in the WVS data, thereby limiting my ability directly to account for variations in such support across administrations.

9. I exclude from the logit model in table 7.1 several extreme outlier observations. Including these observations modestly weakens but does not fundamentally alter the reported results.

10. For a recent study on Korean political parties and regional voting patterns, see W. Moon 2005.

11. In each case, the median value for group involvement is 0. I set "confidence in the military" to its mean of 2.85 (close to the median value of 3) when examining the effects of involvement in other social groups. Being uninvolved with consumer/social or professional groups is relatively common in these data. However, very few respondents expressed no confidence in the military. Consequently, setting confidence in the military to its mean while setting group involvement to 0 arguably has greater face validity.

12. Throughout the discussion of figure 7.3, I vary group involvement from the mean level (labeled "low" in the figure) to two standard deviations above the mean in the data (labeled "high"). I vary confidence in the military from one standard deviation below ("low") to one standard deviation above ("high") the mean level of confidence. In the latter case, this value is approximately equivalent to the maximum value on the confidence in the military scale. These variations are, of course, illustrative. Given variations of similar magnitudes, the overall patterns described in the text remain similar (albeit not identical) regardless of the starting and ending points.

13. All models exclude several extreme outliers; their inclusion modestly affects but does not fundamentally alter the reported results.

14. In 2001, the correlations with confidence in the civil service vary from a low of .12 for the military to a high of .26 for business. The corresponding correlations in 1990 are a low of .27 for the military and a high of .46 for the police.

15. In those years, Korea had freely contested presidential elections without having a real democracy except for 1960–61.

CHAPTER 8

1. In a comparative study of APAs in presidential and parliamentary systems, Jensen and McGrath (forthcoming [2010]) find that parliamentary systems only constrain adjudicative actions while presidential systems constrain both adjudicative actions and rule making.

Bibliography

1999 Who's Who of Republic of China. 2000. Taipei: Central News Agency.

Achen, Christopher H., and Duncan Snidal. 1989. "Rational Deterrence Theory and Comparative Case Studies." *World Politics* 41(2): 143–69.

Ackerman, John. 2003. "Empowered Autonomy: The Politics of Delegation and Accountability in Latin America." Working Paper, FLACSO-Mexico.

Ackerman, John. 2004. "Co-Governance for Accountability: Beyond Exit and Voice." *World Development* 32 (3): 447–63.

Ackerman, John. 2005. *Social Accountability in the Public Sector: A Conceptual Discussion.* Social Development Paper 82. Washington, DC: World Bank.

"The Administrative Procedure Act: A Fortieth Anniversary Symposium." 1986. *Virginia Law Review* 72 (2): 337–61.

Alchian, Armen, and Harold Demsetz. 1972. "Production, Information Costs, and Economic Organization." *American Economic Review* 62 (5): 777–95.

Amorim Neto, Octavio. 1998. "Of Presidents, Parties, and Ministers: Cabinet Formation and Legislative Decision-Making under Separation of Powers." Ph.D. diss., University of California, San Diego.

Amorim Neto, Octavio. 2006. "The Presidential Calculus: Executive Policy-Making and Cabinet Formation in the Americas." *Comparative Political Studies* 39 (4): 415–40.

Amsden, Alice. 1989. *Asia's Next Giant: South Korea and Late Industrialization.* New York: Oxford University Press.

August, Oliver. 2000. "Taiwan's 50-Year Regime Senses Electoral Defeat." *Times of London,* March 16.

Banks, Arthur, and Thomas Muller, eds. 1997. *Political Handbook of the World.* Binghamton, NY: CSA.

Banks, Jeffrey S. 1989. "Agency Budgets, Cost Information, and Auditing." *American Journal of Political Science* 33 (3): 670–99.

Batto, Nathan F. 2005. "The Adverse Consequences of the Trust in Government." Paper presented at the Annual Meeting of the Midwest Political Science Association, Chicago.

Baum, Jeeyang Rhee. 2002. "Presidents Have Problems Too: The Logic of Intra-Branch Delegation in New Democracies." Ph.D. diss., University of California, Los Angeles.

Baum, Jeeyang Rhee. 2005. "Breaking Authoritarian Bonds: The Political Origins of the Taiwan Administrative Procedure Act." *Journal of East Asian Studies* 5 (3): 365–99.

Baum, Jeeyang Rhee. 2007a. "Presidents Have Problems Too: The Logic of Intrabranch Delegation in East Asian Democracies." *British Journal of Political Science* 37 (4): 659–84.

Baum, Jeeyang Rhee. 2007b. "Reining in the Bureaucrats: Democratic Transition and Administrative Procedural Reform in Korea." *Governance: An International Journal of Policy, Administration, and Institutions* 20 (2): 233–54.

Baum, Jeeyang Rhee. 2007c. "The U.S. Administrative Procedure Act from a Comparative Perspective." Paper presented at American Political Science Association, Chicago.

Baum, Jeeyang Rhee. 2009. "The Impact of Bureaucratic Openness on Public Trust in South Korea." *Democratization* 16 (5): 969–97.

Baum, Jeeyang Rhee, and Kathleen Bawn. 2005. "Slowing at Sunset: Administrative Procedures and the Pace of Reform in Korea." Paper presented at American Political Science Association, Washington, DC.

Baum, Jeeyang Rhee, and Christian B. Jensen. 2009. "APAs and Single Party Majority Government: Why Bother?" Paper presented at American Political Science Association, Toronto, Canada.

Bawn, Kathleen. 1995. "Political Control versus Expertise: Congressional Choices about Administrative Procedures." *American Political Science Review* 89 (1): 62–73.

Bawn, Kathleen. 1997. "Choosing Strategies to Control the Bureaucracy: Statutory Constraints, Oversight, and the Committee System." *Journal of Law, Economics, and Organization* 13 (1): 101–26.

Bennett, C. 1997. "Understanding Ripple Effects: The Cross-National Adoption of Policy Instruments for Bureaucratic Accountability." *Governance: An International Journal of Policy and Administration* 10 (3): 213–33.

Bignami, Francesca. 1999. "The Democratic Deficit in European Community Rulemaking: A Call for Notice and Comment Comitology." *Harvard International Law Journal* 40 (2): 451–515.

Brillantes, Alex B., Jr. 1988. "The Executive." In *Government and Politics of the Philippines,* ed. Raul P. De Guzman and Mila A. Reforma, 113–31. Oxford: Oxford University Press.

Brull, Steven. 1994. "Accidents Show the High Cost of Haste: Growth, Now Korea Pays." *International Herald Tribune,* December 8.

Calvert, Randall, Mathew McCubbins, and Barry Weingast. 1989. "A Theory of Political Control and Agency Discretion." *American Journal of Political Science* 33 (3): 588–611.

Campos, José Edgardo, and Hilton L. Root. 1996. *The Key to the Asian Miracle: Making Shared Growth Credible.* Washington, DC: Brookings Institution Press.

Cariño, Ledivina V. 1985. "The Politicization of the Philippines Bureaucracy: Corruption or Commitment." *International Review of Administrative Sciences* 51 (1): 13–18.

Cariño, Ledivina V. 1987. "The Aquino Government and the Civil Service: Lessons for Future Regime-Bureaucracy Interaction." In *A Filipino Agenda for the 21st Century:*

The Papers, Discussions and Recommendations of the Solidarity Conference, ed. F. Sionil José, 271–86. Manila: Solidaridad.

Cariño, Ledivina V. 1989. "Bureaucracy for a Democracy: The Struggle of the Philippine Political Leadership and the Civil Service in the Post-Marcos Period." *Philippine Journal of Public Administration* 33 (3): 207–52.

Cariño, Ledivina V. 1990. "An Assessment of Public Administration in the Philippines, 1986–88." Working Paper Series No. 90-03. January. Philippine Institute for Development Studies.

Cariño, Ledivina V. 1992. *Bureaucracy for Democracy: The Dynamics of Executive-Bureaucracy Interaction during Governmental Transitions.* Philippines: University of the Philippines, International Center for Economic Growth, and Philippine Institute for Development Studies.

Central Election Committee (Zhongyang xuanju weiyuanhui). Various years. *Official Report of the Election* (Xuanju gongbao).

Chen, Shui-Bian. 2000. President Chen Shui-Bian's Inauguration Speech. May 20. Taipei. Available at http://ken.davies.tripod.com/inaugural.html.

Cheng, Allen T. 2000. "The Curse of 'Black Gold': Lee Teng-hui's Darker Legacy May Be a Political Culture Riddled with Corruption and Gangsters." *Asiaweek,* March 17. Available at http://www.cnn.com/asianow/asiaweek/magazine/2000/0317/nat.4taiwan.kmt.html 26(10).

Cheng, Tun-Jen, and Yung-Han Chu. 2002. "State-Business Relations in South Korea and Taiwan." In *Emerging Market Democracies: East Asia and Latin America,* ed. Laurence Whitehead, 31–62. Baltimore: Johns Hopkins University Press.

Cheng, Tun-Jen, and Stephan Haggard. 2001. "Democracy and Deficits in Taiwan: The Politics of Fiscal Policy, 1986–1996." In *Presidents, Parliaments, and Policy,* ed. Stephan Haggard and Mathew D. McCubbins, 183–228. Cambridge: Cambridge University Press.

Chin, Ko-Lin. 2003. *Heijin: Organized Crime, Business, and Politics in Taiwan.* Armonk, NY: Sharpe.

China, Republic of. 1997. *Constitution.* July 18. Available at http://www.taiwandocuments.org/constitution02.htm.

China, Republic of. 1998. *Administrative Litigation Act.* The Gazette of the Office of the President. 6242. October 28. Available at http://www.glin.gov/view.action?glinID=108924.

China, Republic of. 1999. *Administrative Procedure Act.* The Gazette of the Office of the President. 6258. February 3. Available at http://www.glin.gov/view.action?glinID=104537.

Cho, Suk-Chon. 1975. "The Bureaucracy." In *Korean Politics in Transition,* ed. Edward Reynolds Wright, 76–77. Seattle: University of Washington Press.

Chu, Henry. 2000a. "Nationalists Ousted in Taiwan." *Los Angeles Times,* March 19. Available at http://articles.latimes.com/2000/mar/19/news/mn_10449.

Chu, Henry. 2000b. "Taiwan Youth Drifting toward Independence." *Los Angeles Times,* March 12. Available at http://www.international.ucla.edu/eas/newsfile/taiwanyouth/000312_latimes.htm.

Chu, Yun-Han, Larry Diamond, and Doh Chull Shin. 2001. "Halting Progress in Korea and Taiwan." *Journal of Democracy* 12 (1): 122–36.

Chun, Young-Jae. 1998. "Regulatory Reform and Privatization of State-Owned Companies." Samsung Economic Research Institute (*SERI*) 69.

Clark, Cal. 2000. "Taiwan Elections in 2000." *Asia Society*, March. Available at http:www.asiasociety.org/publications/taiwan_elections.html.

Cohen, Jeffrey. 1988. *The Politics of the U.S. Cabinet: Representation in the Executive Branch, 1979–1984*. Pittsburgh: University of Pittsburgh Press.

Conachy, James. 2000. "Corruption and China Policy Dominate Taiwan Presidential Campaign." *World Socialist*, January 14. Available at http://www.wsws.org/articles/2000/jan2000/taiw-j14.shtml.

"Counting the Cost of Corruption." 1998. Janet Matthews Information Services. April 1.

Cox, Gary, and Mathew D. McCubbins. 1993. *Legislative Leviathan: Party Government in the House*. Berkeley: University of California Press.

Dalton, Russell. 2004. *Democratic Challenges, Democratic Choices: The Erosion of Political Support in Advanced Industrial Democracies*. New York: Oxford University Press.

de Figueiredo, Rui J. P., Jr., Pablo Spiller, and Santiago Urbiztondo. 1999. "An Informational Perspective on Administrative Procedures." *Journal of Law, Economics, and Organization* 15 (11): 283–305.

de Figueiredo, Rui J. P., Jr., and Richard G. Vanden Bergh. 2004. "The Political Economy of State-Level Administrative Procedure Acts." *Journal of Law and Economics* 47 (2): 569–88.

Diamond, Larry. 1999. *Developing Democracy: Toward Consolidation*. Baltimore: Johns Hopkins University Press.

Diamond, Larry. 2001. "The Anatomy of an Electoral Earthquake: How the KMT Lost and the DPP Won the 2000 Presidential Election." In *Taiwan's Presidential Politics: Democratization and Cross-Strait Relations in the Twenty-first Century*, ed. Muthiah Alagappa, 48–87. Armonk, NY: Sharpe.

Diamond, Larry, and Do Chull Shin. 2000. "Introduction: Institutional Reform and Democratic Consolidation in Korea." In *Institutional Reform and Democratic Consolidation in Korea*, ed. Larry Diamond and Do Chull Shin, 1–42. Stanford: Hoover Institution Press.

"DPP Launches New Campaign TV Ad Focused on Young People." 2000. *Financial Times Information*. February 10.

Drezner, Daniel W. 2000. "Ideas, Bureaucratic Politics, and the Crafting of Foreign Policy." *American Journal of Political Science* 44 (4): 733–49.

Dubsky, Roman. 1981. "Development and Technocratic Thought in the Philippines." Ph.D. diss., University of the Philippines.

Dunn, John. 2005. "Why Democracy." In *Setting the People Free: The Story of Democracy*, 149–89. London: Atlantic Books.

Eaton, Kent. 2002. *Politicians and Economic Reform in New Democracies: Argentina and the Philippines in the 1990s*. University Park: Pennsylvania State University Press.

Eaton, Kent. 2003. "Can Politicians Control Bureaucrats? Applying Theories of Political Control to Argentina's Democracy." *Latin American Politics and Society* 45 (4): 33–62.

Eckstein, Harry. 1975. "Case Study and Theory in Political Science." *In Handbook of Political Science*, ed. Fred Greenstein and Nelson Polsby, 79–137. Reading, MA: Addison-Wesley.

EIU Country Profile: Taiwan. 1999–2000. London, Economist Intelligence Unit.

Epstein, David, and Sharyn O'Halloran. 1994. "Administrative Procedures, Information, and Agency Discretion." *American Journal of Political Science* 38 (3): 697–722.

Epstein, David, and Sharyn O'Halloran. 1999. *Delegating Powers.* Cambridge: Cambridge University Press.

European Values Study Group and World Values Survey Association. European and World Values Surveys Four-Wave Integrated Data File, 1981–2004, v.20060423, 2006. Aggregate File Producers: Análisis Sociológicos Económicos y Políticos (ASEP) and JD Systems (JDS), Madrid, Spain/Tilburg University, Tilburg, The Netherlands. Data Files Suppliers: Análisis Sociologicos Economicos y Politicos (ASEP) and JD Systems (JDS), Madrid, Spain/Tilburg University, Tilburg, The Netherlands/Zentralarchiv fur Empirische Sozialforschung (ZA), Cologne, Germany. Aggregate File Distributors: Análisis Sociológicos Económicos y Políticos (ASEP) and JD Systems (JDS), Madrid, Spain/Tilburg University, Tilburg, The Netherlands/Zentralarchiv fur Empirische Sozialforschung (ZA) Cologne, Germany.

Eyton, Laurence. 1997. "A Lesson in Democracy." *Asiaweek,* December 12.

Fama, Eugene. 1980. "Agency Problems and the Theory of the Firm." *Journal of Political Economy* 88 (2): 288–307.

Far Eastern Economic Review Asia Yearbook. 1988. Hong Kong: Review Publishing.

Fenno, Richard F. 1959. *The President's Cabinet: An Analysis in the Period from Wilson to Eisenhower.* Cambridge: Harvard University Press.

Ferejohn, John, and Charles Shipan. 1990. "Congressional Influence on Bureaucracy." *Journal of Law, Economics, and Organization* 6 (special issue): S1–S20.

Flanigan, James. 1998. "Asia's Improbable New Strongman." *Los Angeles Times,* April 26.

Francisco, Gregorio A., Jr. 1960. "A Study of Higher Civil Servants of the Philippines." Ph.D. diss., University of Minnesota.

Francisco, Gregorio A., Jr., and Raul P. De Guzman. 1963. "The '50-50 Agreement.'" In *Patterns in Decision-Making: Case Studies in Philippine Public Administration,* ed. Raul P. De Guzman, 91–120. Manila: Graduate School of Public Administration.

Frassrand, Tony. 1998. "Newsroom Worldview." CNN transcript 98042700V05, April 27.

"From Poverty to Power: Chen's Rise to the Presidency." 2000. *Financial Times Information.* November 9.

Gallup Korea Polls. 2007. Available at http://www.gallup.co.kr/english/social.asp. March 15.

Gamson, William. 1968. *Power and Discontent.* Homewood, IL: Dorsey.

Ganz, Susanne. 1999. "Chen Shui-Bian Announces Bid for Taiwan Presidency." Kyodo News Service, Japan Economic Newswire, May 27.

Geddes, Barbara. 1990. "How the Cases You Choose Affect the Answers You Get: Selection Bias in Comparative Politics." *Political Analysis* 2 (1): 131–50.

Geddes, Barbara. 1994. *Politician's Dilemma: Building State Capacity in Latin America.* Berkeley: University of California Press.

Geddes, Barbara. 1999. "What Do We Know about Democratization after Twenty Years?" *Annual Review of Political Science* 2:115–44.

Gewirtz, Paul. 1996. "On 'I Know It When I See It.'" *Yale Law Journal* 105 (4): 1023–47.

Ginsburg, Tom. 2001. "Dismantling the 'Developmental State'? Administrative Procedure Reform in Japan and Korea." *American Journal of Comparative Law* 49 (4): 585–625.

Ginsburg, Tom. 2003. *Judicial Review in New Democracies: Constitutional Courts in Asian Cases.* Cambridge: Cambridge University Press.

"GMA Pledges to Trim Down Bureaucracy." 2004. July 26. Available at http://www.ops.gov.ph/sona2004/news.htm#GMA%20pledges.

Golden, April. 2003. "Electoral Connections: The Effects of the Personal Vote on Political Patronage, Bureaucracy, and Legislation in Postwar Italy." *British Journal of Political Science* 33 (2): 189–212.

Habermas, Jürgen. 1996. *Between Facts and Norms: Contributions to a Discourse Theory of Law and Democracy.* Cambridge: MIT Press.

Haggard, Stephan. 1990. *Pathways from the Periphery: The Politics of Growth in the Newly Industrializing Countries.* Ithaca: Cornell University Press.

Haggard, Stephan, and Robert Kaufman. 1995. *The Political Economy of Democratic Transition.* Princeton: Princeton University Press.

Hahm, Sung Deuk, and L. Christopher Plein. 1997. *After Development: The Transformation of the Korean Presidency and Bureaucracy.* Washington, DC: Georgetown University Press.

Hamilton, James T., and Christopher H. Schroeder. 1994. "Strategic Regulators and the Choice of Rulemaking Procedures: The Selection of Formal vs. Informal Rules in Regulating Hazardous Waste." *Law and Contemporary Problems* 57 (2): 111–60.

Healy, Tim, and Laurence Eyton. 1998. "Old Party, New Face." *Asiaweek,* December 18.

Hicken, Allen, and Yuko Kasuya. 2003. "A Guide to the Constitutional Structures and Electoral Systems of East, South, and Southeast Asia." *Electoral Studies* 22 (1): 121–51.

Hilfe Country Report. 2000a. "Taiwan Politics." Janet Matthews Information Services, January 20.

Hilfe Country Report. 2000b. "Taiwan Politics." Janet Matthews Information Services, July 17.

Hood, Steven J. 1997. *The Kuomintang and the Democratization of Taiwan.* Boulder: Westview.

Huang, Kuo-Tsung. 1999. "Introduction of the APA." *Journal for the Lawyers,* April, 49–51.

Huber, John D. 1998. "How Does Cabinet Instability Affect Political Performance? Portfolio Volatility and Health Care Cost Containment in Parliamentary Democracies." *American Political Science Review* 92 (3): 577–91.

Huber, John D., and Arthur Lupia. 2001. "Cabinet Instability and Delegation in Parliamentary Democracies." *American Journal of Political Science* 45 (1): 18–32.

Huber, John D., and Charles R. Shipan. 2002. *Deliberate Discretion? The Institutional Foundations of Bureaucratic Autonomy.* Cambridge: Cambridge University Press.

Huntington, Samuel P. 1991. *The Third Wave: Democratization in the Late Twentieth Century.* Norman: University of Oklahoma Press.

Hutchcroft, Paul D. 1998. *Booty Capitalism: The Politics of Banking in the Philippines.* Ithaca: Cornell University Press.

Japan. 1993. Administrative Procedure Law. November 12. Law No. 88.

Jensen, Christian B., and Robert J. McGrath. Forthcoming. "Making Rules about Rulemaking: A Comparison of Presidential and Parliamentary Systems." *Political Research Quarterly.*

Johnson, Chalmers. 1982. *MITI and the Japanese Miracle: The Growth of Industrial Policy, 1925–1975.* Stanford: Stanford University Press.

Johnson, Chalmers. 1995. Review of *Korean Dynasty: Hyundai and Chung Ju Yung,* by Donald Kirk. *Journal of Asian Studies* 54 (4): 1103–4.

Kang, David. 2002. *Crony Capitalism: Corruption and Development in South Korea and the Philippines.* Cambridge: Cambridge University Press.

Katz, Richard S., and Peter Mair. 1995. "Changing Models of Party Organization and Party Democracy: The Emergence of the Cartel Party." *Party Politics* 1(1): 5–28.

Kerwin, Cornelius M. 1999. *How Government Agencies Write Law and Make Policy.* Washington, DC: Congressional Quarterly Press.

Key, V. O., Jr. 1942. *Politics, Parties, and Pressure Groups.* New York: Crowell.

Kiewiet, D. Roderick, and Mathew McCubbins. 1991. *The Logic of Delegation.* Chicago: University of Chicago Press.

Kim, Bun Woong. 1991. "An Assessment of Government Intervention in Korean Economic Development." In *A Dragon's Progress: Development Administration in Korea,* ed. G. Caiden and B. W. Kim. Hartford, CT: Kumarian.

Kim, Bun Woong. 1997. "Limits on Administrative Deregulation: The Korean Experience." *Korean Review of Public Administration* 2 (1): 165–92.

Kim, Hyuk-Rae. 2000. "The State and Civil Society in Transition: The Role of Non-Governmental Organizations in South Korea." *Pacific Review* 13 (4): 595–613.

Kim, Jong Yull. 2005. Press statement, June 23. Available at www.jykimi.net.

Kim, Pan S., and M. Jae Moon. 2003. "NGOs as Incubator of Participative Democracy in South Korea: Political, Voluntary, and Policy Participation." *International Journal of Public Administration* 26 (5): 549–67.

King, Gary, Michael Tomz, and Jason Wittenberg. 2000. "Making the Most of Statistical Analyses: Improving Interpretation and Presentation." *American Journal of Political Science* 44 (2): 341–55.

Kitschelt, Herbert P., and Steven Wilkinson, eds. 2006. *Patrons or Policies? Patterns of Democratic Accountability and Political Competition.* Cambridge: Cambridge University Press.

Koh, B. C. 1997. "South Korea in 1996: Internal Strains and External Challenges." *Asian Survey* 37 (1): 1–9.

Koo, Hagen. 2002. "Civil Society and Democracy in South Korea." *Good Society* 11 (2): 40–45.

Korea, Republic of. 1987. Constitution. October 29. Available at http://www.servat.unibe.ch/law/icl/ks00000_.html.

Korea, Republic of. 1994. *Basic Law on Administrative Regulations and Civil Affairs Act.* January 1.

Korea, Republic of. 1996. *Korean Administrative Procedures Act.* December 31. Act No. 5241.

Korea, Republic of. 1997. *Basic Act on Administrative Regulations.* August 22. Act No. 5368.

Korea, Republic of. 1998. *Framework Act on Administrative Regulations.*

Korea, Republic of. Economic Planning Board. 1994. *White Paper on Economy.* Seoul, Korea.

Korea, Republic of. Office of the Prime Minister. 1999. *The Basic Act on Administrative Regulations: Building a Permanent System for Regulatory Reform.* June.

Korea, Republic of. Presidential Commission on Administrative Reform. 1995. *Administrative Reform in Korea: In Search of a New Paradigm.* Seoul: PCAR.

Korea, Republic of. Regulatory Reform Committee. Regulatory Reform in South Korea. August 1998–February 2005. Available at http://www.rrc.go.kr.

Korea, Republic of. Regulatory Reform Committee. 2004. "History: Development of the Regulatory Reform Committee." Available at http://www.rrc.go.kr.

Korea: Imha Multipurpose Dam Project. 2002. Available at http://www.jica.go.jp/english/operations/evaluation/oda_loan/post/2002/pdf/022_full.pdf.

Korea Economic Research Institute. 1996. *A Survey Report on Government Regulation in Korea.* Seoul: KERI.

Lancaster, Thomas D., and Gabriella R. Montinola. 1997. "Toward a Methodology for the Comparative Study of Political Corruption." *Crime, Law, and Social Change* 27 (3–4): 185–206.

Laver, Michael J., and Kenneth Shepsle. 1996. *Making and Breaking Governments: Cabinets and Legislatures in Parliamentary Democracies.* Cambridge: Cambridge University Press.

Lee, Ju-Sun, and Sun-Ok Han, eds. 1999. *Kim Young-sam Jeongbueui Gyujae Wanhwa Shiljuk Pyungga.* Seoul: KERI.

Lee, Sook-Jong, and Celeste Arrington. 2008. "The Politics of NGOs and Democratic Governance in South Korea and Japan." *Pacific Focus* 23 (1): 75–96.

Lee, Young Jo. 2000. "The Rise and Fall of Kim Young Sam's Embedded Reformism." In *Institutional Reform and Democratic Consolidation in Korea,* ed. Larry Diamond and Do Chull Shin, 97–126. Stanford: Hoover Institution Press.

Legislative Reform in Korea 9. 2000. Seoul: Ministry of Legislation.

Lijphart, Arend. 1984. *Democracies: Patterns of Majoritarian and Consensus Government in Twenty-one Countries.* New Haven: Yale University Press.

Lijphart, Arend. 1992. "Democratization and Constitutional Choices in Czechoslovakia, Hungary, and Poland, 1989–91." *Journal of Theoretical Politics* 4 (2): 207–23.

Lim, Joon Hyoung, and Shui-Yan Tang. 2002. "Democratization and Environmental Policy-Making in Korea." *Governance* 15 (4): 561–82.

"Lin Feng-Cheng Becomes KMT Secretary General." 2000. Central News Agency, March 27.

Lin, Jih-Wen. 1996. "Social Cleavage, Electoral Institution, and Political Consequences: The Case of Japan and Taiwan." Ph.D. diss., University of California, Los Angeles.

Linz, Juan J. 1990. "The Perils of Presidentialism." *Journal of Democracy* 1 (1): 51–69.

Linz, Juan J., and Alfred Stepan. 1996. "Toward Consolidated Democracies." *Journal of Democracy* 7 (2): 14–33.

Liu, Shih-Chung. 2000. "The Real Potential for Political Decay." *Taipei Times,* January 23. Available at http://www.taipeitimes.com/news/2000/01/23/story/0000021197.

Lowry, Cameron. 2008. "Civil Society Engagement in Asia: Six Country Profiles." Asia Pacific Governance and Democracy Initiative. East-West Center, Honolulu, July 14–16.

Lupia, Arthur, and Mathew McCubbins. 1994. "Learning from Oversight: Fire Alarms and Police Patrols Reconsidered." *Journal of Law, Economics, and Organization* 10 (1): 96–125.

Lupia, Arthur, and Mathew McCubbins. 1998. *Democratic Dilemma: Can Citizens Learn What They Need to Know?* New York: Cambridge University Press.

Macapagal-Arroyo, Gloria. 2004. Fourth State of the Nation Address. July 26. Available at http://filipinopresidency.multiply.com/journal/item/69.

McCubbins, Mathew. 1985. "Legislative Design of Regulatory Structure." *American Journal of Political Science* 29 (4): 721–48.

McCubbins, Mathew, Roger Noll, and Barry Weingast. 1987. "Administrative Procedures as Instruments of Political Control." *Journal of Law, Economics, and Organization* 3 (2): 243–77.

McCubbins, Mathew, Roger Noll, and Barry Weingast. 1989. "Structure and Process, Politics and Policy: Administrative Arrangements and the Political Control of Agencies." *Virginia Law Review* 75 (2): 431–82.

McCubbins, Mathew, and Thomas Schwartz. 1984. "Congressional Oversight Overlooked: Police Patrols versus Fire Alarms." *American Journal of Political Science* 28 (1): 167–79.

McNollgast. 1999. "The Political Origins of the Administrative Procedure Act." *Journal of Law, Economics, and Organization* 15 (1): 180–217.

Moe, Terry. 1985a. "Control and Feedback in Economic Regulation: The Case of the NLRB." *American Political Science Review* 79 (4): 1094–1116.

Moe, Terry. 1985b. "The Politicized Presidency." In *The New Direction in American Politics,* ed. John E. Chubb and Paul E. Peterson. Washington, DC: Brookings Institution.

Moe, Terry. 1989. "The Politics of Bureaucratic Structure." In *Can the Government Govern?* ed. John Chubb and Paul Peterson, 267–329. Washington, DC: Brookings Institution.

Moe, Terry, and Michael Caldwell. 1994. "The Institutional Foundations of Democratic Government: A Comparison of Presidential and Parliamentary Systems." *Journal of Institutional and Theoretical Economics* 150 (1): 171–95.

Montinola, Gabriella R. 1999. "The Philippines in 1998." *Asian Survey* 39 (1): 64–71.

Montinola, Gabriella R., and Robert W. Jackman. 2002. "Sources of Corruption: A Cross-Country Study." *British Journal of Political Science* 32 (1): 147–70.

Moon, Myung-Jae, and Patricia Ingraham. 1998. "Shaping Administrative Reform and Governance: An Examination of the Political Nexus Triads in Three Asian Countries." *Governance: An International Journal of Policy and Administration* 11 (1): 77–100.

Moon, Woojin. 2005. "Decomposition of Regional Voting in South Korea: Ideological Conflicts and Regional Interests." *Party Politics* 11(5): 579–99.

Müller, Wolfgang C., Torbjörn Bergman, and Kaare Strøm. 2003. "Parliamentary Democracy: Promise and Problems." In *Delegation and Accountability in Parliamentary Democracies,* ed. Kaare Strøm, Wolfgang C. Müller, and Torbjörn Bergman, 3–32. Oxford: Oxford University Press.

Neustadt, Richard E. 1990. *Presidential Power and the Modern Presidents: The Politics of Leadership from Roosevelt to Reagan.* Rev. ed. New York: Free Press.

Niskanen, William. 1971. *Bureaucracy and Representative Government.* Aldine: Atherton.

Noll, Roger. 1971. *Reforming Regulation.* Washington, DC: Brookings Institution.

Noll, Roger. 1976. "Breaking Out of the Regulatory Dilemma: Alternatives to the Sterile Choice." *Indiana Law Journal* 51 (3): 686–99.

O'Donnell, Guillermo. 1994. "Delegative Democracy." *Journal of Democracy* 5 (1): 55–69.

O'Donnell, Guillermo. 1996. "Illusions about Consolidation." *Journal of Democracy* 7 (2): 34–51.

O'Donnell, Guillermo. 1999. "Horizontal Accountability in New Democracies." In *The Self-Restraining State: Power and Accountability in New Democracies,* ed. Andreas Schedler, Larry Diamond, and Marc F. Plattner, 29–52. Boulder: Rienner.

Organisation for Economic Co-Operation and Development. 2000. *Regulatory Reform in Korea: OECD Reviews of Regulatory Reform.* Paris: OECD Publications.

Organisation for Economic Co-Operation and Development. 2005. "Public Sector Modernization: Open Government" (policy brief). OECD Programme on Public Management and Governance. February 16. Available at http://www.oecd.org/dataoecd/1/35/34455306.pdf.

Overholt, William. 1986. "The Rise and Fall of Ferdinand Marcos." *Asian Survey* 26 (11): 1137–63.

Paddock, Richard C. 2001. "Philippine Leader Vows to Crush Rebellion." *Los Angeles Times,* May 2.

Paik, Young-Chul. 1994. "Political Reform and Democratic Consolidation." *Korea and World Affairs* 18 (4): 730–48.

Painter, Martin. 2004. "The Politics of Administrative Reform in East and Southeast Asia: From Gridlock to Continuous Self-Improvement?" *Governance: An International Journal of Policy, Administration, and Institutions* 17 (3): 361–86.

Philippines, Republic of the. 1972. Presidential Decree No. 6. Amending Certain Rules on Discipline of Government Officials and Employees. September 27. http://www.lawphil.net/statutes/presdecs/pd1972/pd_6_1972.html.

Phillippines, Republic of the. 1975. Civil Service Decree of the Philippines. October 6. Available at http://www.chanrobles.com/presidentialdecreeno807.htm.

Philippines, Republic of the. 1986a. Executive Order 17. May 28. Prescribing Rules and Regulations for the Implementation of Section 2, Article III of the Freedom Constitution. Available at http://www.lawphil.net/executive/execord/eo1986/eo_17_1986.html.

Philippines, Republic of the. 1986b. Provisional Freedom Constitution. March 25. Available at http://www.chanrobles.com/aquinoproclamation03.htm.

Philippines, Republic of the. 1987a. Administrative Code. July 25. Available at http://www.chanrobles.com/administrativecodeofthephilippinesfulltext.html.

Philippines, Republic of the. 1987b. Constitution. February 11. Available at http://www.chanrobles.com/philsupremelaw1.htm.

Philippines, Republic of the. Department of Budget and Management. 1989. "Staffing Profile of the Various Departments before and after Reorganization." January 25.

Philippines, Republic of the. Office of the President. 2006. "President Acts to Purge Government Bureaucracy of 'Ghost Workers'." October 25. Available at http://www.op.gov.ph/index.php?option=com_content&task=view&id=6094&Itemid=2.

Philippines, Republic of the. Presidential Commission on Government Reorganization. 1986. *Principles and Policy Proposals, Book I: Provisional Report.* Metro Manila. June 11.

Polsby, Nelson W. 1983. *Consequences of Party Reform.* Oxford: Oxford University Press.

Poole, Keith T., and Howard Rosenthal. 1997. *Congress: A Political-Economic History of Roll Call Voting.* Oxford: Oxford University Press.

Popkin, Samuel L. 2007. "Changing Media and Changing Political Organization: Delegation, Representation, and News." *Japanese Journal of Political Science* 8 (1): 71–93.

Przeworski, Adam, Susan Stokes, and Bernard Manin. 1999. *Democracy, Accountability, and Representation.* New York: Cambridge University Press.

Putnam, Robert. 2000. *Bowling Alone: The Collapse and Revival of American Community.* New York: Simon and Schuster.

Ramseyer, J. Mark, and Frances McCall Rosenbluth. 1993. *Japan's Political Marketplace.* Cambridge: Harvard University Press.

"Rebel Leader Soong Announces Candidacy for 2000 Elections." 1999. *Dow Jones Newswires,* July 16.

Riedinger, Jeffrey. 1994. "The Philippines in 1993." *Asian Survey* 34 (2): 139–46.

Roberts, Dexter, Stuart Young, Mark L. Clifford, and Stan Crock. 2000. "Taiwan: The Reformer in Charge." *Business Week,* April 3. Available at http://www.businessweek.com/2000/00_14/b3675010.htm.

Roeder, Philip G. 1993. *Red Sunset: The Failure of Soviet Politics.* Princeton: Princeton University Press.

Rohde, David. 1994. "The Contemporary Congress, 1930–1990." In *Encyclopedia of the American Legislative System,* ed. Joel Silbey, vol. 1, 157–73. Charles Scribner's Sons.

Romer, Thomas, and Howard Rosenthal. 1978. "Political Resource Allocation, Controlled Agendas, and the Status Quo." *Public Choice* 33 (4): 27–43.

Rose-Ackerman, Susan. 1978. *Corruption: A Study in Political Economy.* New York: Academic Press.

Rose-Ackerman, Susan. 1995. *Controlling Environmental Policy: The Limits of Public Law in Germany and the United States.* New Haven: Yale University Press.

Rose-Ackerman, Susan. 1999. *Corruption and Government: Causes, Consequences, and Reform.* Cambridge: Cambridge University Press.

Rose-Ackerman, Susan. 2005. *From Elections to Democracy: Building Accountable Government in Hungary and Poland.* New York: Cambridge University Press.

Schedler, Andreas. 1998. "What Is Democratic Consolidation?" *Journal of Democracy* 9 (2): 91–107.

Schedler, Andreas. 2001a. "Measuring Democratic Consolidation." *Studies in Comparative International Development* 36 (1): 66–92.

Schedler, Andreas. 2001b. "Taking Uncertainty Seriously: The Blurred Boundaries of Democratic Transition and Consolidation." *Democratization* 8 (4): 1–22.

Schedler, Andreas. 2002. "The Nested Game of Democratization by Elections." *International Political Science Review* 23 (1): 103–22.

Schmitter, Philippe C., and Terry Lynn Karl. 1991. "What Democracy Is and Is Not." *Journal of Democracy* 2 (3): 75–88.

Shapiro, Martin. 1988. *Who Guards the Guardians? Judicial Control of Administration.* Athens: University of Georgia Press.

Shepsle, Kenneth. 1979. "Institutional Arrangements and Equilibrium in Multidimensional Voting Models." *American Journal of Political Science* 23 (1): 27–59.

Shepsle, Kenneth, and Barry Weingast. 1981. "Structure-Induced Equilibrium and Legislative Choice." *Public Choice* 37 (3): 503–19.

Shin, Eui Hang. 2003. "The Role of NGOs in Political Elections in South Korea." *Asian Survey* 43 (4): 697–716.

Shirk, Susan. 1993. *The Political Logic of Economic Reform in China.* Berkeley: University of California Press.

Shugart, Matthew S., and John M. Carey. 1992. *Presidents and Assemblies: Constitutional Design and Electoral Dynamics.* Cambridge: Cambridge University Press.

Shugart, Matthew S., and Stephan Haggard. 2001. "Institutions and Public Policy in Presidential Systems." In *Presidents, Parliaments and Policy,* ed. Stephan Haggard and Mathew McCubbins, 64–102. Cambridge: Cambridge University Press.

Simin-ui Sinmun (*Citizens Times*). 1999. Hanguk min-gan danche chongnam (Directory of Korean NGOs). Seoul: Citizens Times.

Sniderman, Paul, Richard Brody, and Philip Tetlock. 1991. *Reasoning and Choice.* New York: Cambridge University Press.

Song, Young-Il. 2004. "Environmental Impact Assessment in Korea." *Korea Environmental Policy Bulletin* 2 (2): 1–19.

"Soong Laments Downsizing." 1998. Asia Intelligence Wire. September 2.

Soriano, Emanuel. 1986. "Upgrading the Civil Service System." Paper presented at the Colloquium on Public Management, Development Academy of the Philippines and the University of Philippines College of Public Administration.

"South Korean Government to Form Civil Complaints Committee." 2000. *Yonhap News Agency,* December 20.

Spaeth, Anthony. 2005. "Under Siege." *Time Asia,* May 4. Available at http://www.time.com/time/asia/2005/phil_arroyo/story.html.

Steers, Richard, Yoo Shin, and Gerado Ungson. 1989. *The Chaebol: Korea's New Industrial Might.* New York: Harper and Row.

Stokes, Susan. 2001. *Mandates and Democracy: Neoliberalism by Surprise in Latin America.* Cambridge: Cambridge University Press.

Strøm, Kaare. 1990. *Minority Government and Majority Rule.* Cambridge: Cambridge University Press.

Strøm, Kaare. 2000. "Delegation and Accountability in Parliamentary Democracies." *European Journal of Political Research* 37 (3): 261–89.

Strøm, Kaare, Wolfgang C. Müller, and Torbjörn Bergman, eds. 2003. *Delegation and Accountability in Parliamentary Democracies.* Oxford: Oxford University Press.

Suh, Sangwon, Alejandro Reyes, and Allen T. Cheng. 2000. "Seismic Changes." *Asiaweek,* March 31.

"Taiwan's 50-Year Regime Senses Electoral Defeat." 2000. *Times of London,* March 16.

Thies, Michael F. 2001. "Keeping Tabs on Partners: The Logic of Delegation in Coalition Governments." *American Journal of Political Science* 45 (3): 580–98.

Timberman, David G. 1991. *A Changeless Land: Continuity and Change in Philippine Politics.* Armonk, NY: Sharpe.

Treisman, Daniel. 2000. "The Causes of Corruption: A Cross-National Study." *Journal of Public Economics* 76 (3): 399–457.

Tsai, Shi-Yuan. 1998. *A Complete File of Black-Gold.* Taipei: Tsai Shi-yuan Research Office in the Legislature.

U.S. Congress. 1946. Reprinted in Staff of Senate Committee on the Judiciary. *Administrative Procedure Act: Legislative History,* S. Doc. No. 248, 79th Congress, 1944–46.

U.S. Department of State. "Democracy." Washington, DC. Available at http:www.state.gov/g/drl/democ/index.htm.

Valenzuela, J. Samuel. 1992. "Democratic Consolidation in Post-Transitional Settings:

Notion, Process, and Facilitating Conditions." In *Issues in Democratic Consolidation: The New South American Democracies in Comparative Perspective,* ed. Scott Mainwaring, Guillermo O'Donnell, and J. Samuel Valenzuela, 57–104. Notre Dame, IN: University of Notre Dame Press for the Helen Kellogg Institute for International Studies.

Wade, Robert. 1990. *Governing the Market: Economic Theory and the Role of Government in East Asian Industrialization.* Princeton: Princeton University Press.

Wade, Robert. 1992. "East Asia's Economic Success: Conflicting Perspectives, Partial Insights, Shaky Evidence." *World Politics* 45 (2): 270–320.

Weber, Max. 1968. *Economy and Society: An Outline of Interpretive Sociology.* Berkeley: University of California Press.

Weingast, Barry, and Mark Moran. 1983. "Bureaucratic Discretion or Congressional Control? Regulatory Policymaking by the Federal Trade Commission." *Journal of Political Economy* 91 (5): 765–800.

West, James, and Dae-Kyu Yoon. 1992. "The Constitutional Court of the Republic of Korea: Transforming the Jurisprudence of the Vortex." *American Journal of Comparative Law* 40 (1): 73–119.

Wilson, James Q. 1989. *Bureaucracy: What Government Agencies Do and Why They Do It.* New York: Basic Books.

World Bank. 1997. *World Development Report 1997: The State in a Changing World.* New York: Oxford University Press.

Wu, Sofia. 2000. "Taiwan Goes to Polls Amid Sense of Uncertainty." Central News Agency, March 17.

Wu, Yu-Shan. 1998. "Semi-Presidentialism or Imperial-Presidentialism? A Comparison between Constitutional Reforms in the ROC and the Russian Federation." Paper presented at the American Political Science Association, Boston.

Index